ARCHITECT AND ENGINEER LIABILITY

1999 Cumulative Supplement

This supplement supersedes all previous supplements.

ARCHITECT AND ENGINEER LIABILITY
CLAIMS AGAINST DESIGN PROFESSIONALS
SECOND EDITION

1999 Cumulative Supplement

ROBERT F. CUSHMAN
G. CHRISTIAN HEDEMANN

Supplement prepared by
Michael T. Callahan

ASPEN LAW & BUSINESS
A Division of Aspen Publishers, Inc.
Gaithersburg New York

Permissions
Aspen Law & Business
1185 Avenue of the Americas
New York, NY 10036

Printed in the United States of America

ISBN 0-7355-0456-3

1 2 3 4 5 6 7 8 9 0

About Aspen Law & Business

Aspen Law & Business—comprising the former Prentice Hall Law & Business, Little, Brown and Company's Professional Division, and Wiley Law Publications—is a leading publisher of authoritative treatises, practice manuals, services, and journals for attorneys, financial and tax advisors, corporate and bank directors, and other business professionals. Our mission is to provide practical solution-based how-to information keyed to the latest legislative, judicial, and regulatory developments.

We offer publications in the areas of banking and finance; bankruptcy; business and commercial law; construction law; corporate law; pensions, benefits, and labor; insurance; securities; taxation; intellectual property; government and administrative law; real estate law; matrimonial and family law; environmental and health law; international law; legal practice and litigation; and criminal law.

Other Aspen Law & Business products treating construction law issues include:

Alternative Clauses to Standard Construction Contracts (Second Edition)
Calculating Construction Damages
Calculating Lost Labor Productivity in Construction Claims
California Construction Law (Fifteenth Edition)
Construction Bidding Law
Construction Change Order Claims
Construction Claims Deskbook: Management, Documentation, and Presentation of Claims
Construction Defect Claims and Litigation
Construction Delay Claims (Second Edition)
Construction Dispute Resolution Formbook
Construction Documentation (Third Edition)
Construction Industry Forms (Second Edition)
Construction Industry Insurance Handbook
Construction Joint Venture: Forms and Practice Guide
Construction Law Handbook
Construction Law Library on CD-ROM
Construction Litigation: Practice Guide with Forms
Construction Litigation: Representing the Contractor (Second Edition)
Construction Litigation: Representing the Owner (Second Edition)
Construction Management: Law and Practice
Construction Scheduling: Preparation, Liability, and Claims
Construction Subcontracting: A Legal Guide for Industry Professionals
The Construction Subcontracting Manual: Practice Guide with Forms
Design-Build Contracting Formbook
Design-Build Contracting Handbook
Differing Site Condition Claims
Fifty State Construction Lien and Bond Law
Legal Guide to AIA Documents (Fourth Edition)

1999 Wiley Construction Law Update
Practical Guide to Construction Contract Surety Claims
Proving and Pricing Construction Claims (Second Edition)
State-by-State Guide to Architect, Engineer, and Contractor Licensing
Sweet on Construction Industry Contracts: Major AIA Documents (Third Edition)

ASPEN LAW & BUSINESS
A Division of Aspen Publishers, Inc.
A Wolters Kluwer Company

SUBSCRIPTION NOTICE

This Aspen Law & Business product is updated on a periodic basis with supplements to reflect important changes in the subject matter. If you purchased this product directly from Aspen Law & Business, we have already recorded your subscription for the update service.

If, however, you purchased this product from a bookstore and wish to receive future updates and revised or related volumes billed separately with a 30-day examination review, please contact our Customer Service Department at 1-800-234-1660, or send your name, company name (if applicable), address, and the title of the product to:

ASPEN LAW & BUSINESS
A Division of Aspen Publishers, Inc.
7201 McKinney Circle
Frederick, MD 21701

CONTENTS

Note: The following new sections are *additions* to the main volume.

Preface		*xi*
Chapter 1	**Bases of Architects' and Engineers' Liability: An Overview**	**1**
Chapter 2	**The Pros and Cons of Standard Contract Forms**	**8**
§ 2.28	Termination	15
Chapter 3	**Design Professionals' Insurance and Surety Programs**	**17**
Chapter 4	**We Have Been Sued. Is That Attorney Chosen by My Insurance Company My Friend or My Foe? Do I Need My Own?**	**22**
Chapter 5	**Liability on the Contract**	**25**
Chapter 6	**Design Professional's Liability to the Contractor**	**38**
Chapter 7	**Liability for Negligence**	**56**
§ 7.20A	Sick Building Syndrome and Indoor Air Quality	69
Chapter 9	**Miscellaneous Claims**	**80**
Chapter 10	**The Design Professional's Criminal Liability**	**89**
Chapter 11	**Ownership and Reuse of Design Professionals' Designs**	**98**
§ 11.19A	—Reuse Statutes	104
Chapter 12	**Liability for Innovative but Unproven Designs**	**111**
Chapter 13	**The Design Professional as Construction Manager**	**115**
Chapter 14	**Risk Management**	**123**
Chapter 15	**Injuries Resulting in Damage Claims**	**134**
Chapter 16	**Reducing Damages**	**138**
Chapter 17	**Contractual Defenses**	**145**

CONTENTS

Chapter 18 Immunity Defenses **157**

Chapter 19 Statutes of Limitation and Statutes of Repose **164**

Chapter 20 Defending Against a Claim: An Overview **170**

Chapter 21 Preparing for Trial **172**

Chapter 22 Expert Consultants and Witnesses **175**

Chapter 23 Alternate Dispute Resolution: The Pros and Cons **178**

Table of Cases ***184***

Index ***193***

PREFACE

The 1999 supplement to *Architect and Engineer Liability* continues to update the suggestions necessary to prevent and resolve claims against designers. Using the suggestions included in this cumulative supplement can help resolve disputes quicker to keep defense costs down and settlement values accurate. According to Johnson & Higgins's 1996 survey of risk management for designers, *Risk Management Study of Large Design Firms*, annual professional liability losses (including defense and settlement costs) range from 0.73 percent to 2.10 percent of the design firm's revenue. In addition, Johnson & Higgins's survey showed it costs more to defend a claim against a designer than it costs a designer to settle it: designers with revenues below $100 million have defense costs equal to 141 percent of settlements; designers with revenues more than $100 million have defense costs equal to 112 percent of settlements.

By explaining how the supplement's updated suggestions can be successful, more designers may be encouraged to use them, something many designers have not yet discovered. The Johnson & Higgins's 1996 survey also showed design firms are only partially successful at negotiating contract clauses that can reduce their liability. Designers obtained a preferred indemnification clause in 68 percent of their contracts and a preferred limitation of liability clause in only 41 percent of their contracts, and they apparently failed to recognize the importance of the scope of work clause entirely.

The 1999 *Architect and Engineer Liability* supplement adds comments and descriptions of the 1997 revisions to B141, Standard Form of Agreement Between Owner and Architect, by both the AIA and industry commentators. The supplement expands citations concerning the designer's liability for slander, interference with contractual relations, and qualified privileges, including descriptions how the designer's contract with the owner is used to defend the designer's actions and explanations as to what constitutes a designer's malice. It also describes how the industry has reacted to the details for delegating part of the design responsibility to the contractor included in the 1997 revisions to B141. Moreover, it discusses designer liability for incomplete drawings on fast-track, design-build projects. The supplement also continues to expand the new section added in previous supplements for § 11.19A "Reuse Statutes," and begins a new § 2.28 "Termination."

I gratefully acknowledge the significant contributions of Randal Wax at Shapiro, Lifschitz & Schram for Chapter 11 and Gerald Garfield at Day, Berry & Howard for Chapter 13.

Overland Park, Kansas
April 1999

Michael T. Callahan
President
CCL Construction Consultants, Inc.

ARCHITECT AND ENGINEER LIABILITY

1999 Cumulative Supplement

CHAPTER 1

BASES OF ARCHITECTS' AND ENGINEERS' LIABILITY: AN OVERVIEW

§ 1.4 Legal Theories Recognized Against Design Professionals

Page 6, add to note 2:

Thomson v. Espey Huston & Assocs., Inc., 899 S.W.2d 415 (Tex. Ct. App. 1995) (any negligence by engineering consulting firm in performing inspection contract caused no injury beyond economic loss to subject of contract itself, which pursuant to the economic loss rule, did not give rise to tort cause of action).

Page 7, add to note 5:

cert. denied, 642 N.E.2d 1302 (Ill. 1994).

§ 1.5 Contract Documents

Page 7, add after second paragraph:

In *Chesapeake Paper Products Co. v. Stone & Webster Engineering Corp.,* 51 F.3d 1229 (4th Cir. 1995), conflicts between the standard of care contained in contracts submitted by the designer and the owner were resolved by the court. Stone & Webster was hired to design the expansion of a paper mill. It sent to Chesapeake Paper its contract form that provided design services would be provided consistent with "good engineering practices." Chesapeake Paper never signed Stone & Webster's form contract.

Chesapeake later sent a purchase order to Stone & Webster that stated, "all materials and articles covered by this order . . . will be free from defects in material and/or workmanship, and merchantable," a much higher standard than that contained in Stone & Webster's form contract. Stone &

Webster never rejected the terms of Chesapeake's purchase order. Later, Stone & Webster and Chesapeake signed an amendment that modified the Stone & Webster form contract as referenced in Chesapeake Paper's purchase order, but apparently without any change to the form's reference to standards of care.

In a subsequent dispute over Stone & Webster's standard of care, the jury concluded that the amendment modified Stone & Webster's form contract rather than Chesapeake's purchase order, imposing a higher standard than that presented in Stone & Webster's form contract. Clearly, designers should insist on one clear and complete contract document that is signed by all of the parties. Instead of beginning work, Stone & Webster should have waited until a complete contract agreement had been exchanged.

§ 1.7 Design Phase

Page 10, add to note 9:

The *Spearin* Doctrine does not extend to situations in which the design requires a specific product for incorporation into the project but the product turns out to contain a manufacturing defect or has been misrepresented by the manufacturer. Instead, as between the owner and the contractor, liability will be placed on the contractor. The contractor must look to the manufacturer for a remedy. F. Baltz, *The Spearin Doctrine: How Far Does It Go?,* 33 Procurement Law. 11 (No. 1, Fall 1997).

§ 1.9 Construction Phase

Page 12, add to second full paragraph:

Although the contractor is responsible for preparation of the construction schedule, the designer's review and reliance on the contractor's schedule is often a sensitive area. While both B141 and A201 do not require the owner and architect to approve the schedule, the contractor's schedule does constitute an important method of communicating the contractor's expectations concerning the time of the designer's services and the owner's involvement.

By reviewing the contractor's schedule, the designer should be able to determine when site visits are particularly appropriate; determine when the architect's engineering consultants will be required; determine when tests required by the contract documents are likely to occur; determine when governmental inspections will occur; and determine when approved shop drawings will be needed so as to avoid delay in the work. The owner can use the contractor's schedule to forecast cash flow requirements; delivery of owner-supplier equipment; and tenant improvements. Goldberg & Coote, "Reporting and Scheduling Under AIA Documents A201 and B141: The Architect's Viewpoint," 15 *Construction Lawyer* No. 2, at 3 (Apr. 1995).

Although the contractor's A201 schedule is submitted for informational purposes, the owner and designer review the schedule closely. The owner and designer have a strong economic interest in timely completion of the project. The construction schedule is also an essential tool for demonstrating to the architect and owner (and possibly to an arbitrator or court) the contractor's right to an adjustment in contract time or sum resulting from a change or claim.

§ 1.10 Design/Build Arrangements

Page 12, add after first paragraph:

Licensing requirements with respect to design/build vary significantly from state to state. Statutes must be examined to determine whether the design services can or must be performed by a licensed architect or engineer who is an employee of a general contractor; by a licensed architect or engineer who is a subcontractor to the contractor; or by a licensed architect or engineer who is exclusively part of the design/build team itself. Asselin & Stout, "Legal Exposure of the Design/Build Participants: The View of the General Contractor," 15 *Construction Lawyer* No. 3, at 10 (Aug. 1995). Without requisite licenses, it may be necessary to shut down a design/build project. In addition, the failure to fully comply with licensing requirements provides a defense to a dissatisfied owner in an action brought by a design/builder to recover payment.

Page 13, add after carryover paragraph:

The Engineers Joint Contract Documents Committee (EJCDC), comprising the NSPE, the American Consulting Engineers Council, and the American Society of Civil Engineers, have also created a family of design-build contract documents. The documents are to be offered in electronic format. Siegel, "Contract Documents May Ease Design-Build Process," *Engineering Times,* May 1995, at 11.

It is estimated that by 1997, 77 percent of private sector projects will be built using design/build. Typical public sector design/build projects are easily replicated or developed like prisons, housing, educational facilities, and warehouses.

The EJCDC's design/build documents reflect the various types of possible design/build arrangements. These different types of arrangements all call for different types of contracts. The design/builder may be any of the following:

- A company that can perform both in-house design and construction;
- A joint venture between an engineer performing design services and a contractor providing construction;
- A general contractor or specialty contractor who subcontracts design services to an engineer;
- An engineer who subcontracts construction to a contractor; or
- A developer or entrepreneur who subcontracts both design and construction.

The *Guide to the Use of EJCDC Design-Build Documents* provides guidance on preparing requests for proposals, proposal language, proper use of the documents, and supplementary conditions.

Because laws that apply to design/build projects vary from state to state, EJCDC recommends that at a minimum prospective participants look into licensing laws, contractor licensing and bonding, qualifications-based selection for design professionals, and competitive bidding for public construction.

Page 13, add after first full paragraph:

The design/builder may be required to provide a performance bond that covers not only the construction function, but also the design function. Bonding companies may be reluctant to provide surety bonds for design/build projects because designers often do not have sufficient assets to guarantee performance. In addition, by expanding the coverage of their bonds to include defective design, sureties may increase coverage for design defects to the full amount of the contract price for the design/build project. Design firms are often partnerships of design professionals that distribute income among the partners and maintain small retained earnings. Construction companies are more likely to maintain large retained earnings, capital improvements, and construction equipment. This makes contractors more desirable to bonding companies because of their greater financial ability to indemnify the bonding company. Asselin & Stout, "Legal Exposure of the Design/Build Participants: The View of the General Contractor," 15 *Con-*

struction Lawyer No. 3, at 12 (Aug. 1995). Because sureties may consider the general contractor to be the dominate participant in design/build, the contractor must recognize that it may be undertaking a greater share of the risk on paper than the designer because the surety company may rely more upon the general contractor with respect to the surety's willingness to bond the project and the surety's right to be indemnified. *Id.* at 13.

Sureties may also be reluctant to provide surety bonds if the design/ build price is to be determined later. The surety may not be able to determine the size of the bond. Incremental bonding or bonding one phase of a project at a time may put the owner at risk if the surety refuses to continue the process when a subsequent increment is needed. *Id.* at 12–13.

Definitions in commercial general liability insurance, professional liability insurance, and builder's risk insurance have been designed with the concept that the design and build function will be separate. By placing design/build responsibilities in the same entity, insurance coverage may have either gaps or overlaps in coverage. Traditional methods of categorizing the design and build functions may also create conflicts among insurance coverage whether the damage has resulted from negligent design, which is covered by professional negligence insurance, or a construction defect, which may or may not be covered by some sort of liability insurance or performance bond. Contractor's commercial general liability insurance generally excludes coverage for claims that result from negligent design. *Id.* at 14.

Construction exclusions in most professional liability policies leave the execution of the design to the contractor. These also exclude design/build activities. Design/builders tend to be contractors with staff architects. However, a contractor's ordinary CGL coverage does not cover design/build risks either. The design/builder needs special coverage, such as contractor's design professional liability insurance, to protect its design-related risk. Chemers & Knox, "When Designs Don't Work: Professional Liability Coverage of Architects and Engineers," 15 *Construction Lawyer* No. 1, at 17 (Jan. 1995).

Owner contracts with a design/build contractor who, in turn, contracts with the architect, have no special consequences to the professional liability insurer. However, professional liability insurance may be unavailable for some parts of the designer's work when the owner contracts with an A/E to provide design/build services, and the A/E in turn has contracted with the contractor to provide construction services. The A/E, being prime, needs professional liability coverage should the construction differ from the documents in quality, technicalities, or construction due to designer negligence during construction observation. Yet, most insurers, because of their fear of inviting claims by providing this coverage, do not offer it. Abramowitz, "Professional Liability Insurance in the Design/Build Setting," 15 *Construction Lawyer* No. 3, at 4 (Aug. 1995). In 1980, CNA/Schinnerer first began insuring design/build, excluding primarily "any faulty workmanship, construction or work not in accordance with the design of the project or the construction documents." *Id.* at 5.

If the owner contracts with an A/E-contractor joint venture, neither the A/E nor the joint venture will have any professional liability protection because under most policies, design professionals can get joint venture coverage only with other design professionals. *Id.* See **§ 3.6**.

Design/build has traditionally been covered on a project-by-project basis, with the professional liability insurer underwriting each "exposure" by determining how the owner has contracted for the design/build services, evaluating what is being designed and constructed, and then picking and choosing which of the projects it is willing to insure. Abramowitz, "Professional Liability Insurance in the Design/Build Setting," 15 *Construction Lawyer* at 5.

Under CNA/Schinnerer's new policy, insureds who perform occasional design/build services will automatically be covered for their "wrongful acts" in connection with their design/build professional services during all phases of services, including construction observation. The cost to repair or replace faulty workmanship will still be excluded, but now only if the faulty workmanship that is not in accordance with the design of the project or the construction documents was performed directly by the insured firm itself. Joint ventures with non–design professionals will be covered automatically, but the standard for coverage will remain "wrongful acts" in the delivery of professional services. If past is prologue, other professional liability insurers will develop language that mirrors the new CNA policy. *Id.* at 6.

The design/build function invites an expectation by an owner that the design function will carry with it a kind of warranty and guarantee that exceeds the minimum standard of professional care. The design/builder may also obtain construction manager's liability insurance or contractor's malpractice insurance to cover its design liability and not wholly rely on insurance obtained by the design professional. Asselin & Stout, "Legal Exposure of the Design/Build Participants: The View of the General Contractor," 15 *Construction Lawyer* No. 3, at 21 (Aug. 1995).

Page 13, add at end of section:

The design function is a creative process. Delays may occur because of the additional time needed for that creativity, ensuring the resulting ideas are acceptable to the owner, and then working with the contractor part of the design/build entity to value engineer the design may jeopardize the overall success of the project. It is vital to monitor and control the designer's work to make certain that it stays on schedule and within the budgets for design and construction. A key element to coordinate the interrelated performance of the owner, designer, and contractor in a design/build arrangement is a detailed schedule that binds all of them. A detailed CPM schedule for both design and construction will alert all parties to their responsibilities and to the potential adverse consequences of a failure to perform in a timely manner.

CHAPTER 2

THE PROS AND CONS OF STANDARD CONTRACT FORMS

§ 2.5 —Architect's Services

Page 22, add at end of section:

Among the many items that designers may consider when drafting their contracts is a detailed description of their scope of work. Because designers may make their own claims for additional performance costs, consideration should be given to describing each part of the intended performance in such a way that owner changes, delays, or extras *to the design preparation* may be readily demonstrated and able to support a designer's claims. For example, instead of only saying that the designer will "prepare specifications," describe which specifications will be prepared, how many specifications are included, and how long the owner has to review them. Then, if the owner adds specifications, delays the review process, or changes them, the designer will be in a better position to demonstrate additional performance and support claims for additional performance costs.

§ 2.6 —Schematic Design

Page 24, add at end of section:

Designer's also have a significant role in the time of project delivery. Paragraph 2.2.4 of the AIA's 1987 standard form B141, Standard Form Agreement Between Owner and Architect, provides that the architect shall prepare for approval by the owner, schematic design documents consisting of drawings and other documents illustrating the scale and relationship of project components based on the mutually agreed program, schedule, and construction budget requirements. Yet the only "deliverables" required by the 1987 version are the drawings, even though the architect has reviewed the program furnished by the owner to ascertain the requirements of the project under paragraph 2.2.1; provided a preliminary evaluation of the owner's program schedule and construction budget requirements under paragraph 2.2.2; reviewed with the owner alternative approaches to design and construction of the project under paragraph 2.2.3; and arrived at a mutually agreed program, schedule, and construction budget requirements under paragraph 2.2.4. D. Scotti, "*Reporting and Scheduling Under AIA Documents A201 and B141: The Owner's Viewpoint*," 15 *Con. Law*. 9, 11 (No. 2, April 1995). In contrast, the 1997 version of B141's Article 1.1 contains sixteen blanks on two pages that allow the parties to describe the time periods for the project, including a current schedule at the time the agreement is executed (if the schedule is not yet established, the identifies major time milestones, such as targeted construction start date or a facility opening date). American Institute of Architects, "*Promises, Promises: Forging Healthy Project Relationships*," at 6 (1997) (hereafter *Promises, Promises*).

Neither the 1987 nor the 1997 versions of B141 describes how these "reviews" should be conducted or the schedule of approval. Although mutual understandings must be arrived at on critical aspects of the project, no writing is required in B141 in order to proceed effectively and efficiently into the design development phase. There should be a formal document generated at the end of the schematic design phase to capture and describe where the project stands, including a review of the project schedule, construction schedule, and the design schedule. Scotti, at 11.

The design development documents are to be based on approved schematic design documents and any adjustments authorized by the owner in the program, schedule, or construction budget under paragraph 2.3.1. Once again, B141 does not provide any description of how this information is to be communicated or the time of this communication. At the conclusion of the design development phase, the architect should conduct a meeting during which the design development documents should be presented, including schedules for remaining design and construction. Scotti, at 11–12.

Similarly, owners will find no defined periods within which shop drawings and other submittals must be turned around, no language specifying the frequency with which the architect and its consultants will visit the project, and no requirement that the architect take meeting notes. P. Cobey, "*The New B141: An Owner's Manual*," 3 *The Construction Forum News* 2, at 4 (No. 2, Jan. 1998).

§ 2.8 — Construction Documents Phase

Page 24, add after third sentence in first paragraph:

Standard form specifications may present as many problems to a designer as do standard form contracts or errors and omissions in the drawings. References to industry standards in the specifications are used to measure whether a contractor's workmanship or materials constitute a defect. However, many times the standards indicated are out of print, out of date, or not familiar to the various trades. For example, "The Painting and Decorating Contractors of America" standard may be referenced, but it includes three different levels of work and is no longer in print. To avoid this type of potential problem, current, known, realistic standards should be utilized and care taken to spell out which levels of work within the standard are expected. Siegel, "Contract Documents May Ease Design-Build Process," *Engineering Times,* May 1995, at 11.

§ 2.12 —Visits and Inspections

Page 28, add after third paragraph:

Early AIA standard form contracts gave architects the express duty of "supervision." "Supervision" was then changed to "observation" in later versions. In the 1997 edition, AIA has deleted the term "observation." According to the AIA, the change does not alter the architect's responsibilities during the construction process, but rather disposes of language that seemed to place a passive connotation on the architect's role at the site. *Promises, Promises*, at 12. As the AIA's standard forms move away from imposing on the architect any duty to oversee construction, some courts refuse to impose such liability on the architect. The court in *Jones v. James Reeves Contractors, Inc.*, 701 So. 2d 774 (Miss. 1997), *see* **§ 7.20**, ruled that a designer had no duty to warn of a dangerous site condition the designer knew existed. The *Jones* court seemed to agree that, by distancing themselves from the product of the work or funding, parties can avoid designer liability for problems arising from known hazards. D. Murphy, "*A&E's Limited Duty to Warn of Hazard,*" 12 *Common Sense Contracting* 9 (No. 3, Summer 1998).

§ 2.14 —Rejection of Work

Page 30, add at end of section:

Provisions that limit the designer's responsibility for construction are often enforced. *See Block v. Lohan Associates, Inc.,* 159 Ill. 2d 583, 645 N.E.2d 207 (1993) (architect could not be held liable in negligence action arising when subcontractor's employee fell from ladder, based on its alleged failure to supervise and coordinate work of its consulting structural engineer, where contract documents limited architect's responsibility to design and determination as to design conformance, and did not extend to worker safety) (engineers hired to design precast concrete panels and their connections, and the structural frame of building at construction project did not have duty to consider, during design stage, manner in which precast column covers and their welded connections could be appropriately erected; engineer's contract stated that it was responsible only for specifications pertaining to structural integrity of precast concrete and required no participation of engineer at construction project, and placed no duty on it to supervise construction means, manners, and methods).

§ 2.15 —Shop Drawings

Page 31, add to third full paragraph:

In 1997, the AIA revised A201, Paragraph 3.12 to remove the contractor's obligation to first "approve" shop drawings and to require a change order for shop drawings that deviate from the contract documents. The revised Paragraph 3.12.5 eliminates the contractor's obligation to approve shop drawings and now states that the purpose of the contractor's review of shop drawings is only for compliance with the contract documents. Paragraph 3.12.8 was revised to require a change order to authorize any deviation from the contract documents except for a minor change, which can be approved by the designer in writing.

§ 2.16 —Change Orders

Page 33, add at end of section:

Many jurisdictions do not protect designers from liability if a design is changed without knowledge or approval of the designer. Situations in which unauthorized changes may be made are frequent. Contractors may consider "harmless" changes to make installation of a difficult detail easier. Building inspectors may suggest an alternate approach to a contractor. Owners' in-house designers may modify a design to fit a particular need. Developers may make changes to accommodate site differences. To avoid responsibility for unauthorized changes, add a contract clause that both prohibits changes without the knowledge and consent of the designer and absolves responsibility for the design if the work is completed by another. Design Professional Insurance Corp., "Unauthorized Changes to Plans," *Structural Engineering Forum* Dec./Jan. 1995, at 38.

Designers that take over incomplete work have a similar problem. Partially completed designs may be evaluated on a time and material basis to discover errors. The client may permit discussions with the prior designer. The designer that completes the design of another may get an indemnity for any services performed by the prior designer or for information provided by others. If a client objects to or forbids consulting with the previous designer, chances are that either the other designer knows something the client does not want the designer to know or money may be owed. The project may not be worth undertaking. *Id.*

§ 2.17 Additional Services

Page 34, add at end of section:

The term "additional services" is gone—there are only "services" and "changes in services." The agreement no longer contemplates a standard scope, but encourages each owner and architect to tailor a scope services to the needs of the project. Cobey, at 2–3.

The new B141 broadens the basis on which an architect may claim an increased fee. Any change to the detailed project information in Article 1.1 is compensable. In many cases, responses to RFIs will be compensable under paragraph 2.8.2. Reviews of submittals out-of-sequence are compensable under paragraph 2.8.2. The old list of "contingent additional services" survives as the basis for the list of compensable "changes in service" described in subparagraph 1.3.3.2 and 2.8.2. B141 continues to provide that all changes in services are deemed compensable, under subparagraph 1.3.3.1, unless the owner specifically objects. Cobey, at 2–3.

§ 2.20 Ownership and Use of Documents

Page 35, add at beginning of section:

Paragraph 1.3.2 of B141 (1997) gives the owner a limited right to use the architect's documents for construction of the project, but this license now terminates immediately on termination of the contract for any reason. If the contract ends, the owner must return the architect's documents and all copies within seven days. If the architect is ever "adjudged in default" at the completion of formal dispute resolution proceedings, a second license begins and the documents are presumable shipped back to the owner, who may then use them to complete the project without the architect. Cobey, at 2.

It is difficult to imagine an owner who will accept these provisions in unaltered form. Many owners will simply require ownership of all rights to the project documents from the outset. An owner-oriented compromise could provide that owners have the right to use the documents to complete the project, provided the architect is released from any claims arising out of such use without the architect's participation. Cobey, at 2.

In addition to limiting the terminated designer's liability, the owner should indemnify the architect or engineer from claims arising from any modifications or deviations from its plans and specifications. This obligates the owner to insulate the design professional from claims that result from the work of the owner's new design team and other contractors. A sample indemnification provision reads as follows:

> The Owner agrees to hold harmless and indemnify the Architect from and against all liability, loss, damages, costs, and expenses, including reasonable counsel fees, which the Architect may at any time incur by reason of any demands, claims, causes of action, or legal proceedings arising out of or in connection with any revision, addition, misuse, alteration, or deviation from the Documents occuring subsequent to the termination of the Agreement. If the Owner utilizes the Documents for any addition, extension, modification, or remodeling of the Project or for completion of the Project by others, then the Owner agrees to delete any and all references to the Architect from all drawings and specifications used therein.

Patterson, at N7.

In addition to the limitation of liability and indemnification, a design professional may ask the owner to acknowledge that it shall not be held responsible for minor errors or ambiguities in its documents that could have been addressed easily through clarifications had it remained involved in the project. This additional qualification may have limited value if a claim arises, since parties are not likely to agree whether a particular problem could have been easy to correct as a routine matter. Nevertheless, it can be important for the owner to acknowledge that the architect's documents are not being held to a higher standard as a result of the termination of the parties' agreement. Patterson, at N7.

To minimize the risk of third-party claims, the designer should promptly advise authorities with jurisdiction over the project that it is no longer involved in the work. The owner should agree that the successor will assume full responsibility for the public filings required to complete the project. To avoid future confusion regarding the terminated architect's responsiblities, the owner should also agree to remove the architect's name and title block from the project documents. Patterson, at N7–N8.

The termination agreement should also clearly specify the scope of the owner's right to use and modify the design professional's plans. Since design professionals' documents reflect a unique approach to a project's design, they are often unwilling to transfer their copyright interest to others. By granting the owner a license to use its drawings to construct and perhaps subsequently alter the completed project, a design professional can permit the flexibility the client needs while avoiding the risk that the owner or others can use the design for other projects. Any termination agreement should acknowledge the departing designer's copyright interest in its plans, the scope of the owner's license, and the owner's obligation to require all recipients to limit their use of the documents to the purposes specified in the license. Patterson, at N8. *See also § 7.22*.

§ 2.24 —Insurance

Page 38, add after first paragraph:

B141 contains no insurance requirements. Owners will want to add specific coverage requirements as well as stipulations regarding length of coverage, naming of the owner as an additional insured, and so forth. There is no express representation or warranty that the design will not infringe on any other copyright and no obligation to indemnify and defend the owner against infringement claims. Cobey, at 4.

§ 2.25 Limitation on Amount or Type of Damages

Page 40, add to note 18:

Valhal Corp. v. Sullivan Assocs., Inc., 1995 WL 2621 (3d Cir. Jan. 3, 1995) (court of appeals distinguished between exculpatory, hold harmless, and indemnity clauses and limitation of liability clauses. Although limitation of liability clauses are not favored and must meet stringent conditions to be enforceable, they are enforced and are a part of businesses and commercial life. Because the liability cap was seven times greater than designer's fee, limitation of liability clause did not immunize the designer from consequences of its own actions and was not against public policy as expressed under Pennsylvania statute).

Some states have statutes that prohibit limitation of liability clauses. For example, Wisconsin (Wis. Stat. § 895.49 (1994)) expressly prohibits any provision that limits or eliminates tort liability in construction contracts. Limitation of liability agreements are prohibited for architects or engineers under the Virginia statute (Va. Code Ann. § 54.1-411 (Michie 1994)). See also **§ 17.8**.

Potter-Shackelford Constr. Co. v. Law Eng'g, Inc., 1996 U.S. App. LEXIS 33368 (4th Cir. Dec. 6, 1996) (written proposal for both testing and evaluations, which included limitation of liability clause, applied to both testing and evaluations because one invoice was sent for both services and other circumstances relating to the contract demonstrated that both services were part of a single contract to which the limitation of liability provision applied); Marbro, Inc. v. Borough of Tinton Falls, 297 N.J. Super. 411, 688 A.2d 159 (1996) (limitation of liability clause did not act as disincentive for design professional to perform its contract properly and was enforceable).

§ 2.28 Termination (New)

B141 recognizes the commercial reality that the owner may terminate the agreement for convenience in subparagraph 1.3.8.5. In 1.3.8.7, however, the architect shall be compensated for all lost profits on services not performed. Owners will undoubtedly accept the new termination right, and strike the lost-profits clause. Cobey, at 3.

Paragraph 1.3.2 of B141 (1997) gives the owner a limited right to use the architect's documents for construction of the project, but this license now terminates immediately on termination of the contract for any reason, whereon the owner must return the architect's documents and all copies within seven days. Cobey, at 2. A terminated designer without default may permit the owner to use the drawings. Although the departing design professional may obtain assurance that it will not be responsible for the errors or omissions of its successor, the owner is likely to want to continue to hold it responsible for its own work. But any residual liability may depend on the level of completion of the design at the time of termination. If the agreement is terminated in the schematic design phase, the architect may have no continuing liability for the project because the successor is likely to modify the design so substantially that the successor should assume full design responsibility for the project. If the design is complete, the designer should stand behind its work, especially if the designer has been paid. In either situation, the owner should acknowledge that the designer is not liable for the design services, errors, or omissions of its successors, or for deficiencies in the work of the contractors. Patterson, C., "*Construction Tips from Division 5: Protecting the Design Professional*," 3 *Construction Forum News* N6, at N6–N7 (July, 1998).

CHAPTER 3

DESIGN PROFESSIONALS' INSURANCE AND SURETY PROGRAMS

§ 3.1 Introduction

Page 44, add to note 2:

The 1996 American Consulting Engineers Council survey reported that costs declined almost universally among the various disciplines, with the exception of structural engineers. The survey showed them paying an average of 2.3% of gross annual billings in 1996, down from 2.4% in 1995 and 2.6% in 1994. The ACEC estimates the national total for all construction design firms to be $1 billion. Krizan, *Costs Decline for Engineers,* 238 Eng'g News-Rec. 22 (No. 9, Mar. 3, 1997).

Page 45, add after first full paragraph:

The cost of engineer's professional liability insurance, as a percentage of billings, continues to fall even as the litigation risk continues to rise. The cost of premiums dropped to 2.42 percent in 1995, according to the 17th annual liability survey conducted by the American Consulting Engineers Council (ACEC). The survey was based on responses from 985 ACEC members. "Insurance Costs Drop Again," 236 *Engineering News-Record* 16 (No. 11, Mar. 18, 1996).

The decrease in relative expense of liability insurance has much to do with growing revenues among consulting engineers, but also with increasing competitiveness among insurers. Many design firms have instituted risk avoidance programs that have cut claims and insurance costs.

The number of claims made against surveyed firms increased in 1995, although half of all claims were resolved without any payment to the claimant. There were 522 claims filed against the 985 responding firms, compared with 446 claims against 934 firms in 1994. Nearly two-thirds of all firms with 100 or more employees had at least one claim filed against them. Firms with fewer than 10 employees had only about a 5 percent chance of being sued. The average firm devoted 183 personnel hours to defending claims, on top of litigation and insurance costs. "Insurance Costs Drop Again," 236 *Engineering News-Record* 16 (No. 11, Mar. 18, 1996).

Six of seven firms surveyed said they have turned work down at least once because of concern over potential liability. Seventy-two percent said that the threat of litigation stifles innovative design approaches or attempts to hold down costs. *Id.*

Is it fair to attribute the decline in relative cost of designer's professional liability insurance solely to increased billings, competition among insurers, and risk avoidance programs? Should not some of the credit be given to the attorneys who successfully defended claims against the designers, reducing recovery and saving the professional liability insurers money? These savings would return to the designers in the form of reduced rates.

§ 3.4 — Claims-Made Provision

Page 51, add after first paragraph:

In *Calocerinos & Spina Consulting Engineers, PC v. Prudential Reinsurance Co.,* 856 F. Supp. 775 (W.D.N.Y. 1994), expiration of the period in which claims may be presented in a claims-made policy was found to prevent coverage. In January 1984, a contractor notified the engineer, Calocerinos & Spina, that it encountered a site condition different than those indicated in the contract documents. In December 1988, the contractor sued the engineer for negligent design and failure to discover and report excessive water flows in the tunnel drilling line. The engineer notified Prudential, its malpractice insurance carrier, about the lawsuit, also in December 1988.

Unfortunately, the engineer had a "claims-made" policy that had been canceled at the termination of the policy in 1984. Although the claims-made policy had a "discovery" endorsement that covered all claims made within three years of the cancellation, the engineer's notice to the professional liability insurer was after the three-year discovery period.

The court found that the liability insurer had no duty to cover the claims against the engineer after the expiration of the discovery period, despite the fact that the claim arose in January 1984, within the original claims-made period. The court felt it was inappropriate to extend the period of protection by allowing coverage for any and all claims that arose during the policy period but that went unreported until after the period has elapsed, even when extended by the discovery endorsement.

In *Calocerinos & Spina,* the engineers were notified of the contractor's differing site claim, a claim normally brought against the owner. Four years later, the contractor sued the engineer. How many designers with claims-made coverage would expect to notify their professional liability insurer for every disputed change order or claim *against the owner*? The court in *Calocerinos & Spina* warned that designers that do not may risk losing their insurance protection.

Sad but true—if a designer buys a claims-made policy, it has bought coverage for only those claims that are made during the policy period. If the act giving rise to the claim occurred during the policy period, but no claim was made until after the policy period—even if the period is extended by a "discovery" period—the claim is not covered.

At one time, the designer could have purchased an "occurrence" policy instead. An occurrence policy provides coverage if the act or omission occurred during the policy period, regardless when the claim was reported. Although occurrence policies are now rare, "retroactive" coverage may be available, regardless when the act occurs, as long as the designer has no knowledge of any facts that could give rise to a claim at the time the retroactive coverage begins. If the designer was aware of any facts that might suggest a claim, even if no claim actually had been made, even retroactive coverage will not provide coverage. See §§ **4.4** and **14.8**.

§ 3.6 —Exclusions

Page 54, add to carryover paragraph:

Exclusions can be clustered into six broad categories: contractual liability; high-risk design; construction; employer liability; nonprofessional negligence; and other tort liability. Chemers & Knox, "When Designs Don't Work: Professional Liability Coverage of Architects and Engineers," 15 *Construction Lawyer* No. 1, at 17 (Jan. 1995).

Page 54, add after second full paragraph:

An example of a one-sided arrangement under which the engineering firm is asked to indemnify the owner regardless of the fault of the engineering company is:

> The Engineers will assume the defense of and indemnify and save harmless the Owner from any claims or liabilities of any type or nature from any person, firm or corporation, arising in any manner from the Engineers' performance of the work covered by the engineering contract, and will pay any judgment obtained or growing out of said claims or liabilities or any of them.

National Society of Professional Engineers, "For the Clients," 35 *Private Practice News* No. 6 at 4 (July 1995).

Page 58, add at end of section:

Recently, design services for condominiums have also been considered high-risk design and excluded from inclusion in a professional liability policy. Many carriers refuse to provide errors and omissions insurance for companies providing services for condominium projects because of successful condominium defect litigation in California. Aharoni, "Misconceptions Concerning E & O Insurance for Condominium Reconstruction," 5 *Condo Management* No. 57, at 28 (May 1995). Level of risk associated with errors and omissions insurance for reconstruction is often lumped with the risk associated with new condominium design and construction. However, errors and omissions insurance costs for reconstruction projects should not be included in the exclusions for condominium design. Errors and omissions insurance costs for reconstruction projects should be reconsidered for responsible reconstruction firms because risk for reconstruction is substantially less than for new construction.

There are many reasons why risks for reconstruction of a defectively built condominium are less than for a new condo project. A condominium reconstruction project is usually well-defined and limited. Reconstruction projects are often inspected, analyzed, and dissected extensively by qualified professionals. When ready for reconstruction, more is known about the project than when the project was originally constructed. Furthermore, new defects discovered during reconstruction are not part of the responsibility of the reconstruction designer or contractor. Also, chances of repeat failure are greatly minimized by the analysis included in the reconstruction effort. In addition, a designer in a reconstruction program often has an additional role as manager, while observation of construction is rarely part of the designer's service for new condominium construction. After defect litigation, association management is more likely to correct future problems while they are still small instead of letting them grow into larger ones.

Insurance carriers could ensure that their interest will be protected in a reconstruction project by requiring a comprehensive reconstruction plan; qualifying professionals associated with the project; encouraging designer observation; and demanding that a list of defects be agreed upon and documented. Aharoni, "Misconceptions Concerning E & O Insurance for Condominium Reconstruction," 5 *Condo Management* No. 57, at 28 (May 1995).

Although the architect's traditional function as an agent of the owner to implement the plans and specifications is generally within professional liability coverage, less conventional roles for an architect such as construction manager, design/builder, or supervisor are often specifically excluded. Construction exclusions leave the execution of the design to the contractor. This also excludes design/build activities. Design/builders tend to be contractors with staff architects. However, a contractor's ordinary CGL coverage does not cover design/build risks either. The design/builder needs special coverage such as contractor's design professional liability insurance. Chemers & Knox, "When Designs Don't Work: Professional Liability Coverage of Architects and Engineers," 15 *Construction Lawyer* No. 1, at 17 (Jan. 1995).

CHAPTER 4

WE HAVE BEEN SUED. IS THAT ATTORNEY CHOSEN BY MY INSURANCE COMPANY MY FRIEND OR MY FOE? DO I NEED MY OWN?

§ 4.2 Sources of Conflict: Policy Language Covering Errors, Omissions, or Negligent Acts

Page 66, add after third sentence:

Many activities of the designer may not be included in professional liability insurance. In *Bell Lavalin Inc. v. Simcoe & Erie General Insurance Co.,* 61 F.3d 742 (9th Cir. 1995), the Ninth Circuit Court of Appeals determined that a $7 million award against a design/builder that had been defended by the design/builder's professional liability insurer was not covered by the professional liability policy. Bell Lavalin subcontracted with Conam Alaska for construction services related to the design and building of several crude oil tanks. After the work fell behind schedule and went over budget, Conam requested a six-month time extension. Bell Lavalin refused the time extension and Conam left the job site. Bell later terminated Conam, which sued Bell for its cost overruns. Bell tendered the defense of Conam's claim to its professional liability insurer, Simcoe and Erie General Insurance Company. The insurer accepted the defense with a reservation of its right to later deny coverage. Conam was awarded more than $7 million on its breach of contract and abandonment of contract claims by the court.

Bell Lavalin's professional liability insurance policy required the insurer, Simcoe and Erie, to pay Bell's damages for performance of professional services as architect, engineer, land surveyor, project manager, construction manager, and inspector. The court of appeals determined that the professional liability insurer would be liable for the breach of contract and abandonment award if three requirements were met. First, that a judgment was for damages. Second, that the liability for the damages resulted from Bell Lavalin's performance of professional service for others. Finally, that the liability was caused by an error, an omission, or a negligent act. The court determined that Conam's award related to the value of the unpaid work that Conam had performed, rather than from the failure to grant a time extension. As a result, the court concluded that the third requirement needed to trigger coverage under Simcoe and Erie's policy—that the liability was caused by an error, an omission, or a negligent act—was not met because the cause of the damage was that Conam had performed 87 percent of the work and Bell Lavalin had refused to pay. The court determined that even if Bell Lavalin had not refused the time extension, Bell would still have owed Conam the value of the 87 percent of the work completed.

§ 4.3 —Was Claim Made During the Policy Period?

Page 67, add after first paragraph:

In *Brown Daltas & Associates, Inc. v. General Accident Insurance Co.,* 48 F.3d 30 (1st Cir. 1995), the designer initially operated as a partnership when it contracted with the Saudi Arabian Monetary Authority (SAMA) to design branch bank buildings in various Saudi cities. The designer completed its work in 1978, but by that time it was incorporated. The designer then formed a joint venture with a Saudi company to administer and supervise the construction of the banks. In 1983, the joint venture and SAMA entered into a second supervision contract. From 1979 through 1986, the joint venture was covered for liability arising out of its supervision of the banks' construction under consulting engineer's indemnity policies issued by the underwriters at Lloyd's of London. From 1978 through 1985, the insured and, in some cases, the joint venture was insured for liability arising out of the design of the banks under various professional liability policies. The policies were written on a claims-made basis and provided coverage only for claims first made against the insured during the coverage period. The policies also contained a discovery clause which required that notice be given to the insurer when the designer first became aware of circumstances that might subsequently give rise to a claim.

At some point between 1978 and 1981, when the banks were under construction, the contractor advised the designer that the heating, ventilation, and air conditioning system was defectively designed. Following meetings with the contractor, the insured notified the insurer of the possibility of a claim at one branch bank being built. In April 1982, the joint venture also gave written notice to another insurer of the possibility of claims and listed the date of discovery as October 1981. However, no claim was actually made against the insured or the joint venture prior to the insureds' completion of its design and supervision work in November 1986. The underlying claim made by SAMA was raised in April 1987, five years after the expiration of the policy coverage triggered by the discovery clause.

The First Circuit reversed the judgment entered for the designer, holding that it had failed to establish that the contractor's complaints of the mechanical systems (discovery) first occurred during the policy period and that it had complied with the discovery provisions.

CHAPTER 5

LIABILITY ON THE CONTRACT

§ 5.4 Formational Issues and Incorporation by Reference

Page 83, add after carryover paragraph:

In *Chesapeake Paper Products Co. v. Stone & Webster Engineering Corp.*, 51 F.3d 1229 (4th Cir. 1995), Stone & Webster was hired to design the expansion of a paper mill. It sent to Chesapeake Paper its contract form that provided design services would be provided consistent with "good engineering practices." Chesapeake Paper never signed Stone & Webster's form contract.

Chesapeake later sent a purchase order to Stone & Webster that stated, "all materials and articles covered by this order . . . will be free from defects in material and/or workmanship, and merchantable." Stone & Webster never rejected the terms of Chesapeake's purchase order. Later, Stone & Webster and Chesapeake signed an amendment that modified the Stone & Webster form contract as referenced in Chesapeake Paper's purchase order.

In a subsequent dispute over Stone & Webster's standard of care, the jury concluded that the amendment modified Chesapeake's purchase order rather than Stone & Webster's form contract, imposing a higher standard than that presented in Stone & Webster's form contract. Clearly, designers should insist on one clear and complete contract document that is signed by all of the parties. Instead of beginning work, Stone & Webster should have waited until a complete contract agreement had been exchanged.

Questions can also arise as to fundamental issues such as the amount of fees. Designers who get ahead of the contracting process and work without a written contract may discount their earned fee in order to avoid litigation to enforce an oral contract. Architects often work with clients for long periods, expecting that contracts eventually will be executed and a fair fee paid. The experience of Bermello, Ajamil & Partners, Inc., Miami, illustrates the designer's risk: the Broward County Commission had never approved changes to an original contract to design parking and baggage-handling areas to match the growth of the assignment to a $4.3 million fee.

"Designer Settles Airport Fee Flap," 237 *Engineering News-Record* 17 (No. 21, Nov. 18, 1996).

Every firm working on the airport had provided service without a formal contract, said a partner in the firm. Because airports must respond quickly to changing economic conditions, it works against the owner's interests for a project to be put on hold until a consultant's contract is approved. It made sense for the airport authority to continue with design at the time, and the designers were assured verbally that the firm would be paid. But Broward County regulations required county commissioners to approve contract increases, and approval can take months. If a designer declines to work without a contract, it may be quickly ostracized and cut from consideration for the next airport project. Although the county eventually paid the designers $4.1 million ($200,000 less than the architect requested), much of the airport design plan will probably never be used.

Page 83, add after second sentence in first full paragraph:

Failure to list the documents intended to be incorporated and ambiguity among the contract clauses were determined to have eliminated the standard general conditions in *Atlantic Mutual Insurance Co. v. Merton Engineering & Construction Co.,* 83 F.3d 897 (7th Cir. 1996). Merton, the construction manager, executed an AIA Standard Form of Agreement Between Owner and Construction Manager, Document A101/CM, with Intercommunity Charitable Trust (ICT). In a dispute over damages arising from a fire, Merton claimed that the AIA's Construction Management Edition Standard General Conditions, Document A201/CM, had been incorporated into the ITC contract. Atlantic Mutual Insurance claimed that the General Conditions had not been made a part of the contract.

The first page of A101/CM states that it is "intended to be used in conjunction with AIA Documents A201/CM," but the court found that that language simply informs the user that the American Institute of Architects has created a document that can be used in conjunction with A101/CM to provide general conditions. Further, the introductory language or recitals are not a binding part of a contract unless expressly made so in the operative portion of the contract.

The court explained that the contract's Article 1 did not incorporate the disputed general conditions because the provision simply indicated that the parties *could* incorporate any other conditions they desired into their contract. Article 1 provided:

> The Contract Documents consist of this Agreement, the Conditions of the Contract (General, Supplementary and other Conditions), the Drawings, the

> Specifications, all Addenda Issued prior to and all Modifications issued after execution of this Agreement. These form the contract, and all are as fully a part of the Contract as if attached to this Agreement or repeated herein. An enumeration of the Contract Documents appears in Article 7.

The court also explained that Article 7.1 stated that the terms of the agreement were defined in the "Conditions" of the contract. This suggested that the parties had relied on some document entitled "Conditions of the Contract," but because there was no reference to "General Conditions," the intent was unclear.

The court found another ambiguity in Article 7.2, which said:

> the Contract Documents, which constitute the entire agreement between the Owner and the Contractor, are listed in Article 1 and, except for Modifications issued after execution of this Agreement, are enumerated as follows. (List below the Agreement, the Conditions of the Contract [General, Supplementary and Other Conditions], the Drawings, the Specifications, and any Addenda and accepted alternates, showing page or sheet numbers in all cases and dates where applicable.)

The parties listed 23 documents, but they did not list the A201/CM General Conditions or the Agreement. Although the court found that the omission of the General Conditions did not necessarily mean that the parties did not intend to incorporate the General Conditions, the court did find the intent of the provision unclear. Although Article 7.2 stated that the Contract Documents were those documents identified in Article 1, Article 1 referred back to Article 7. Because Article 7.2 indicated that all the documents constituting the parties' agreement would be listed, including the A101/CM Agreement, the omission suggested either that the Agreement was not included or that the list was not exhaustive. The court concluded that the list was not exhaustive because to omit the Agreement would be "silly." As a result of the ambiguities in the A101/CM, the court concluded that the contract was ambiguous as to whether the General Conditions were incorporated.

§ 5.7 Third-Party Concerns

Page 86, add at beginning of note 23:

Jim's Excavating Serv. v. HKM Assocs., 878 P.2d 248 (Mont. 1994) (contractor may recover purely economic loss against an engineer when the design professional knew or should have foreseen that contractor was at risk in relying on the information designer supplied).

Page 87, add after "Illinois" in note 26:

Fireman's Fund Ins. Co. v. SEC Donohue, Inc., 176 Ill. 2d 160, 679 N.E.2d 1197 (1997) (economic loss doctrine bars recovery in tort against engineers for purely economic losses).

Page 87, add before "Virginia" in note 26:

Texas (Thomson v. Espey Huston & Assocs., Inc., 899 S.W.2d 415 (Tex. Ct. App. 1995) (any negligence by engineering consulting firm in performing inspection contract caused no injury beyond economic loss to subject of contract itself, which, pursuant to the economic loss rule, did not give rise to tort cause of action)).

Page 87, add to carryover paragraph:

The trend seems to be to expand recovery for economic loss and to ease the limitation of the economic loss rule as it applies to designers. Bell, "Eroding Foundations: Increased Liability of Construction Design Professionals," 32 *Procurement Lawyer* 3 (No. 2, Winter 1997).

Page 87, add at beginning of note 28:

Thomson v. Espey Huston & Assocs., Inc., 899 S.W.2d 415 (Tex. Ct. App. 1995) (any negligence by engineering consulting firm in performing inspection contract caused no injury beyond economic loss to subject of contract itself, which, pursuant to the economic loss rule, did not give rise to tort cause of action).

Page 87, add to note 30:

DIC Commercial Construction Corp. v. Broward County, 668 So. 2d 697, 1996 Fla. App. LEXIS 1619 (1996) (contract and facts showed sufficienct supervisory control in the architect to permit contractors claim for negligence to proceed under A.R. Moyer Inc. v. Graham).

§ 5.8 Statutes of Limitation Considerations

Page 89, add to note 38:

Republic Contracting Corp. v. S.C. Dept. of Highways and Pub. Transp., 332 S.C. 197, 503 S.E.2d 761, 1998 S.C. App. LEXIS 88 (1998) (Contractor sued owner, DOT, and engineer for damages from defective bridge design. Because the discovery rule applied, the cause of action accrued when contractor encountered construction and installation problems in the field. The claim against the owner did not accrue until Republic had exhausted its remedies under the contract or Republic was denied payment under the contract on final completion. Even though the claims arose from the same set of operative facts, the claims against the engineer were time-barred, while the claim against the owner was not).

Page 90, add to note 41:

O'Reilly v. Dock, 929 S.W.2d 297 (Mo. Ct. App. 1996) (in Missouri, the time in which an action for breach of contract may be brought begins when "the damage resulting . . . is sustained and is capable of ascertainment." Ascertainment of some damage or injury is all that is required to commence the running of the statute of limitations; ascertainment occurs when a person has some awareness that either an injury has been suffered or that another person has committed a legal wrong that may result in harm. When the breach is not known and there is delayed manifestation of damage resulting from the breach that cannot reasonably be discovered by a lay person, "capable of ascertainment" applies if some knowledge of the damage was known five years before the suit was filed, even though the specific breach of contract was not known; thereafter, a lawsuit that seeks recovery of any resulting damage may be precluded. If the manifestation of the defect is not known or is not reasonably ascertainable by a lay person, damages may be recovered as long as a lawsuit is initiated within five years). See § **19.5**.

Page 91, add at end of section:

The New York Court of Appeals dismissed a lawsuit brought by a public library against a general contractor, an architect, and an engineer for damage from a burst pipe, which occurred 15 years after construction of the building, as time-barred by the six-year statute of limitations for breach of contract actions. *City School District v. Hugh Stubbins & Associates, Inc.*, 85 N.Y.2d 535, 650 N.E.2d 399 (1995). Recognizing the potential statute of limitations problem, the library owner based the lawsuit on negligence rather than breach of contract, contending that because it was not the party that had contracted with the contractor and the designers, the applicable statute of limitations should not start to run until the date the pipe burst and should be governed by the 3-year statute of limitations for negligence. The court disagreed and dismissed the lawsuit because, although the library owner was not the contracting party, the relationship was the "functional equivalent" of a contractual relationship; the library owner was the intended beneficiary of the contract.

AIA form B141 provides at ¶ 9.3 that substantial completion begins the statute of limitations for claims against the designer. This clause eliminates the uncertainty of the "discovery" rule, which may extend the potential liability of the architect indefinitely, subject only to any applicable statute of repose. *Oriskany Central School District v. Edmond J. Booth Architects,* 206 A.D.2d 896, 615 N.Y.S. 2d 160 (1994), enforced this provision. Because virtually all states hold that the parties to an agreement are free to structure their own affairs and can freely contract for different limitations periods applicable to their own particular needs, including shortening the otherwise applicable statutory time period, it is highly probable that a limitations accrual provision that does not shorten the statutory time period will be enforced between the parties by most courts. Wright & King, "Design Professional Liability: Applicability of the A.I.A. Contractual Limits on the Operation of the Statute of Limitations to Members of the Design Team Not in Privity with the Owner," 15 *Construction Lawyer* No. 4, at 43 (Nov. 1995).

It is common practice for the architect to engage special consultants to assist in the design. These commonly are structural engineers, mechanical engineers, and electrical engineers. Can an owner who discovers an alleged latent defect chargeable to the work done by the architect's consultant avoid the limitations provision in the architect's contract by suing the consulting engineer in negligence? At present, no case is known to discuss this issue.

The consultants enter into their contracts with the architect in express reliance on the covenants and promises that were made between the owner and architect, both with respect to dispute resolution and with respect to the statute of limitations. The architect's consultants are privy to the promises of the owner and entitled to rely on them as demonstrated by reference to both the architect's prime agreement in the consultant's contract and the ability of the architect to warrant the performance obligations of the owner to the engineer. The architect may compel the owner to furnish property and topographic surveys; data pertaining to existing improvements and trees; information on service and utility lines; soil consultants; test bodings; and other data. Similarly, the engineer relies on the owner's promise to pay the architect when it agrees to condition its own receipt of payment on the owner's fulfillment of this promise. The consultant's agreement accepts and repeats the limitations/accrual provisions of the prime agreement. *Id.* at 44.

Three legal theories support the position that the owner may not avoid the accrual of limitations provisions by a direct suit against the consultant in negligence.

1. Estoppel Based on the Contractual Relationships of the Parties. When there is a close contractual relationship of the entities involved in a dispute and the allegations are intimately founded in, and intertwined with, underlying contractual obligations, the courts have refused to allow a claimant in the contractual chain to assert the lack of a direct written contract as a defense to defendants in the chain without contracts with the claimant. 44–45 (citing *Hughes Masonry Co. v. Greater Clark County School Building Corp.,* 659 F.2d 836 (7th Cir. 1981) (relationship among masonry contractor, owner, and construction manager so intertwined that masonry contractor could not deny arbitration with construction manager even though no arbitration agreement existed); *McBro Planning & Development Co. v. Triangle Electrical Construction Co.,* 741 F.2d 342 (11th Cir. 1984) (electrical contractor could not deny arbitration of its claim against construction manager because of absence of arbitration clause with owner because of intimate relation among electrical contractor, construction manager, and owner); *Dunn Construction Co. v. Sugar Beach Condominium Ass'n, Inc.,* 760 F. Supp. 1479 (S.D. Ala. 1991) (bank bound to arbitrate dispute with contractor because of contractor's arbitration clause with owner)).

   Language in the contract in *Hughes Masonry, McBro Planning,* and *Dunn* stated that nothing in the contract created a contractual relationship with any third party, but the contract was not deemed to prevent the application of estoppel and the terms of the contract against the claimant.

   The principles applied in *Hughes Masonry, McBro,* and *Dunn* apply with equal force to members of the architect's design team in contractually time-barred actions brought by the owner.
2. The application of equitable estoppel precluding the owner from asserting that it is not bound by the provisions of the consultant's contract is appropriate and fully justified by the owner's status as a third-party beneficiary. The owner is a creditor beneficiary of the consultant's contract because performance of the consultant's promises satisfies the duty of the architect to the owner to provide engineering services. Wright & King, "Design Professional Liabil-

ity: Applicability of the A.I.A. Contractual Limits on the Operation of the Statute of Limitations to Members of the Design Team Not in Privity with the Owner," 15 *Construction Lawyer* No. 4, at 46 (Nov. 1995).

3. Through Article 9 of A.I.A.'s B141 Agreement Between the Owner and the Architect, the owner agrees and consents to the assignment of the engineering portion of the architect's contract to the consultant. Furthermore, the "flow down" provision in paragraph 1.1.2 of the AIA's standard form consultant's agreement C141 requires the consultant to "perform the services undertaken according to this Agreement with the Architect in the same manner and to the same extent that the Architect is bound by the attached Prime Agreement to perform such services for the Owner." *Id.* at 47.

4. Accruing the statute of limitations as of the date of substantial completion actually allows the owner substantially more than the applicable limitations time period to check the work product of the architect and the design team. The design documents are generally completed prior to the start of construction, which, in most cases, is months or years prior to substantial completion. The design team's work product is not hidden and covered, but is open and apparent by reason of the plans and specifications that they produce. *Id.*

§ 5.12 Claims Based on Cost Estimating Problems

Page 93, add after second paragraph:

In *C.L. Maddox Inc. v. Benham Group, Inc.,* 88 F.3d 592 (8th Cir. 1996), Maddox, a general contractor, asked Benham, an engineering firm, to provide drawings and specifications to bid for a design-build project to remodel a coal-processing system at an electric power plant. Without a written agreement, Benham provided Maddox with estimated quantities, along with necessary design drawings, from which Maddox prepared and submitted its proposal. Maddox's design-build proposal was accepted by the owner. Maddox later contracted with Benham to perform the design work for the project.

Maddox's work overran the bid quantities; the project also experienced delays and other inefficiencies due to design omissions. In addition to delays and overruns, the new computerized control system never performed as required and was replaced by the owner. Further, there were defects and deficiencies in Maddox's work.

At trial, Maddox sought damages for breach of contract for Benham's failure to guard Maddox against defects and deficiencies in Maddox's work, for Maddox's overruns caused by Benham's bid quantities, and for other claims. The jury found for Maddox and against Benham. Benham appealed, arguing that the court erred in not setting aside that portion of the judgment relating to Benham's failure to protect Maddox against its own deficiencies and that Benham had never warranted the accuracy of the take-off quantities.

The appellate court ruled that Benham had warranted the accuracy of the bidding information because it had repeatedly assured Maddox that it was qualified to do the work and that it had the expertise and resources to perform satisfactorily. Further, Maddox's witnesses had testified that Maddox had had to rely on Benham's bidding information to bid the project because only Benham knew what was to be designed.

Page 95, add after carryover paragraph:

At subparagraph 2.1.7.6, if bids come in high, the architect must, at no extra charge, revise the documents so as to generate bids that come in within the owner's budget. The value of this clause to owners is considerably reduced by subparagraph 2.1.7.3, which gives the architect unilateral control over the "materials, equipment, component systems and types of construction" to be included in the contract documents, as well as the ability to make "reasonable" unilateral adjustments in project scope. Owners will want to exert considerably more control over the redesign process if this purported risk-sharing is to have any real value. P. Cobey, "*The New B141: An Owner's Manual*, 3 *The Construction Forum News* 2, at 3 (No. 2, Jan. 1998).

§ 5.15 Insurance Coverage Considerations

Page 96, add after second sentence in section:

For example, in *Hurst-Roche Engineers, Inc. v. Commercial Union Insurance Co.,* 51 F.3d 1336 (7th Cir. 1995), Quality Granite sued Hurst-Roche, an engineering firm engaged to design and administrate the construction of a 22-building apartment complex, alleging that a letter written by an engineer contained defamatory statements imputing a lack of ability to perform its trade or business. At the time, Hurst-Roche had two commercial liability policies. The engineer tendered the defense of the action to the insurers. The insurers disclaimed coverage and refused to provide a defense. Hurst-Roche paid for the defense of the libel suit by Quality Granite and commenced an action against the insurers. Quality Granite recovered $430,000 in compensatory damages and $100,000 in punitive damages at trial of the libel suit.

Both of Hurst-Roche's commercial liability policies covered *personal injuries,* which was defined in the policies to include libel and slander. However, the policies also contained a professional liability exclusion clause. Although the language was different in each policy, both clauses excluded from coverage claims arising from the rendering or failure to render professional engineering services.

The court in Hurst-Roche determined that the letter was written by the engineer as part of the professional services provided to the owner; therefore, it was not covered by the commercial liability policies. The court concluded that the insurers were correct to deny coverage.

§ 5.16 Considerations Regarding Confusion in Jury Instructions

Page 98, add at end of section:

A judge in a state court in Oakland, California, instructed the jury that under the typical American Institute of Architects agreement, the designer was a fiduciary to the building owner, whose duties went beyond informing the client of problems the designer had observed and required the designer to see that the problems were corrected. A fiduciary responsibility goes beyond a professional standard based on how other professionals would act in a similar situation, or a fitness standard under which negligence need not be proved but only that the desired results were not achieved. A fiduciary standard imposes a greater liability on a design professional and changes the traditional relationship between architects, engineers, and clients. "Jury's $7-Million Verdict Based on Designer's 'Fiduciary' Role," 238 *Engineering News-Record* 11 (No. 26, June 30, 1997).

§ 5.17 Considerations Regarding Indemnity, Limitations of Liability, and Exculpatory Provisions

Page 98, add to note 72:

National Hydro Sys. v. M.A. Mortensen, 529 N.W.2d 690 (Minn. 1995) (indemnification clause in engineer's agreement not favored and must be clearly expressed; because clause was equivocal as to whether it applied to claims occasioned by indemnitee's own negligence, subcontractor claim against engineer for negligent preparation of equipment specifications was not covered by indemnity).

Page 99, add at end of section:

Ambiguities may also allow a court to ignore a limitation of liability clause. In *CRS Sirrine, Inc. v. Dravo Corp.,* 445 S.E.2d 782 (Ga. Ct. App. 1994); 464 S.E.2d 897 (Ga. Ct. App. 1995), Dravo, a construction company, agreed to jointly pursue a United States Navy contract to construct a large, technically complex power plant at the Norfolk Navy Shipyard in Virginia with Sirrine, an engineering firm. Sirrine prepared the technical proposal, including quantity estimates, and Dravo prepared the bid based on Sirrine's proposal and quantities. The Sirrine-Dravo Joint Venture was awarded the contract.

The power plant was a design-build project. The design-builder's bid was submitted on the basis of preliminary design and engineering done by the bidders. The detailed design and engineering work was to be done after the award of the contract on a fast-track basis as the project was constructed.

Construction cost $30 million more than anticipated. Numerous changes in the project had to be made as the result of problems with Sirrine's design that delayed completion of the project and increased the cost of the work. Dravo sued Sirrine for $12.5 million for breach of contract and fiduciary duties, including material overruns that far exceeded the quantities in the technical proposal.

The trial court found that Sirrine had breached its contractual and fiduciary duties by failing to provide sufficient, accurate information on which to base the bid; failing to make reasonable efforts to design the project within budgeted quantities; failing to track quantities in its own design; and failing to promptly notify its partners that budgeted quantities would be exceeded.

Sirrine believed that, under § 9.3 of the joint venture agreement, it was not responsible for any damage resulting from increases in material quantities. Section 9.3 stated:

> Notwithstanding any of the foregoing, Sirrine shall have no risk, liability, or accumulation will occur of error and omission charges for construction material quantity variations if the actual quantities are different from those in the bid to the Navy. W/L will provide Sirrine with budget quantities for all functional areas of Project and Sirrine's detail design will make every reasonable effort to stay within these quantities within the requirements of the Prime Contract. W/L will be notified promptly if Sirrine believes quantities will be exceeded.

The court of appeals found the first sentence of § 9.3 ambiguous on its face. That provision did not shield Sirrine from all responsibility as to increases in construction material quantities even if such increase were caused by errors or omissions in its prebid or postbid design and engineering work.

After the trial court awarded Dravo $5,518,000, Sirrine twice appealed the judgment's calculation. Sirrine challenged the manner in which the amount of the award was determined, claiming that the award should have been limited to specific increases in costs that could be attributed solely to specific breaches of Sirrine, because the trial court had found that some of the cost overruns were caused by Dravo. The appellate court ruled that Dravo had shown the damages with a reasonable degree of certainty and had satisfactorily demonstrated the portion attributable to Sirrine.

§ 5.19 Site Visits

Page 99, add to note 75:

The 1997 edition of AIA B141 permits the parties to limit the visits to the site during construction administration in article 2.8.1.

Page 100, add after "But see" in note 81:

Gables CVF, Inc. v. Bahr, Vermeer & Haecker Architect, Ltd., 506 N.W.2d 706 (Neb. 1993) (AIA Doc. B141 para. 1.5.5 (1977), requiring only periodic site visits, does not absolve the architect from liability for a breach of the architect's contractual duty to inform the owner of deviations from the building plans when the architect has agreed to make periodic observations, if the architect had a duty to report deviations from the architect's plans. Deletion of paragraph 1.5 from contract except for subparagraph

1.5.5 and substitution of fee for "observation of construction" did not define the precise nature of such duties, and factual question existed regarding contractual obligation that architect understood to observe construction of condominium units.).

Page 100, add to note 81:

C.L. Maddox Inc. v. Benham Group, Inc., 88 F.3d 592 (8th Cir. 1996) (designer was not responsible for not guarding contractor against defects and deficiencies in designer's work, despite provisions in contractor-designer contract that required designer to keep contractor informed of the progress and quality of the work, and to endeavor to guard contractor against defects and deficiencies in the contractor's work, because contract also included a provision that designer shall not be responsible for construction means, methods, techniques, sequences or procedures, or for acts or omissions of contractor or its subcontractors. Court found that designer had duty to visit the site and make recommendations to contractor, but did not impose duty to guarantee that contractor would not make any errors).

§ 5.20 Means and Methods

Page 101, add to note 84:

C.L. Maddox Inc. v. Benham Group, Inc., 88 F.3d 592 (8th Cir. 1996) (designer was not responsible for not guarding contractor against defects and deficiencies in designer's work, despite provisions in contractor-designer contract that required designer to keep contractor informed of the progress and quality of the work, and to endeavor to guard contractor against defects and deficiencies in the contractor's work, because contract also included a provision that designer shall not be responsible for construction means, methods, techniques, sequences, or procedures, or for acts or omissions of contractor or its subcontractors. Court found that designer had duty to visit the site and make recommendations to contractor, but did not impose duty to guarantee that contractor would not make any errors).

CHAPTER 6

DESIGN PROFESSIONAL'S LIABILITY TO THE CONTRACTOR

§ 6.6 Comparative Fault in a Contract Case

Page 110, add to note 42:

But see Gateway W. Ry. v. Morrison Metalweld Process Corp., 46 F.3d 860 (8th Cir. 1995) (comparative fault extends to contract case when issue of plaintiff's mitigation of damages is at issue).

Page 110, add after second full paragraph:

However, in *Gateway Western Railway v. Morrison Metalweld Process Corp.,* 46 F.3d 860 (8th Cir. 1995), the federal court permitted comparative fault to be used in a claim against a welding contractor for defective repair of track. The railroad had brought suit for both breach of contract and negligence for the contractor's defective work that had caused a train to derail. The federal court held that comparative fault could also be used to assess the damages in the breach of contract claim. The Eighth Circuit Court of Appeals stated frankly that it was uncertain whether the Missouri Supreme Court would broadly extend comparative fault to contract damages, but decided to do so anyway.

§ 6.9 — Consequential Damages

Page 111, add to note 46:

Stonecipher v. Mitchell, 655 So. 2d 1381 (La. Ct. App. 1995) (jury awarded $25,000 in nonpecuniary damages to homeowner. Whether gratification of some nonpecuniary interest is principal object of a contract is question of fact; jury was not clearly wrong in determining that not only was Stonecipher's intellectual enjoyment the principal or exclusive purpose of contract to build residence, but also whether designer or contractor knew or should have known it. Verdict of jury affirmed).

§ 6.10 —Economic Damages

Page 112, add at beginning of note 48:

Boston Inv. Property No. 1 State v. Burman, 658 A.2d 515 (R.I. 1995) (building purchaser sued general contractor in negligence for cost to remedy defects and the additional depreciation in the value of the building. Shortly following the purchase of building from developer, Boston Investment learned that the windows of the building leaked when it rained and that erosion problems were present with the parking lot. Rhode Island Supreme Court held that in absence of privity of contract with general contractor, subsequent purchaser of commercial office building in Rhode Island is not entitled to recover economic damages it alleges were proximately caused by negligence of general contractor).

Page 112, add to note 51:

Thomson v. Espey Huston & Assocs., Inc., 899 S.W.2d 415 (Tex. Ct. App. 1995) (to extent that alleged inadequacies resulting from engineering consulting firm's allegedly negligent performance of contract to perform variety of engineering and design services in connection with construction of apartment complex caused damage to parts of property beyond contract, such negligence would give rise to tort clam; firm's alleged negligence in designing drainage system and testing soil quality had allegedly caused damage to other parts of apartment complex, specifically resulting in cracking walls, doors that would not fit properly, mildew, standing water, shifting, and formation of water pools in one area of complex, blocking street and spilling into adjacent property).

Page 113, add after carryover paragraph:

However, in *Edgeworth Construction v. N.D. Lea & Assoc.*, [1993] 3 S.C.R. 206, 12 C.L.R. (2d) 161, [1993] 8 W.W.R. 129, 83 B.C.L.R. (2d) 145, 107 D.L.R. (4th) 169, the Supreme Court of Canada took a general look at the way the construction industry conducts its business and allowed a contractor to brings its claims against a designer if the designer prepared the bid documents negligently and caused the contractor financial loss. The Canadian Supreme Court found the following policy reasons permitted the contractor's appeal:

- if the designer had no liability to the contractor, contractors would be obliged to do their own engineering and each bidder would be obliged to repeat a process already undertaken by the designer;
- from an economic point of view, it makes more sense for one engineering firm to do the engineering work and for the contractors to rely on that work. In addition, designers may protect themselves by a clear disclaimer of liability;
- the risk of liability to third parties for design error will be reflected in the cost of the engineers' services to the owner and that was much better than requiring the owner to pay indirectly for the additional engineering which all bidders would be forced to perform;
- in the typically short period allowed for the filing of bids, the contractor would have to do the work that took engineers months or even years and this would be an almost impossible task.

As a result, the Canadian Supreme Court imposed a major new liability on architects and engineers for policy reasons that were based on how the court perceived how the construction industry operated. P. Sandori, "*Lost Money on a Project? Sue Somebody! Economic Loss in Construction Litigation in Canada*," 16 *Const. Law*. 30, at 34 (No. 3, July 1996).

Page 113, add at beginning of note 56:

Lippy v. Society Nat'l Bank, 100 Ohio App. 3d 37, 651 N.E.2d 1364 (1995) (any duty owed to land purchaser by consultant hired to perform environmental site assessment of property was one owed under contract with consultant, and thus there was no action in tort for economic losses suffered as a result of any alleged breach of contract).

Page 114, add after second full paragraph:

For example, the decision by the South Carolina Supreme Court in *Griffin Plumbing & Heating Co. v. Jordan, Jones & Goulding,* 463 S.E.2d 85 (S.C. 1995), found that the contractor could recover extra costs incurred in performing a contract with the County of Charleston, South Carolina, due to alleged false interpretations of the contract by the designer. The court reversed a summary judgment granted by the trial court in favor of the designer and held that the contractor could recover economic losses, if proven, for professional malpractice and breach of implied warranty. A careful reading of the decision reveals a fundamental misunderstanding of the nature of economic loss. It appears from the *Griffin* decision that the court treated economic loss as loss of money, as opposed to physical damage or personal injury, and did not recognize that economic loss means loss of expectation or failure to receive the benefit of one's bargain. "A breach of a duty which arises under the provisions of a contract between the parties must be redressed under contract, and a tort action will not lie." Bell, "Eroding Foundations: Increased Liability of Construction Design Professionals," 32 *Procurement Lawyer* 5 (No. 2, Winter 1997).

Notwithstanding the court's statement, it is difficult to understand what is a duty "which arises under the provisions of a contract" so that it must be "redressed under contract," because, at least in the construction arena, there appear not to be any decisions finding only a contractual duty. Every opinion in South Carolina in which a third-party action for economic loss arising from construction has been considered has found a breach of a general duty rather than a contractual duty, thus allowing maintenance of an action in tort. *Id.*

Page 114, add to note 60:

See also Tommy L. Griffin Plumbing & Heating Co. v. Jordan, Jones & Goulding, Inc., Op. No. 24328 (S.C. filed Oct. 16, 1995) (where the engineer designed the project for the county and supervised construction, facts supported a duty to the contractor (even in the absence of privity) not to negligently design or supervise the project and a refusal to apply economic loss rule).

§ 6.12 Site Safety and Workers' Injuries

Page 119, add after carryover paragraph:

The Engineers' Joint Contract Documents Committee (comprising the American Society of Civil Engineers (ASCE), the National Society of Professional Engineers, and the American Consulting Engineers Council) construction general conditions explicitly state that the owner and the engineer are not responsible for safety precautions and programs. The rationale behind these standard contract provisions is that the contractor—the party with authority and accountability who supervises and directs the work and controls the site—should have sole responsibility for ensuring safety. The American Institute of Architects' construction general conditions contain similar language. T. Smith,"*Site Safety: Rights, Risks and Responsibilities*," 68 *Civil Eng'g* 55, at 56 (No. 5, May 1998).

However, the proposed new version of the ASCE's policy says that a project owner should take a significant, if not leading, role in ensuring workers' safety on construction sites. According to the proposed policy statement, the owner must assign project safety duties to a specific organization or individual or retain that responsibility itself. The proposed policy also states that the owner should make prior safety performance a criterion in selecting a contractor and should monitor safety performance during construction. Critics of the revised policy said that requiring owners to assign responsibility for site safety will shift the burden to engineers, who often act as owners' representatives. "*Construction Site Safety: Whose Job Is It Anyway?*," 23 *ASCE News* 1 (No. 4, 1998).

Page 119, add at beginning of note 75:

Block v. Lohan Assocs., Inc., 159 Ill. 2d 583, 645 N.E.2d 207 (1993) (architect could not be held liable in negligence action arising when subcontractor's employee fell from ladder, based on its alleged failure to supervise and coordinate work of its consulting structural engineer, where contract documents limited architect's responsibility to design and determination as to design conformance, and did not extend to worker safety) (engineers hired to design precast concrete panels and their connections, and structural frame of building at construction project did not have duty to consider, during design stage, manner in which precast column covers and their welded connections could be appropriately erected; engineer's contract stated that it was responsible only for specifications pertaining to structural integrity of precast concrete and required no participation of engineer at construction project, and placed no duty on it to supervise construction means, manners, and methods); Ivanov v. Process Design Assocs., 267 Ill. App. 3d 440, 642 N.E.2d 711 (1993) (design professional who has been hired to perform usual on-site observation and construction management activities for project that it designed generally does not owe contractor's employees a duty to ensure safe jobsite conditions, but one must look to the contract to determine respective liability).

Page 119, add at beginning of note 76:

Ivanov v. Process Design Assocs., 267 Ill. App. 3d 440, 642 N.E. 2d 711 (1993) (fact that site construction manager that was also engineering firm agreed to act as agent or representative of the owner and be responsible for continuously inspecting or supervising the work of the contractor was sufficient to permit finding that it had authority coexistent with that of the owner to require that contractors comply with safety requirements and that it was thus responsible for safety conditions on the project) (language in manufacturing facility construction contract between owner and the engineering and design firm that imposed on the firm the "duty to supervise" could be found to mean that firm had assumed a duty to provide safe workplace to the contractors' employees).

Page 120, add to note 79:

Yocum v. City of Minden, 649 So. 2d 129 (La. Ct. App. 1995) (contractor's employee injured in excavation sued designer for failure to exercise due care to prevent dangerous condition; court found no legal duty because designer's contract with owner prohibited designer from advising on safety precautions and programs in connection with the construction).

Page 120, add to note 82:

But see Peck v. Horrocks Eng'g, 106 F.3d 949 (10th Cir. 1997) (despite limited support in other states, Utah would not impose duty on engineer for site safety based on knowledge of the unsafe condition and inaction, when engineer contractually declined to accept responsibility for work safety and did not in fact exercise control over worker safety at jobsite).

Page 120, add after second full paragraph:

As in *Balagna,* the New Jersey Supreme Court in *Carvalho v. Toll Bros. & Developers,* 278 N.J. Super. 451, 651 A.2d 492 (App. Div.), *certification granted,* 140 N.J. 326 (1995), *aff'd & remanded* 143 N.J. 565, 675 A.2d 209 (1996), ruled that a project engineer had a legal duty to exercise reasonable care for the safety of construction workers. It so held even though the contract made the contractor solely responsible for means and methods of construction, stated that the project engineers shall not have control over the construction means and methods or the contractor's safety precautions, and stated that the contractor "alone" shall be responsible for the safety and adequacy of equipment and methods, including OSHA compliance.

The New Jersey Supreme Court found the designer responsibility for safety on the jobsite because of an overlap between work-progress and work-safety. The court found that matters of construction safety bore directly on the engineer's contractual responsibility for supervising the progress of the work. The court reasoned that if safety conditions could affect work progress, the engineer had the authority and control to take or require corrective measures to address safety concerns. The court imposed a legal duty to exercise reasonable care for the safety of workers on a construction site when the engineer has responsibility for the progress of the work—but not for safety conditions—yet is aware of working conditions on the construction site that create a risk of serious injury to workers.

Page 121, add to note 83:

Yocum v. City of Minden, 649 So. 2d 129 (La. Ct. App. 1995) (contractor's employee injured in excavation sued designer for failure to exercise due care to prevent dangerous condition; court found that designer had moral duty to warn employee if it knew of existence of unreasonably dangerous condition, despite contract clause that prohibited designer from advising on safety precautions and programs in connection with the construction).

Page 121, add to note 85:

Suriano v. City of N.Y., 658 N.Y.S.2d 654 (App. Div. 1997) (New York appellate court found that engineer on municipal project did not owe duty to injured worker because engineer did not actually exercise control over site, even though engineer's contract with city provided that engineer was to inspect site and report safety violations like the one that caused plaintiff's injury).

Page 121, add after first full paragraph:

In *McAninch v. Robinson,* 942 S.W.2d 452 (Mo. Ct. App. 1997), McAninch died when a trench collapsed at a construction site. McAninch's survivors sued the architect, claiming that the architect was in charge of the manner and method of compaction of the fill; solving the settling and sinking problems of the building; designing and establishing specifications for the safe and proper methods of trench digging; notifying and warning workers about the dangers of working in a trench that was not braced or shored; and requiring use of safe methods in constructing the trench. The trial court granted the architect's summary judgment motion and the court of appeals affirmed. The court noted that one of the elements a plaintiff must establish in a negligence case is a legal duty to conform to a certain standard of conduct to protect others against unreasonable risks. The existence of a duty is a matter of law to be determined by the court. The architect submitted an affidavit and the contract with the owner, both of which indicated that the scope of work on the project did not include any direction of construction, including jobsite safety. Because McAninch had no evidence to the contrary, the court held that the architect owed no duty to McAninch.

In *Peck v. Horrocks Engineering,* 106 F.3d 949 (10th Cir. 1997), on the day of a trench collapse, a Horrocks Engineering employee helped decide what to do about a steel culvert that obstructed the path of the pipeline being laid. The decision was to dig the pipeline trench deeper to go under the culvert. Peck, an employee of the contractor, was working in a seven-foot trench about 20 feet from the culvert when the trench collapsed. In violation of OSHA regulations, the trench in which Peck was killed had been neither sloped nor shored. The fact that Horrocks was consulted about the trench that collapsed was not, in itself, sufficient to make the engineering firm liable for work safety, the court said.

In *Peck,* the engineering agreement between Horrocks and the water district explicitly disavowed any responsibility for maintaining worker safety on site. In addition, the construction contract specified that the contractor would be responsible for all safety precautions and required the contractor to carry appropriate insurance.

The court noted that there is a split of authority regarding whether an engineer who contractually assumes a responsibility to the owner for general supervision of a construction project thereby assumes a duty of care to the employees of the general contractor to supervise the safety of their working conditions. The minority rule imposes a standard of care, whereas the majority rule denies contractual liability. The federal court determined that Utah follows the majority rule. The court also found that the disavowal provision agreed to by Horrocks was added to the standard engineering form by the American Institute of Architects specifically to avoid liability under the minority rule. The court concluded that Utah would not impose a duty on an engineer on the basis of knowledge and inaction alone, when the engineer contractually declined to accept responsibility for worker safety and did not exercise control over worker safety at the jobsite.

§ 6.14 Contract Administration

Page 125, add to note 97:

C.L. Maddox Inc. v. Benham Group, Inc., 88 F.3d 592 (8th Cir. 1996) (designer was not responsible for guarding contractor against defects and deficiencies in designer's work, despite provisions in contractor-designer contract that required designer to keep contractor informed of the progress and quality of the work, and to endeavor to guard contractor against defects and deficiencies in the contractor's work, because contract also included a provision that designer shall not be responsible for construction means, methods, techniques, sequences, or procedures, or for acts or omissions of contractor or its subcontractors. Court found that designer had duty to visit site and make recommendations to contractor, but did not impose duty to guarantee that contractor would not make any errors).

Page 126, add to note 100:

DIC Commercial Construction Corp. v. Broward County, 668 So. 2d 697, 1996 Fla. App. LEXIS 1619 (1996) (contract and facts showed sufficient supervisory control in the architect to permit contractor's claim for negligence to proceed under A.R. Moyer Inc. v. Graham).

Page 127, add to note 104:

See also Dehnert v. Arrow Sprinklers, Inc., 705 P.2d 846 (Wyo. 1985) (construction contract specified brass sprinkler heads or an approved equal that any changes in the work, including the substitution, had to be approved by a written change order. Without written change order, contractor installed plastic sprinkler heads that had been indicated on a shop drawing approved by the architect but which the architect did not take specific exception to the substitution. The architect directed contractor to replace the heads. When contractor refused, the architect recommended the board terminate the contract. Contractor sued the architect for intentional interference with a contractual relationship. The court noted that the architect had a contractual duty to reject nonconforming work and to advise and protect the owner. The court held that no liability attached where an individual charged with protecting the interests of a third person justifiably acts to cause that person not to perform a contract. An architect who acts within the scope of its employment is not liable for advising an owner to terminate unless it acts with malice or bad faith. The court distinguished malice or bad faith from negligence, poor judgment, or inflexibility, and stated that failure to reject the plastic heads at the outset and resolution of the resulting impasse may have reflected negligence and poor judgment, but not malice or bad faith necessary to hold the architect liable); Waldinger Corp. v. CRS Group Engineers, Inc., 775 F.2d 781 (7th Cir. 1985) (contractor sued subcontractor for breach of contract after subcontractor was unable to supply specified sludge dewatering equipment. Subcontractor claimed impracticability of performance due to the engineer's intentional or negligent drafting of inordinately restrictive specifications. Contractor also sued the engineer for intentional interference with the subcontract because engineer unreasonably insisted on strict compliance by the subcontractor with the restrictive specifications. Contractor argued that the engineer, while performing its contractual duties, was not conditionally privileged to interfere with subcontracts. The court found designer possessed a conditional privilege to interfere with the principal's contract by enforcing specifications but declined to recognize a conditional privilege to enforce compliance with the same specifications in a subcontract. While holding that the engineer was conditionally privileged to interfere with the subcontract, the court remanded to determine whether the engineer's insistence on strict compliance with the restrictive specifications was intended to injure the subcontractor or to further the engineer's personal goals).

§ 6.15 Arbiter of Performance and Related Matters

Page 128, add after first full paragraph:

The owner's power to terminate under AIA A201, Paragraph 14.2.2, requires that the architect certify "that sufficient cause exists to justify such action." The design professional's influence on the decision to terminate carries with it enormous responsibility and the potential for professional liability. Commentators have suggested that the decision to terminate, although involving some issues for which the architect may be trained, requires legal expertise rather than design skill, and that it would be better to have the owner's attorney make the termination decision, especially if the architect's conduct is itself an issue in the termination. J. Sweet, Legal Aspects of Architecture, Engineering and the Construction Process 748 (5th ed. 1994). Under the current AIA forms, however, whether serving as arbiter or as representative of the owner, the design professional is inescapably intertwined in the termination process. M. Heley & M. Bloomquist, "The Design Professional's Role in Termination of the Contractor," 17 *Construction Lawyer* 3 (No. 2, Apr. 1997).

The AIA General Conditions Paragraph 14.2.2 explicitly acknowledges the architect's involvement in the termination process by conditioning the owner's right to terminate the contract on receipt of a certification by the architect that sufficient cause exists to terminate the contractor on the project. When determining whether delay constitutes a material breach, the design professional must examine not just the extent of the delay but also the cause of the delay. Delays caused by the owner, or other circumstances outside the contractor's control, could excuse the delay. The design professional should also consider whether the owner has waived its right to enforce any contract provisions regarding delay. Consenting to a delay or making progress payments without objecting to delays can be construed as a waiver of the owner's right to enforce the time provisions in the contract.

Termination would not be appropriate under these circumstances. Heley & Bloomquist at 5.

If the contract includes a substantial completion date and further states that time is of the essence, then the failure to finish by that date will be deemed a substantial breach and sufficient cause for termination. The contractor's abandonment of the project will also justify termination. Although it might seem a simple task, it is not always clear when an abandonment has occurred. The design professional should consider the contractor's motivation in leaving the project. A contractor who walks off the job for two weeks over a payment dispute may not have abandoned the project. *Id.*

Courts have found a contractor's failure to complete the work as required by the contract to be a material breach when the defects cannot be cured or when the defective work related to the essence of the contract. In evaluating a contractor's defective or nonconforming work, the design professional should consider not only the extent of the departure but also the number of errors. It appears that in most instances a breach will not be deemed substantial if there are still reasonable means to cure the default. *Id.*

The designer must articulate specifically and objectively the nature of the deficiency or deficiencies that are to be corrected. Failure to satisfy this requirement can be a defense to termination. Just as important, the design professional's notice can also create liability exposure for defamation or tortious interference with business relations if not handled appropriately.

Page 128, add after second full paragraph:

The contractor's deficiencies must be tied directly to the contract documents and explained in such a way that any reasonable person would understand what is deficient. Attaching a copy of meeting minutes that include a discussion of work deficiencies to a termination notice letter may fail to provide proper notice of the terms of default. Heley & Bloomquist at 9.

There are countless other ways a contractor may substantially breach its contract and permit owner termination. Some of the more common examples of substantial breaches include failure to pay suppliers; failure to respond to the architect's requests for information, thereby impairing other contractors' work; failure to obtain insurance when required by contract; and failure to remain within the designated budget. *Id.* at 6.

Most contractual default provisions do not require that there be a substantial or material breach to trigger a right of termination. Traditional contract law permits termination for any contract default, regardless of whether the default affects the essence of the contract or substantially alters the rights of the parties. However, the design professional should be aware that contractual default provisions will typically be narrowly construed, if possible, against termination. The owner/designer must follow the contract's procedural requirements to the letter to accomplish termination. The design professional must be satisfied that under any reasonable interpretation of the facts and the contract documents, there is no basis to contest that a default has occurred. If the parties dispute the facts supporting the default or if the contract provisions are susceptible to more than one meaning, the design professional should be cautious in certifying a default or recommending termination. *Id.*

The design professional should also be aware of the good faith requirement that pervades the entire termination process. Even if the contractor is in default, the owner or design professional may not use the termination process for retribution or other purposes. The designer must consider whether the owner caused or contributed to the breaches and whether the owner has waived its right to strictly enforce the contract. Before making these decisions, the design professional must analyze the contract documents, conduct an appropriate inquiry and investigation, and then make an impartial determination. It is absolutely critical that the design professional substantiate the conditions that support any potential termination, through photographs, letters, reports, or investigation by independent consultants. Heley & Bloomquist at 6–7.

Perhaps the best practice is for the design professional to keep its statements to a minimum, expressing only information that is necessary to identify the nonconforming work items and to describe what must be cured. Extraneous opinions should be avoided. If the design professional confines statements to matters within the scope of its work and if the statements are not knowingly false or made without any investigation to verify their truth or falsity, the design professional should be able to avoid liability to the contractor for its statements critical of the contractor's work that are made in the termination process. *Id.* at 10.

No recent cases have addressed whether an absolute privilege should apply when the design professional is acting in a quasi-judicial role in judging a contractor's work before a potential termination. A strong argument exists that the absolute privilege should apply if the design professional's decision is required at a time when the owner and contractor are engaged in litigation or where there is a bona fide threat of litigation. *Id.* at 11.

In *Ashco International, Inc. v. Westmore Shopping Center Associates,* 42 Va. Cir. 427, 1997 Va. Cir. LEXIS 158 (1997), the contractor alleged that architect caused delays in performance of the contract; failed and refused to approve proper change orders requested by contractor; entered incorrect information into minutes of all meetings concerning the status and quality of contractor's performance; and incorrectly certified that contractor breached the contract. The contractor claimed tortious interference and conspiracy to interfere with a contractual relationship.

The architect in *Ashco* had authority to act on behalf of the owner only to the extent provided in the contract. The contract established architect's duty to provide for administration of the contract, to review and certify amounts due to the contractor, to reject nonconforming work, to decide matters concerning performance under requirements of the contract, and to order minor and written changes to the work. The *Ashco* court found the acts attributable to the architect fell within the architect's duties to administrate the contract and approve changes to the work.

The court explained that tortious interference with contract and common-law conspiracy both require the presence of two or more persons acting to interfere with a valid contractual relationship or conspiring to accomplish an unlawful purpose, and that an architect acting within the scope of an agency could not constitute the second person necessary to state a claim. The court dismissed the contractor's claims for tortious interference with contract and conspiracy.

The contractor in *Ashco* had argued that the architect constituted a second person because the architect had an independent stake in achieving the conspiracy's objective. The court rejected application of the doctrine in the present case, however, because contractor had failed to allege any fact supporting the inference that the architect gained any direct personal benefit from the alleged conspiracy.

In *Kerr Contruction and Paving Co. v. Khazin, et. al.*, 961 S.W.2d 75, 1997 Mo. App. LEXIS 2079 (Mo. Ct. App. 1997), as a result of an inspector's report, a contractor was not permitted to finish its work under the contract. The court upheld the verdict in favor of the contractor and against an inspector and the inspector's supervisor who worked for the state Department of Transportation, finding that the evidence supported a reasonable inference that the inspectors had intentionally misled the city with an erroneous report designed to create problems for the contractor.

See also Somers Construction Co. v. Board of Education, 198 F. Supp. 732 (D.N.J. 1961) (architect tabulated the bids and alternates for a public construction contract and determined that a contractor other than Somers was the low bidder. After a notice to proceed was issued and work had been commenced, Somers advised the architect that there was an error in the tabulation, and Somers was in fact the low bider. The awarding authority rescinded the award, but reconsidered the previously selected alternates. Declining one alternate for which the price of the other contractor exceeded

Somers's price and reinstating the award to the other contractor as new "low" bidder. Somers alleged that the architect's initial mistabulation of bids and the architect's subsequent advice to the awarding authority constituted tortious interference with prospective economic advantage. The court dismissed the tortious interference claim because under the law of New Jersey, malice is an essential element for a toritious interference and Somers had failed to allege that the mistabulation was malicious. However, Somers did allege that the architect's advice was maliciously given, and the court declined to grant summary judgment on the factual issue of whether or not malice existed); *Ballou v. Basic Construction Co.*, 407 F.2d 1137 (4th Cir. 1967) (architect for hospital insisted on literal compliance with specification requiring a certain thickness of concrete over reinforcing steel in concrete columns. The architect rejected 41 of the first 50 columns installed by the subcontractor. In the course of the ensuing dispute, subcontractor went bankrupt. The trustee of the bankrupt subcontractor claimed that the architect's rejection of the columns constituted tortious interference with the contract between the subcontractor and the general contractor. The architect claimed quasi-judicial immunity, under contract provisions giving the architect the right to determine the acceptability of work, to reject defective work, and to have defective work replaced without charge. The court adopted the trial court's finding that the architect was immune from suit unless the plaintiff could show that fraud or bad faith motivated the decision and found the architects' decision to enforce literal compliance with the contract may have reflected poor judgment or excessive rigidity, but was no evidence or even suggestion that they were motivated by malice or bad faith); *Kecko Piping Co. v. Town of Monroe,* 172 Conn. 197, 374 A.2d 179 (1977) (subcontractor named in the general contractor's successful bid not accepted for a school construction project sued the architect for tortious interference with the contract between it and the general contractor. The architect's duties included obtaining bids, preparing, and awarding contracts. The architect and the owner had urged the subcontractor to provide information to substantiate its qualifications to perform the work because of concern about the subcontractor's ability to perform. The architect later advised the town to require the general contractor to select a different subcontractor. The Connecticut Supreme Court confirmed that the architect was under an obligation to advise the owner as to the suitability of contractors and subcontractors and accordingly enjoyed a qualified privilege under *Restatement (Second) of Torts*, § 772, and the architect had not exceeded the limits of its qualified privilege); *Joba Construction Co. v. Burns & Roe, Inc.,* 329 N.W.2d 760 (Mich. Ct. App. 1982) (contractor sued engineer for tortious interference with prospective economic relations because the engineer had wrongfully persuaded the owner not to award Joba the general contract on one project for which Joba submitted the lowest bid, and to have Joba removed as excavation and piling subcontractor on another project. The engineer's responsibilities included preparation of construction specifications, evaluation of bids, and recommendations of which contractor should be awarded contracts. The court determined that a presumption of good faith arose once qualified privilege was established, but that the presumption could be overcome with evidence of bad faith or dishonest purpose. The court stated whether the engineer's conduct was privileged is a factual issue to be decided under all the circumstances, including whether the conduct was fair and reasonable. The court upheld the instruction that if the purpose of the advice was malevolent, instead of protecting a legitimate interest, the defendant is liable for the harm done regardless of the apparent existence of privilege); *George A. Fuller Co. v Chicago College of Osteopathic Medicine,* 719 F.2d 1326 (7th Cir. 1983) (general contractor for new clinic brought an action for tortious interference with contract against the owner and the project architect because it was terminated before the clinic was completed. The court concluded that, under Illinois law, an architect would be afforded a conditional privilege to interfere in a construction contract of its principal. The acts of interference alleged by the contractor were all held to fall within the architect's contractual duties, and there was no allegation that the architect acted contrary to the owner's best interest. The architect's motion to dismiss was affirmed); *Santucci Construction Co. v. Baxter & Woodman, Inc.*, 502 N.E.2d 1134 (Ill. App. Ct. 1986) (municipality brought suit against Santucci Construction, general contractor on a sewer project. Santucci filed third-party complaint against Baxter & Woodman, municipality's designer and supervising engineer. Santucci alleged negligent and intentional interference with a contractual relationship and prospective advantage resulting from engineer's direct communication with Santucci's suppliers, purportedly to determine the status of their accounts with Santucci, and encouraged the suppliers to terminate delivery of material and services. Santucci further claimed that Baxter abused its responsibility to administer the project by persuading the municipality to treat the actions of the suppliers as grounds to terminate Santucci's contract. Santucci alleged that these actions were done with malice or negligently and carelessly in violation of engineer's duty to administer Santucci's work. The appellate court followed *George A. Fuller v. Chicago College of Osteopathic Medicine* in holding that Illinois would allow an engineer or an architect a conditional privilege to interfere with the construction contract of its principal, which otherwise would be improper interference with contractual relationship. To establish the privilege, designer must act to protect a conflicting interest of a value equal to or greater than contractor's contractual rights and acts that bring about the breach must be legal acts and must not be unreasonable in the circumstances. Because the full extent of the duties of engineer had not been defined, the court remanded for determination whether the actions complained of fell within the engineer's conditional privilege); *Certified Mechanical Contractors, Inc. v. Wight & Co.*, 515 N.E.2d 1047 (Ill. App. Ct. 1987), a contractor claimed that an architect interfered with its contract by causing the owner to suspend the project to test the contractor's work. The architect's report of the test results outlined problems with the poured-in-place concrete work and was critical of the general contractor's performance. The suspension also caused a six-month delay. The contractor claimed that the architect desired to injure it for reasons unrelated to a desire to advise the owner properly and attempted to have it removed from the project to conceal the architect's own mistakes and omissions. The court stated contractor must show actual malice may exist. To demonstrate malice, evidence must establish the designer acted with a desire to harm unrelated to an interest to protect. If an architect induced a breach of contract with intent to harm the other party or to further its personal goals, the architect is liable for tortious interference. The court found no factual support that architect was motivated by a desire to harm the contractor or to further its own personal goals and affirmed summary judgment for the architect).

Page 128, add to note 112:

cert. denied, 642 N.E.2d 1302 (Ill. 1994).

Page 129, add at end of section:

In *Riblet Tramway Co. v. Ericksen Associates, Inc.*, 665 F. Supp. 81 (D.N.H. 1987), the State of New Hampshire engaged Ericksen as an engineering consultant to renovate and repair ski lifts. Ericksen's duties included reviewing bids for compliance with specifications. At a public hearing before the governor and executive council, the engineer had stated there was a risk to the public safety if the State awarded Riblet the contract. Riblet claimed that the engineer slandered it and tortiously interfered with its prospective agreement.

The court ruled that the engineer was entitled to summary judgment on both the defamation and intentional interference claims. The statements were held to be the nondefamatory opinion of an expert consultant based on fully disclosed, undisputed facts. On the intentional interference count, the court found that the facts alleged by Riblet were sufficient to make out a claim of tortious interference with Riblet's prospective agreement with the State, but were privileged or otherwise justified. The court applied *Restatement (Second) of Torts,* § 772, Comment c (1979), to find a qualified privilege because the engineer's advice was requested by the terms of its contract and by the council's specific question; the response was within the scope of the request, and there was no dispute as to the honesty of the advice.

See also Vojak v. Jensen, 161 N.W.2d 100 (Iowa 1968) (Vojak, doing business as United Roofing Company, sought a subcontract on a school construction contract for which Jensen was the architect. Several years before, United had installed a roof on another school project designed by the architect and the roof had failed. The architect wrote letters to the general contractor and the awarding authority, rejecting United as a subcontractor unless the general contractor would "assume complete responsibility" for the roofing work and give the awarding authority "complete protection." The general contractor thereupon cancelled its contract with United. United sued the architect for libel. The Iowa Supreme Court ruled a statement attributing business incompetence or lack of skill to another is libelous per se, from which a presumption of malice, falsity, and damage arises; but if made under a qualified privilege, such libelous statement is not actionable unless actual malice nullifies the immunity of a qualified privilege. The court held that the architect's letters to the contractor and owner were libelous per se but that the architect had pleaded and proven a qualifed privilege. For actual malice there was evidence from which the jury might find the defendant was seeking to relieve its own failures by falsely accusing plaintiff of incompetence; that the architect unreasonably refused to give considerations to suggestions submitted by plaintiff concerning the cause and possible cure of the prior roof problem; that the architect recklessly accused plaintiff of incompetence without making any bona fide investigation to determine the basis for such charges. However, the court found that trial judge's instruction with respect to these issues to be so confusing, inconsistent, and misleading as to justify the granting of a new trial); *Alfred A. Altimont, Inc. v. Chatelain, Samperton & Nolan,* 374 A.2d 284 (D.C. 1977) (when construction of a church project was behind schedule, the architect wrote to the contactor's surety and indicated that the contractor was not promptly and faithfully performing the contract and might be in default. In a second letter the architect blamed the contractor for the delays and stated that it considered it "extremely negligent." Architect refused to retract the statements and stated that it thought the contractor should get out of the construction business. The contractor sued the architect for defamation, interference with its business with bonding companies, and intentionally or maliciously interfering with its contract with the church. The court upheld a directed vedict on the defamation claim because it found that the architect's statements to the bonding company were subject to a qualified privilege as defined in § 596 of the *Restatement (Second) of Torts*, and that the architect acted in good faith and within the scope of its duty in communicating with the bonding company. The court found that the architect's antagonistic and resentful acts to contractor was as consistent with the nonexistence of malice as with its existence. The court recognized the existence of privilege as a defense to the interference claims, but did not reach this issue because it found that the contractor failed to extablish a prima facie case of interference with contractual relations. There was no evidence that the architect intentionally induced the church to breach its contract with the contractor or interfered with business relations with the bonding companies because both had rejected the contractor before the letters were written based on the contractor's past history and financial background).

CHAPTER 7

LIABILITY FOR NEGLIGENCE

§ 7.2 Governmental, Professional, and Industry Standards

Page 133, add after second sentence in fourth paragraph:

Licensing statutes may distinguish between architecture and engineering and regulate the type of work that engineers and designers may perform. Although many states have no statutory difference between the engineering and architecture acts, Arkansas does. Architects are the only ones in Arkansas who can design buildings for human occupancy or habitation according to an interpretation of Arkansas law by the Arkansas Attorney General. "Arkansas AG Says PEs Can't Design Some Buildings," 35 *Private Practice News* 1 (NSPE's Professional Engineers in Private Practice Jan. 1995). Although they will lose future work, professional engineers in Arkansas currently designing buildings for human habitation, such as churches, office buildings, hotels, and schools, are not violating the law according to the Attorney General's interpretation.

The differences between the abilities of architects and engineers to design buildings for habitation may reflect the jealousy between the two disciplines rather than any real differences in training. National Society of Professional Engineers (NSPE) asked the Justice Department to conduct an antitrust investigation of various state and national architectural organizations. The society claims those organizations have conspired to restrain engineers' ability to provide building design services. Korman, "Why NSPE Wants a Probe," 234 *Engineering News-Record* No. 10, at 10 (Mar. 13, 1995).

NSPE seeks to connect the American Institute of Architects' national policy, legislative activity by its chapters, and the National Council of Architectural Registration Boards (NCARB). In 1988, NCARB published a plan to stamp out what it perceived as illegal architectural practice, including that by engineers. After Maine adopted NCARB guidelines as architectural law, local building code officials began refusing to accept submissions from engineers that lacked an architectural stamp. Engineers eventually won back that right, but the effort was costly.

§ 7.5 STANDARD OF CARE

The U.S. Department of Justice has decided not to act on the NSPE's antitrust complaint against the national architectural organizations. Following an announcement that the Justice Department's investigation had ended, the AIA in a statement pointed out that there are significant differences between architecture and engineering that affect public health, safety, and welfare. Most state statutes define *architecture* as the design of structures for human habitation or use, and *engineering* as the design of systems and structures. State law, according to the AIA, should allow each professional to practice the other discipline only to the extent that he or she is qualified and to the extent that it is incidental to each project. Korman, "Architects Feel 'Vindicated,' " 236 *Engineering News-Record* 12 (No. 13, Apr. 1, 1996).

§ 7.5 Reasonable Standard of Care

Page 138, add after first sentence in first full paragraph:

For example, in *City of York v. Turner-Murphy Co.,* 452 S.E.2d 615 (S.C. Ct. App. 1994), the City of York, South Carolina, hired the engineering firm of Mayes, Sudderth and Etheredge, Inc. for design of a wastewater treatment plant. The engineer agreed to provide detailed inspection of the construction work for general compliance with contract documents.

During construction, the engineer's inspector noticed leaks in a concrete wall in the filter structure. After forms were stripped, honeycombing was discovered. The contractor repaired the wall, and the city accepted the plant. A year later, a hole developed in the wall. Another engineer hired by the city took core samples and found extensive voids. The second engineer recommended replacement of the wall.

The city sued Mayes, Sudderth for negligence. At trial, the city presented expert testimony that established that Mayes had a duty to notify the city of defective work during construction. However, the city's expert did not testify that Mayes had violated its duty to notify the city of the contractor's defective work.

The court of appeals ruled that the jury was not equipped to decide whether Mayes violated its duty to notify the city of defective work because the voids in the concrete could not be discovered except through destructive testing. Expert testimony was needed to prove whether Mayes violated its duty to destructively test the concrete walls.

The designer's decision to destructive test for hidden defects requires evaluation of many subjective factors. These factors include past conformance of the contractor's completed work to the contract requirements; the importance of the portion that is suspected to be defective; the cost of the destructive test; and the stage of construction of the project. These factors are better evaluated by experts familiar with design and construction.

Page 138, add to note 42:

Edgewater Apartments v. Flynn Consulting Eng'rs, 216 A.D.2d 53, 627 N.Y.S.2d 385 (1995) (architect was competent to testify as expert in building owners' negligence action against consulting engineers because architect was familiar with leakage problems and had stopped water seepage that defendant's engineers had failed to halt); Yantzi v. Norton, 927 S.W.2d 427 (Mo. Ct. App. 1996) (testimony of two foundation repair experts was found sufficient to establish applicable standard of care for professional engineer, because homeowner's claim of negligence was based on standard of care of a foundation specialist (not an engineer), foundation repair experts were qualified to engage in same line of work, and foundation expert had corrected problem).

§ 7.8 Warranties and Estimates

Page 141, add to second paragraph:

This is especially troubling because designers inherently cannot warrant a successful outcome unless their plans, advice, or prescriptions are accepted and followed. Bell, "Eroding Foundations: Increased Liability of Construction Design Professionals," 32 *Procurement Lawyer* 5 (No. 2, Winter 1997).

Page 146, add at end of section:

In *Darell Thacker v. Menards, Inc.,* 105 F.3d 382 (7th Cir. 1997), the federal court enforced a disclaimer on a written estimate that expressly disclaimed any warranty of fitness for a purpose. In *Darell Thacker,* homeowners selected plans from several choices offered by National Plan Service for a vacation home. The selected plan included an estimate indicating that \$13,398.40 worth of materials would be required. The homeowners actually purchased \$147,398.40 worth of material, including 2 x 12s and windows missing from the materials list. The homeowners sued Menards, the building supply company that offered the National Plan Services's plans, and National Plan Service, claiming that the oral assurances of completeness they received from Menards became part of the contract.

Each page of the $13,398.40 estimate contained the following disclaimer:

> This is an estimate. It is given only for general price information. This is not an offer, and there can be no legally binding contract between the parties based upon this estimate. The prices stated herein are subject to change depending upon the market conditions. The prices stated on this estimate are not firm for any time period unless specifically written otherwise on this form. The availability of materials is subject to inventory conditions. MENARDS IS NOT RESPONSIBLE FOR ANY LOSS INCURRED BY THE CUSTOMER WHO RELIES ON PRICES SET FORTH HEREIN OR ON THE AVAILABILITY OF ANY OF THE MATERIALS STATED HEREIN. All information on this form, other than price, has been provided by customer, and Menards is not responsible for any errors in the information on this estimate, including but not limited to quantity, dimension and quality. Please examine this estimate carefully. MENARDS MAKES NO REPRESENTATIONS, ORAL, WRITTEN OR OTHERWISE, THAT THE MATERIALS ARE SUITABLE FOR ANY PURPOSE BEING CONSIDERED BY THE CUSTOMER. BECAUSE OF WIDE VARIATIONS IN CODES, THERE ARE NO REPRESENTATIONS THAT THE MATERIALS LISTED HEREIN MEET YOUR CODE REQUIREMENTS.

The court noted that the disclaimer was relatively inconspicuous, appearing on the estimate in type one-half the size of the other printing on the form. Nevertheless, the court found that the written estimate expressly disclaimed any warranty of fitness for a purpose and that there was nothing indicating that the parties had intended the oral assurances to be part of the contract.

§ 7.10 The Economic Loss Rule

Page 148, add after "E.g.," in note 97:

Boston Inv. Property No. 1 State v. Burman, 658 A.2d 515 (R.I. 1995) (building purchaser sued general contractor in negligence for cost to remedy defects and the additional depreciation in the value of the building. Shortly following the purchase of the building from the developer, Boston Investment learned that the windows of the building leaked when it rained and that erosion problems were present with the parking lot. Rhode Island Supreme Court held that in absence of privity of contract with general contractor, subsequent purchaser of commercial office building in Rhode Island is not entitled to recover economic damages it alleges were proximately caused by negligence of general contractor).

Page 149, add before "Donnelly" citation in note 101:

Jim's Excavating Serv. v. HKM Assocs., 878 P.2d 248 (Mont. 1994) (contractor may recover purely economic loss against an engineer when the design professional knew or should have foreseen that contractor was at risk in relying on the information designer supplied).

Page 149, add to note 101:

Edgeworth Construction v. N.D. Lea & Assoc., [1993] 3 S.C.R. 206, 12 C.L.R. (2d) 161, [1993] 8 W.W.R. 129, 83 B.C.L.R. (2d) 145, 107 D.L.R. (4th) 169 (claims may be brought against designer by contractor if the contractor or subcontractor has reason to believe that the designer's negligent preparation of bid documents caused them financial loss);

Page 149, add after "See, e.g.," in note 102:

Tommy L. Griffin Plumbing & Heating Co. v. Jordan, Jones & Goulding, Inc., Op. No. 24328 (S.C. filed Oct. 16, 1995) (if a party furnishes plans and specifications for a contractor to follow in a construction project, the party thereby impliedly warrants their sufficiency for the purpose in view and cannot take advantage of economic loss rule).

Page 149, add after "But see" in note 103:

Tommy L. Griffin Plumbing & Heating Co. v. Jordan, Jones & Goulding, Inc., Op. No. 24328 (S.C. filed Oct. 16, 1995) (where the engineer designed the project for the county and supervised construction, facts supported a duty to the contractor (even in the absence of privity) not to negligently design or supervise the project and refused to apply economic loss rule).

Page 149, add after "See, e.g.," in note 104:

Fireman's Fund Ins. Co. v. SEC Donohue, Inc., 176 Ill. 2d 160, 679 N.E.2d 1197 (1997) (economic loss doctrine bars recovery in tort against engineers for purely economic losses); Thomson v. Espey Huston & Assocs., Inc., 899 S.W.2d 415 (Tex. Ct. App. 1995) (any negligence by engineering consulting firm in performing inspection contract caused no injury beyond economic loss to subject of contract itself, which pursuant to the economic loss rule, did not give rise to tort cause of action); Lippy v. Society Nat'l Bank, 100 Ohio App. 3d 37, 651 N.E.2d 1364 (1995) (any duty owed to land purchaser by consultant hired to perform environmental site assessment of property was one owed under contract with consultant, and thus there was no action in tort for economic losses suffered as a result of any alleged breach of contract).

Page 150, add at end of note 104:

Following the majority rule, Missouri courts have held that recovery in tort for pure economic damage is limited to cases in which there is personal injury, damage to property other than that sold, or destruction of the property sold due to some violent occurrence. McCarter, *Economic Loss Doctrine: Is Privity Required?,* 53 J. Mo. B. 23 (No.1, Jan.-Feb. 1997), *citing* Bryant v. Murray-Jones-Murray, Inc., 653 F. Supp. 1015 (E.D. Mo. 1985); Aetna Ins. Co. v. Hellmuth, Obata & Kassabaum, Inc., 392 F.2d 472 (8th Cir. 1968); Annotation, *Tort Liability of Project Architect for Economic Damages Suffered by Contractor,* 65 A.L.R.3d 249 (1996). In Fleischer v. Hellmuth, Obata & Kassabaum, Inc., 870 S.W.2d 832 (Mo. Ct. App. 1993), the contractor had no contract with the designer. The court held that for claims asserted against participants in a construction project, the designer owes no tort duty of care and is not liable to a party with which it has no contract. The *Fleischer* court adopted the reasoning from other jurisdictions, which have held that for claims arising out of a construction project resulting from defects in the construction, a party to the project owes no duty of care to parties with whom it has not contracted; the absence of privity of contract is an absolute defense to such claims. McCarter at 24–25. In St. Denis v. Department of Hous. & Urban Dev., 900 F. Supp. 1194 (D. Alaska 1995), the federal district court came to the same conclusion. Under Alaska law, a plaintiff who claims that a product is defective and seeks only damages for economic loss must sue on a contract and has no independent action in tort unless the plaintiff can show that the defect created a significant risk of personal injury or property damage.

Page 149, add at end of section:

In some jurisdictions, courts have created an exception to the economic loss rule for claims to recover damages arising from inherently dangerous products, such as when a building has been contaminated by toxic materials. Claims asserted against a designer who specifies toxic or contaminated materials are based on the theory that such materials create a risk of physical injury and make the building unsafe for use. Alternatively, claims such as this could be supported under the damage to other property exception, on the basis of contamination to the building and its contents from the toxic materials. McCarter, *supra* note 104, at 27–28, *citing Northridge Co. v. W.R. Grace & Co.,* 471 N.W.2d 179 (Wis. 1991) (asbestos contamination caused by defendant caused injury to other property—the building and its contents). Missouri courts appear to have recognized an exception to the economic loss doctrine when a defective product contaminates other property and endangers life or health. McCarter at 27–28.

Three major lines of cases address recovery of economic losses from a designer or other third party on a tort theory of negligence. One theory allows recovery of economic losses in tort when it is foreseeable that a third party might be injured due to the designer's negligent performance. A second theory also considers foreseeability but requires that the negligent designer intend a party or a class of parties to rely upon that faulty information. This is the rule of the *Restatement (Second) of Torts* § 552 (1977). The third theory does not permit recovery of economic loss in tort. These cases require privity of contract to recover a loss of the benefit of the bargain. Bell, "Eroding Foundations: Increased Liability of Construction Design Professionals," 32 *Procurement Lawyer* 3 (No. 2, Winter 1997), *citing East River Steam Ship Corp. v. Transamerica Delaval, Inc.*, 476 U.S. 858 (1986); see also § **6.10**.

§ 7.11 Contractor

Page 150, add at end of section:

For example, in *Jim's Excavating Service v. HKM Associates,* 878 P.2d 248 (Mont. 1994), the Lockwood Water Users Association hired HKM Associates to design plans and specifications for construction of a water pipeline. HKM also acted as project engineer through the completion of construction. Jim's Excavating Service was awarded the construction contract.

Jim's Excavating sued HKM for economic loss on the project because of HKM's negligence in preparing the plans and specifications, the project design, and the direction, supervision, and administration of the construction contract. A jury awarded Jim's Excavating $400,000.

On appeal, the engineer argued that it could not be liable to the contractor for purely economic damages. The Montana Supreme Court said that a contractor may recover for purely economic loss against an engineer when the design professional knew or should have foreseen that an identifiable class of plaintiffs was at risk in relying on the information the designer supplied and so affirmed the jury award.

§ 7.13 Injured Employees

Page 151, add to note 111:

Carvalho v. Toll Bros. & Developers, 278 N.J. Super. 451, 651 A.2d 492 (App. Div.), *certification granted,* 140 N.J. 326 (1995), *aff'd & remanded,* 143 N.J. 565, 675 A.2d 209 (1996) (engineer had legal duty to exercise reasonable care for the safety of workers on a construction site when engineer had a responsibility for the progress of the work but not for safety conditions yet was aware of working conditions on the site that created a risk of serious injury to workers).

§ 7.15 Adjoining Landowner

Page 152, add after last sentence:

See **§ 15.4**.

Page 152, add at end of section:

In *Johnson v. Board of County Commissioners,* 21 Kan. App. 2d 76, 897 P.2d 169 (1995), the Board of County Commissioners of Pratt County hired Mid-Continent Engineers to design a bridge to replace an old wooden bridge over the river that ran through the Johnsons' property. Shortly after completion of the new bridge, the river flooded and damaged the Johnsons' property. The Johnsons argued that the new bridge caused the flood damage because it prevented water from diverting into the flood plain and kept more water in the channel, where it could erode the north bank of the river on the Johnsons' property.

The court of appeals determined that one who undertakes to render services to another, which he should recognize as necessary for the protection of a third person, is subject to liability to the third person for physical harm resulting from a failure to exercise reasonable care if (1) the failure to exercise reasonable care increases the risk of harm to the third person, or (2) he has undertaken to perform a duty owed by the other party to the contract to the third person, or (3) the harm is suffered because of reliance of the other contracting party or the third person upon the work.

The court of appeals applied these tests and stressed expert testimony to the effect that a fundamental part of bridge design is the consideration that the bridge could cause possible damage to the property of landowners on the river. The court held that Mid-Continent should have recognized that its engineering services for the design of the bridge were necessary for the protection of those landowners, and that by failing to foresee or advise the county of the effect of the bridge on the landowners' property, Mid-Continent Engineers increased the risk of harm to the landowners. The court of appeals concluded that Mid-Continent Engineers owed a duty and could be found liable in negligence to the landowners.

§ 7.17 Design Phase

Page 153, add after carryover paragraph:

For example, in *Housing Vermont v. Goldsmith & Morris,* 685 A.2d 1086 (Vt. 1996), the Davis Company hired Goldsmith & Morris (G&M) to design the Salmon Run housing project. Krebs and Lansing was selected as the civil engineer. G&M produced a site plan containing grading information, which was used by Krebs and Lansing to construct the grades in the courtyard. After the project was completed, Davis Company sold Salmon Run, along with the contract rights with G&M and Krebs and Lansing. Salmon Run was eventually acquired by Housing Vermont. Subsequently, the slopes depicted in the site plan had to be redesigned and stabilized.

Housing Vermont sued G&M for the cost of the redesign. G&M claimed that it was not responsible for producing the final grading plan and that the fault lay with Krebs and Lansing; G&M's contract did not require it to produce a final site plan but only a grading plan "to date." The Vermont Supreme Court noted that G&M had signed an acknowledgment on the site plan that stated it was Goldsmith & Morris's professional opinion that soil and ground conditions would not impair the project's structural soundness. Although G&M knew that its site plan had been used, it did not warn anyone that the plan was preliminary. The supreme court concluded that G&M was responsible for the site plan and required it to pay damages to Housing Vermont.

Page 154, add after carryover paragraph:

There are many different expressions of defective specification claims. Another example is the inability of a "designated" supplier to perform. The specifications may also name or designate certain suppliers to provide the required equipment. When the designated supplier fails to perform, the contractor may claim any additional cost from the owner, who in turn may claim the money from the designer. *See Edward M. Crough, Inc. v. Department of General Services,* 572 A.2d 457 (D.C. 1990). Courts have recognized only a limited warranty for suppliers designated in specifications. The owner warrants that the supplier is capable but does not warrant the supplier's willingness to meet time requirements, nor does the owner warrant that the designated supplier will agree to the contractor's conditions for performance. The warranty does not include an assurance that the supplier will perform. Sweet, *Legal Aspects of Architecture, Engineering and the Construction Process* 411–12 (5th ed. 1994).

§ 7.18 Construction Phase

Page 154, add after third paragraph:

Many claims against designers can be traced to delays caused by the designer's reluctance to make a decision. The inability to decide may stem from the designer's fear to "tell the contractor what to do," the designer explaining that the decision really relates to the contractor's "means and methods." Other times, the designer may avoid a decision by continuously judging the contractor's justification "insufficient" no matter how detailed or persuasive. Pronouncing any situation "means and methods" and any justification "insufficient" to avoid a decision may result from the designer's fear of a malpractice claim. Avoiding a decision may or may not eliminate a malpractice claim but may certainly delay the contractor or cause a claim against the owner.

For example, in *MKK Technologies, Inc./Northstar Construction v. Scott,* 63 F.3d 402 (5th Cir. 1995), the contractor on a prison project submitted its claim for delays and cost overruns to the Texas Department of Criminal Justice's designated representative, pursuant to the contract's dispute resolution clause. Six months later, the contractor brought a § 1983 suit in federal district court against the department, contending that the department had instructed the designated representative not to decide the claim, in an effort to deprive the contractor of its right to payment under the contract. The district court dismissed the complaint for failure to state a § 1983 claim and the contractor appealed. Before the appellate court heard the contractor's appeal, the department's designated representative issued its decision and awarded the contractor a maximum of $2.1 million.

The contractor claimed in its appeal that it had been deprived of a property interest—a "timely" decision by the owner's designated representative—without due process. The court of appeals disagreed, concluding that the representative's decision was timely and that the contractor had suffered no deprivation. The court further held that even if it had found the representative's decision untimely and even if the court had found that the delay would have entitled the contractor to some relief, a resolution passed by the Texas Senate authorizing an award of damages of up to $5 million to the contractor would have provided an adequate postdeprivation remedy for any injury caused by the designated representative's "untimeliness."

Both the designer's contract with the owner and the owner's contract with the contractor *require* the designer to make many decisions. A designer's decision is required in the changes clause, the disputes clause, and the differing site conditions clause, among others. Other clauses prevent the contractor from proceeding without direction of the designer. The contractor cannot substitute materials, violate construction limits, increase excavation depth, or change the design without the designer's direction.

A designer's pronouncing a contractor's submission insufficient and ignoring other information the designer has, avoids a decision as much as if the designer refused to respond. The justification for a designer's decision may not be limited to the material submitted by the contractor. The designer may also use the information it learned in school, from past projects, from observations on the project, from attendance at meetings, or from conversations with participants.

If the contractor has problems performing and requests changes in materials, depths, or design, the designer must not ignore its role, raise the "means and methods" shield, and avoid a decision. The contractor cannot make these changes without permission.

Page 155, add at end of section:

Designers are generally reluctant to serve as arbitrators between the owner and contractor. University of Kentucky law professor Thomas J. Stipanowich reported that designers want to move away from their quasi-adjudicative role specified in American Institute of Architects' form contracts. Nearly 75 percent of designers said they should not be the "final judge" in disputes between owners and contractors. McManamy, "Dispute Resolution Gaining," 233 *Engineering News-Record* 16 (Oct. 24, 1994). Stipanovich also reported that designers are much less aware than contractors of the many claims prevention and dispute resolution techniques available.

The design professional's evaluation can have a direct impact on whether the client chooses to terminate the contract and whether the client chooses to hire that contractor in the future. These evaluations can affect the contractor's business reputation and the contractor's future business with other persons. Contractors have sued designers that participated in the termination process for defamation or tortious interference with contract or prospective business advantage. However, if the designer's statements to its client are truthful and its assessment of the contractor's compliance with the contract is accurate, there can be no action. It is not difficult to take precautions to ensure that every decision a design professional makes will be indisputably truthful and accurate. Nevertheless, the design professional will have to take a position as to the adequacy of the work and cannot escape expressing statements of both fact and opinion. M. Heley & M. Bloomquist, "The Design Professional's Role in Termination of the Contractor," 17 *Construction Lawyer* 3, 10 (No. 2, Apr. 1997).

Stipanowich's report indicates that designers and their attorneys need to pay more attention to training and instruction not only in the claims procedures in the contractor's contract, but also for the resolution of the designer's disputes with clients.

Ignoring the claims procedures in the contract can create claims against the designer and inconvenience for the owner and contractor. For example, in *MECO Systems, Inc. v. Dancing Bear Entertainment, Inc.,* No. 21209 (Mo. Ct. App. June 25, 1997), a Missouri appellate court stated that the designer's failure to require compliance with the contract's requirements (for the contractor to substantiate its claims for time extensions under Paragraph 4.4.1 of AIA A201) raised genuine issues of fact regarding the architect's partiality and good faith.

The contractor in *Dancing Bear* had agreed to build a theater for Dancing Bear Entertainment. Dancing Bear sued the contractor, claiming liquidated damages for late completion. The contractor claimed that the architect had granted additional time to complete construction because of rain and other excusable delays. Dancing Bear filed a cross-claim against the architect, alleging that it breached its obligations when it granted the contractor extra time to complete construction. The trial court granted summary judgment because it concluded that the delay was as a matter of law excused by the architect's grant of additional time, which the trial court found was final and binding on Dancing Bear. The Missouri appellate court reversed the trial court because there was a genuine dispute as to whether the decision of the architect was intended to be final and binding.

The appellate court in *Dancing Bear* held that Paragraph 2.6.18 of the A201 General Conditions, 1987 Edition, was ambiguous as to whether an architect's decisions regarding time extensions are final and binding. The court held that parol evidence was essential to resolve the ambiguity in these contracts, preventing summary judgment.

Dancing Bear's cross-claim against the architect claimed that the architect had breached its contractual duty to act impartially and in good faith by granting the contractor's time extension. The trial court had also granted the architect's motion for summary judgment because Dancing Bear had failed to plead that the architect acted fraudulently, with gross mistake, or in bad faith. The appellate court also reversed the trial court's summary judgment for the architect. The court rejected the architect's argument that decisions of design professionals are final and binding on owners and contractors in the absence of fraud or gross mistake. The architect had not required the contractor to strictly comply with the procedural requirements in the contract for time extension requests. The appellate court stated that the failure to require compliance with the contract's requirements for the contractor to substantiate its claims for time extensions, with cost estimates or data indicating that the experienced weather conditions were abnormal under Paragraph 4.4.1 of AIA A201, raised genuine issues of fact regarding the architect's partiality and good faith required under Paragraph 4.2.12. The appellate court further suggested that the architect may have acted with a conflict of interest because some aspects of the claimed delays were allegedly attributable to the architect and the architect had failed to rule with respect to those claims. The court stated that this type of selective decision making raised genuine fact issues about the architect's impartiality and good faith.

Stipanowich's survey also emphasizes earlier discussion that designers generally are reluctant to make decisions, especially those that involve contractor's means and methods. To deal with this, contracts may be revised both to eliminate the designer's final decision in all but those changes that affect the integrity of the building (can the designer decide which disputes involve the integrity of the building and which do not?), and also to identify an alternate "neutral" decision maker as a substitute for the designer. If the designer is unwilling or unable to make hard decisions, the contract may provide for another who can.

§ 7.20 Duty to Warn

Page 157, add at end of section:

In *Jones v. James Reeves Contractors, Inc.*, 701 So. 2d 774 (Miss. 1997), the court held that an architect has no common law duty to warn about dangerous site conditions known to the architect. The court placed only two limitations on this rule: If the architect undertakes, by contract or conduct, a supervisory role, or if there is a defect in the architect's plans, then the architect may have some liability. D. Murphy, "A&E's Limited Duty to Warn of Hazard," 12 *Common Sense Contracting* 9 (No. 3, Summer 1998).

Although the facts do not make it clear, it appears that the architect and possibly the county knew of a dangerous condition at the site known as "water sand." The specifications apparently did not disclose the existence of the water-sand condition. While the contractor was excavating, employees of a subcontractor jumped into the hole to ascertain its depth. One of the workers sank to his knees and two coworkers attempted to help him out of the hole. The hole collapsed, suffocating all three men. The estate of one of the workers sued the architect and contractor. The trial court rendered summary judgment in favor of all defendants. On appeal, the Mississippi Supreme Court upheld summary judgment in favor of the architect.

The architect was absolved from liability because it did not engage in supervisory functions, and its plans were not defective. The court based its decision on § 314 of *Restatement (Second) of Torts*, "[t]he fact that the actor realizes or should realize that action on his part is necessary for another or protection does not of itself impose upon him duty to take such action." The Mississippi court also asserted that its "sister states" were unlikely to impose liability on an architect although no cases or statutes were cited in direct support of this contention. The court stated that the architect was not on site on the day of the accident, but did not state whether the architect had been onsite during any of the construction work. No attempt at defining "supervision" was made by the court. As a result, the question of what constituted "supervision" was left open. The court never addressed the potential issue of defective design. Murphy, at 9–10.

§ 7.20A Sick Building Syndrome and Indoor Air Quality (New)

The 500,000-square-foot Polk County Courthouse in Bartow, Florida, cost the county $37 million to build in 1987. After five years of operation, the county faces a $37 million retrofit, including replacement of all the ductwork, and temporary lease and relocation costs due to air quality problems. The county has sued all parties to the construction, including interior designers and material manufacturers. The Polk County Courthouse problem was the result of interdisciplinary error: bad design; bad construction; deficient specifications for the envelope and interior spaces; poorly positioned air intakes and exhausts; HVAC that was oversized by a factor of three and had no dehumidification controls; poor filtration; improper space planning; and lack of circulation and ventilation systems. Bledel, "Indoor Air Quality Defects," *Urban Land,* June 1995, at 37.

Design and construction defects that lead to sick building syndrome (SBS) and building-related illnesses (BRI) are all too common. The Occupational Safety and Health Administration (OSHA) estimated that 30 percent of the nation's 4.5 million existing commercial buildings have indoor air quality (IAQ) problems of varying degrees. The U.S. Environmental Protection Agency has defined *sick building syndrome* as a situation in which building occupants experience acute health problems linked to time spent in a building but for which no specific illness or cause can be identified. A second characteristic is that the affected occupants experience relief soon after leaving the building. The complaints of those affected by SBS typically include headaches, fatigue, nausea, mucous membrane (eye, nose, and throat) irritation, coughs, and muscle pain. Carey, "Indoor Air Quality," 14 *Construction Lawyer* 29 (No. 2, Apr. 1994).

The recognition of SBS has prompted a legislative and regulatory response at both the federal and state levels. One approach has been to require agencies to review existing building codes and standards as they relate to energy conservation efforts and indoor air quality. For example, California's legislature directed its Public Resources Commission to factor indoor air pollution problems into any energy conservation assessment of new building standards and existing building codes for residential and nonresidential buildings. Oregon directed its administrator of the Building Codes Agency to adopt ventilation standards for public areas and office workplaces and to adopt building codes and building products standards that will protect indoor air quality of private residences. Oregon's Occupational Safety and Health Division adopted the ventilation standards of the American Society of Heating, Refrigeration and Air Conditioning Engineers (ASHRAE) for acceptable indoor air quality in workplaces. This regulation requires a conscious selection of building materials, treatments, and furnishings to prevent indoor air quality problems. Carey, "Indoor Air Quality," at 29–30.

Although the majority of states currently do not have statutes or regulations directly addressing indoor air quality, many states do recognize indoor air quality as an issue that ought to be addressed. The current manner of regulating indoor air quality varies considerably among states, with a handful addressing it head-on, but with most starting slowly and using roundabout methods. It seems likely, however, that the federal government and more states will enact legislation in the near future to address indoor air quality issues.

On April 5, 1994, OSHA published a 70-page proposed IAQ rule (59 Fed. Reg. 15,968 (1994) (to be codified at 29 C.F.R. pts. 1910, 1915, 1926, and 1928) (proposed April 5, 1994)) that will provide the overall regulation of indoor air quality in nonindustrial buildings affecting more than 70 million workers. OSHA estimated a \$8.1 billion cost for compliance with only the IAQ aspects of the proposed rule. Icard & Wright, "Sick Building

Syndrome and Building-Related Illness Claims: Defining the Practical and Legal Issues," 14 *Construction Lawyer* No. 4, at 1 (Oct. 1994). OSHA's recommended and proposed indoor air quality standards elicited more than 100,000 written responses from real estate interests, corporations, and associated industries. Even if OSHA's proposed IAQ standards are not put fully into effect, IAQ litigants may hold up the proposed standards as the current minimum "standard of care" for building owners, designers, and contractors. Bledel, "Indoor Air Quality Defects," *Urban Land*, June 1995, at 37.

Because SBS is creating a new wave of regulation, and because the regulators are beginning to regulate substances often linked to the construction industry, liability exposure for architects, builders, general contractors, subcontractors, and suppliers is likely to increase. This is especially true in states that have effected changes to their building codes to incorporate specific indoor air quality standards. Carey, "Indoor Air Quality," 14 *Construction Lawyer* 31 (No. 2, Apr. 1994).

To date, few sick building syndrome cases have gone to trial, but one professional liability insurer reported a dozen designers now facing sick building claims in the Southeast. McManamy, "Trial Jury Finds Designers Not Responsible for Bad Air," 234 *Engineering News-Record* No. 2, at 9 (Jan. 16, 1995). Most defendants settle out of court to escape media coverage and avoid establishing legal precedents. Bledel, "Indoor Air Quality Defects," *Urban Land,* June 1995, at 37.

Much of the SBS law was developed in the context of asbestos contamination. Although sick building syndrome claims are treated by the courts as less severe subsets of the 1980s asbestos-related claims, it is also fair to say that the law in this area is evolving with the science. Icard & Wright, "Sick Building Syndrome and Building-Related Illness Claims: Defining the Practical and Legal Issues," 14 *Construction Lawyer* No. 4, at 27 (Oct. 1994).

There are two primary sources of IAQ-related problems: microbial contamination and volatile organic compounds. Microbial contamination is often associated with excessive moisture within the building envelope. Typically, this problem is the result of improper drying-in during the construction process, faulty roof or curtain wall construction, improper design, or a lack of proper cleaning and maintenance of HVAC systems. Volatile organic compounds are invisible and odorless fumes associated with almost any synthetic product in a confined space. *Id.* at 1.

There are many causes for SBS and IAQ-related problems, not all of which are the responsibility of the designer: improper building and systems design, management decisions to cut costs, inadequate due diligence, and the building owner's and manager's failure to institute internal environmental management processes. Bledel, "Indoor Air Quality Defects," *Urban Land,* June 1995, at 37. A circuit court jury in Lake County, Illinois, for example, found the designers and builders of a four-year old courthouse *not* liable for the building's indoor air quality problems. Rather, the jury determined that the county's maintenance crews had damaged the air quality by pouring cleaning chemicals into a steam generator and accidentally dropping antifreeze into the building's air ducts. The courthouse opened in the fall of 1991 and started experiencing problems the following spring. After several hundred employees complained of dizziness, nausea, and headaches, the facility was shut down for a $3.4 million overhaul of the HVAC system. McManamy, "Trial Jury Finds Designers Not Responsible for Bad Air," 234 *Engineering News-Record* No. 2, at 9 (Jan. 16, 1995).

However, the design of the HVAC system often has much to do with SBS and other IAQ-related problems. Both microbial contamination and volatile organic compounds can cause sick building syndrome (SBS) if the ventilation system does not provide a sufficient outside air flow. In addition, indoor air pollution generally increases when the ventilation air flow rate falls below design conditions. Gardner, "Is the Design Architect or Engineer Liable for Sick Building Syndrome Damages?," 11 *Construction Lawyer* No. 4, at 31 (Oct. 1991).

In 1985, the HVAC system triggered a sequence of events that resulted in health problems among the tenants in a 24-story office building in El Segundo, California. A month after they moved in, tenants began to experience dizziness, nose bleeds, disorientation, breathing difficulties, numbness, anxiety, and drowsiness. The premises had to be evacuated during acute episodes, and several windows were removed in an effort to provide additional ventilation. The IAQ problems were never resolved, and the tenants moved out within a year. In a lawsuit that followed, *Call v. Prudential* (unreported), the tenants claimed that the HVAC system was defective in design and installation, that certain building products and construction materials emitted toxic substances, and that building management waited too long to act to correct the problems. Bledel, "Indoor Air Quality Defects," *Urban Land,* June 1995, at 37.

Call v. Prudential is significant because it was the first IAQ/SBS case to reach a jury. Also a first was the judge's ruling that those involved in the design, construction, and installation of an HVAC system could be held liable under the theory of strict product liability. In addition, the general contractor ultimately was forced to bear the cost of the settlement due to the standard indemnity agreement it had signed with the developer. Bledel, "Indoor Air Quality Defects," *Urban Land,* June 1995, at 37.

§ 7.20A SICK BUILDING SYNDROME

Claimants bringing actions resulting from problems with IAQ who have a contract with the party they view as responsible can recover their expectancy damages—that is, to be made whole under the contract. These damages should include the loss in value of the structure, remediation and tenant relocation costs, as well as lost profit. If the contract limits damages, then the parties may be required to live with their bargained-for exchange. See §§ **17.4** through **17.9**. Attempts to circumvent such contractual limitations by bringing an action in negligence are not permitted in many jurisdictions. Icard & Wright, "Sick Building Syndrome and Building-Related Illness Claims: Defining the Practical and Legal Issues," 14 *Construction Lawyer* No. 4, at 30 (Oct. 1994). In addition, the economic loss rule may prohibit recovery in tort for those without a contract with the designer. See §§ **6.10**, **7.10**, and **13.12**.

However, some jurisdictions have created an exception to the economic loss rule for claims to recover damages arising from inherently dangerous products, such as when a building has been contaminated by toxic materials. Claims asserted against a designer who specifies toxic or contaminated materials are based on the theory that such materials create a risk of physical injury and make the building unsafe for use. Alternatively, claims such as this could be supported under the damage to other property exception, on the basis of contamination to the building and its contents from the toxic materials. McCarter, "Economic Loss Doctrine: Is Privity Required?," 53 *Journal of the Missouri Bar* 23, 27–28 (No. 1, Jan.-Feb., 1997), *citing Northridge Co. v. W.R. Grace & Co.,* 471 N.W.2d 179 (Wis. 1991) (asbestos contamination caused by defendant caused injury to other property—the building and its contents). The damage to other property exception permits recovery in tort for pure economic damage in cases in which there is personal injury, damage to property other than that sold, or destruction of the property sold due to some violent occurrence. Missouri courts appear to have recognized an exception to the economic loss doctrine when a defective product contaminates other property and endangers life or health. McCarter at 27–28. In *St. Denis v. Department of Housing & Urban Development,* 900 F. Supp. 1194 (D. Alaska 1995), the federal district court came to the same conclusion. Under Alaska law, a plaintiff who claims that a product is defective and seeks only damages for economic loss must sue on a contract, and has no independent action in tort unless the plaintiff can show that the defect created a significant risk of personal injury or property damage.

In typical indoor pollution contexts, even if a contract exists, claims against design professionals are often based on negligent design of the structure or specification of improper materials. The duty of a design professional to use the standard of skill and care employed by others engaged in the same profession in the same locality is implied in every contract. This implied contractual liability attaches when the designer's professional conduct falls below the local standard of skill and care. Contract-related tort duty limited by the obligations defined in the professional services agreement has consistently been applied to third-party malpractice claims against the designer. Therefore, an architect or engineer who designs a ventilation system owes a duty of competency (to adhere to the standard of care and skill practiced by others engaged in the same profession in the same locality) not only to those in privity but also to tort claimants. Gardner, "Is the Design Architect or Engineer Liable for Sick Building Syndrome Damages?," 11 *Construction Lawyer* No. 4, at 32 (Oct. 1991). However, design conformance with a customary local practice is not always a bar to liability. A designer's duty extends beyond local custom and requires sound engineering practice. A duty to design according to sound engineering practices harmonizes with those decisions that refuse to shield professionals from liability who adopt either negligent local or substandard conduct as a design practice. Accordingly, a minimum level of competence in the local professional community is required for conformance to preclude negligence liability. *Id.* at 31.

A designer's standard of care for a ventilation system to avoid microbial contamination and volatile organic compounds may be influenced by federal and state legislation, building codes, a state's regulation of professionals, and industry standards. Among the extensive legislation at the federal level is the National Environmental Policy Act, the Clean Air Act, the Toxic Substances Control Act, the Asbestos Hazard Emergency Response Act, the Federal Insecticide, Fungicide and Rodenticide Act, the Safe Drinking Water Act, and the Radon Abatement Act of 1988. Failure to comply with these minimum standards as they pertain to permitting, construction, and remediation can result in criminal liability, fines, forfeitures, and jail sentences. There are also significant regulatory requirements at the state and local level, in addition to building codes and industry standards. Icard & Wright, "Sick Building Syndrome and Building-Related Illness Claims: Defining the Practical and Legal Issues," 14 *Construction Lawyer* No. 4, at 27 (Oct. 1994).

Building codes usually disclose little ventilation guidance for the designer. Some codes address only the outdoor air requirements for limited areas of buildings. Other codes define ventilation rates based upon expected occupancy levels. Neither formula addresses the root cause of ventilation deficiencies that occur when a building is fully occupied but the variable air volume (VAV) system is circulating a reduced outdoor air flow rate. A

VAV HVAC air distribution system usually circulates less supply air than a constant volume system. VAV systems circulate a reduced ventilation air flow rate during most periods of occupancy because power consumption is related to the air flow rate circulated in a building. Gardner, "Is the Design Architect or Engineer Liable for Sick Building Syndrome Damages?," 11 *Construction Lawyer* No. 4, at 31 (Oct. 1991).

A designer's ventilation design duty may also be influenced by the applicable professional registration requirements. The California attorney general has taken the public safety duty even further by suggesting that an engineer owes a duty to notify third parties upon the discovery of building conditions including IAQ that may cause SBS, which may present an imminent risk of serious injury. *Id.* at 32.

Industry standards are hard to apply to HVAC design because the standards changed so dramatically with the publication of the 1988 revisions to the 1981 ventilation standards of the American Society of Heating, Refrigeration, and Air Conditioning Engineers (ASHRAE). ASHRAE Ventilation Standard 62-1981 established the minimum ventilation design criteria from 1981 to April 1991 and expressly purported to define minimum building ventilation requirements. There were several problems with ASHRAE Standard 62-1981. First, a designer using the outdoor air flow rate tables mechanically introduced only 25 percent of the ventilation that ASHRAE recommends today. Second, ASHRAE Standard 62-1981 did not specifically address VAV ventilation performance. Finally, Standard 62-1981 was based on 50-year-old ventilation test data. Published technical criticism describing all of these IAQ problems began to appear in trade journals during the early 1980s. *Id.* at 31.

In April of 1991, the American National Standard Institute (ANSI) adopted revised ASHRAE Standard 62-1989. The significant changes in design criteria contained in ASHRAE Standard 62-1989 suggest that this ventilation criteria will be the benchmark against which all designs will likely be measured. This Standard addressed both the rate of outdoor air flow and the maintenance of minimum ventilation rates in VAV systems. *Id.* at 32.

During the early 1980s, there were bright-line minimum ventilation design criteria. ASHRAE Standard 62-1981 was the only guideline accepted by the technical society, and building codes generally required even less ventilation. However, there was a steady stream of ventilation design criticism warning of underventilated buildings. Criticisms of the 1981 standards appeared frequently in trade journals during the 1980s. Therefore, because the technical design criteria were in a state of flux, a duty determination was complex. Accordingly, a designer's duty to avoid an SBS condition was unclear as the indoor air quality phenomenon only began to be recognized in the late 1970s and early 1980s. *Id.* at 33.

In addition to the designer's negligent design that may either cause or aggravate sick building syndrome claims, issues can arise regarding whether the designer has a duty to abate a known or suspected IAQ hazard. An action for abatement costs against a design professional will, in all probability, be based on the negligent design or negligent approval of construction. Icard & Wright, "Sick Building Syndrome and Building-Related Illness Claims: Defining the Practical and Legal Issues," 14 *Construction Lawyer* No. 4, at 30 (Oct. 1994) (citing *Evanston Insurance Co. v. Treister,* 794 F. Supp. 560 (D.V.I. 1992)). Generally, strict liability is not applicable to persons providing professional services. *Id.* (citing *Chubb Group of Insurance Cos. v. C.F. Murphy,* 656 S.W.2d 766 (Mo. Ct. App. 1983) (strict liability does not apply to architect of commercial building)).

When a professional's conduct is clearly improper and manifestly below reasonable standards, negligence may be proved by the application of ordinary intelligence to the facts. See § **22.4**. However, the SBS technical ventilation facts and a plethora of other possible causes appear to be too complicated for a lay jury finding of negligence. Gardner, "Is the Design Architect or Engineer Liable for Sick Building Syndrome Damages?," 11 *Construction Lawyer* No. 4, at 33 (Oct. 1991).

A designer's insurance may provide funds to correct any IAQ-related problems in addition to providing a defense. Under policies with no pollution exclusion clauses, the insurer would be liable to defend and indemnify the design professional for damages for cost of repair, loss of use of the facility, and personal injury. Icard & Wright, "Sick Building Syndrome and Building-Related Illness Claims: Defining the Practical and Legal Issues," 14 *Construction Lawyer* No. 4, at 33 (Oct. 1994). However, in order to limit the insurer's exposure, some professional liability policies contain pollution exclusion clauses. See §§ **3.6** and **14.8**. Even with pollution exclusion clauses, significant questions may arise regarding whether the loss was caused by the pollution or by the negligent design or approval of construction.

Design/builders may be covered by commercial general liability policies. When seemingly innocuous building materials or HVAC installations are found to emit into the air space within a building envelope particulate that is harmful to human health, the cost of abating that condition is arguably a loss within coverage of a standard CGL insurance policy. Courts addressing this issue have uniformly held that CGL policies cover damages arising from asbestos exposure. *Id.* at 30.

§ 7.22 Problems with Electronic Media

Page 158, add at end of list in second paragraph:

4. The original designer's CAD system requires special consideration if the designer is changed for any reason, and a new designer is to complete the design. Since changes to documents on CAD can be undetectable, an architect or engineer that allows its clients to continue to use its CAD disks may be included in an action resulting from the errors or omissions of its successor. The termination agreement should obligate the owner to acknowledge that the documents on CAD are provided as an accommodation. The owner should obligate recipients of the disks to acknowledge that translation errors resulting from differences in computer software, hardware, and related equipment, disk malfunctions, and user error may cause data errors. The recipient should also acknowledge that, as a result of these factors, the design professional has no responsibility for, and makes no representations regarding, the accuracy of the information contained on the CAD disks. Patterson, C., "Construction Tips from Division 5: Protecting the Design Professional," 3 *Construction Forum News* N6, at N7 (July 1998).

The signature and stamp of a professional engineer are not easily translated into computer terms. When you create an engineering document and send it to someone, the recipient wants to know several things about the document: the identity of the sender, whether the document was signed by the sender, and whether the document was altered after being signed. The digital signature process provides all that information. J. Orr, "Identity Crisis," 68 *Civil Engineering* 52, at 53 (No. 6, June 1998).

Signing a digital file requires hashing the file and then encrypting the hash. The selected file is decompressed to a temporary file and then hashed. Then the private key is used to encrypt the hash. The encrypted hash and the key file name are then stored with the file. As long as a secure hash function is used, someone's digital signature may not be removed from one document and attached to another or a signed message altered in any way. The slightest change in a signed document will yield a different message digest when the document is hashed. Orr, at 53–54.

A "hash" is a function that takes a message of any length and yields a message digest, a unique string of characters or symbols related to the content of the message. A secure hash will never yield the same string for different messages, and is as unique as a fingerprint. The recipient of a message can hash the received document and compare the result with the hash attached to the document as an identifier. If the two are not exactly the same, the document has been altered. Verifying a signature means hashing the file again after decompression, using the public key to decrypt the signature (or encrypted hash), and the key file name is then stored with the file. Orr, at 53–54.

One organization, the Department of Energy's Savannah River Site, is moving toward broad-based application of digital signature technology. One problem the Department of Energy encountered was the lack of a single major supplier of digital signature technology. The Department of Energy warns vendors and users of the need to integrate a single digital signature technology across business processes and applications to create electronic approval systems. Orr, at 54.

§ 7.23 Liability Concerns

Page 159, add after first full paragraph:

Contractors bidding projects with drawings prepared using CADD systems should be aware that spatial data comprising CADD files may not accurately reflect dimensions. Disclaimers, such as the one below, caution contractors to use the dimensions on the drawings and not to rely on scaled dimensions because of the CADD's inaccurate spatial representations:

> The Department of Transportation makes no representation or warranties, express or implied, with respect to the reuse of the data provided herewith, regardless of its format or the means of its transmission. There is no guarantee or representation to the user as to the accuracy, currency, suitability, or reliability of this data for any purpose. The user accepts the data "as is" and assumes all risks associated with its use. By acceptance of this data, the user agrees not to transmit this data or provide access to it or any part of it to another party unless the user shall include with the data a copy of this disclaimer. The Department of Transportation assumes no responsibility for actual or consequential damage incurred as a result of any user's reliance on this data.

Page 163, add after first full paragraph:

The greatest potential for misappropriation of a trade secret comes when a key employee leaves one company to work for a competitor. Noncompete agreements, in which employees agree not to work for any competitors within a reasonable geographic area for a specified time period after leaving their original employers, are one of the best ways to guard against the loss of trade secrets. The agreements are usually binding, unless an employee can prove that a particular agreement is unreasonably restrictive. Even if the employee does not quit to work for another company, if the employee provides a competitor with confidential information, the noncompete agreement will help prove a misappropriation of trade secrets. J. Lester, "Staking Your Claim," 68 *Civil Engineering* 65, at 66 (No. 7, July 1998).

Many engineering companies today are also software publishers. Proprietary software, an area of growing concern for many companies, can be protected as a trade secret if distribution is limited and controlled carefully. Many software developers have been able to maintain trade secrets by placing restrictions in license agreements and by distributing only the object code, or machine language, versions of their programs. In *Trandes Corp. v. Guy F. Atkinson Co.*, 996 F.2d 655 (4th Cir. 1993), Atkinson received permission to use Trandes Corp.'s subway tunnel design software during a legitimately licensed job. Atkinson made an illegal copy of the software during the job and subsequently used it again without permission. The jury found that Atkinson had misappropriated Trandes's trade secrets and fined Atkinson $17,000 in actual damages and $34,000 in punitive damages. The *Atkinson* case demonstrates that companies should draft their licenses carefully to protect proprietary software against unauthorized copying. Lester, at 66–67.

Unauthorized copying of computer software is an issue of increasing concern. The Software Publishers Association (SPA), Washington, D.C., has filed hundreds of lawsuits against businesses that have permitted employees to distribute illegal copies of software. In one case, the SPA recovered $498,000 from a company that had permitted its employees to make multiple copies of a particular program. Lester, at 67.

CHAPTER 9

MISCELLANEOUS CLAIMS

§ 9.2 Implied Warranties: Traditional Rule

Page 200, add to note 2 after La Rossa citation:

La Rossa rationale also followed in Snyder v. ISC Alloys, Ltd., 772 F. Supp. 251 (W.D. Pa. 1991).

Page 201, add to note 5 after Prier citation:

Federal Mogul Corp. v. Universal Constr. Co., 376 So. 2d 725 (Ala. Ct. App. 1979) (court admitted that, under proper circumstances, an architect impliedly warrants that plans and specifications for the construction of a building are sufficient to make the structure reasonably fit for its intended purpose; because no proof existed that architects' plans were defective in this case, court refused to apply this theory).

Page 203, in note 12, add to Georgetown citation:

rev'd, 7 F.3d 223 (4th Cir. 1993) (without opinion)

§ 9.3 — Justification for Traditional Rule

Page 203, add to note 14 after Tamarac citation:

Zenda Grain & Supply v. Farmland Indus. Inc., 894 P.2d 890 (Kan. Ct. App. 1995) (court extended implied warranty of workmanlike performance to management agreement; court cited professions to which this warranty has been held to apply (*id.* at 891): installation and service of fire and burglary alarms, engineering and architecture, building contractors and subcontractors, insurance investigation and claims handling).

Page 205, add to note 23:

See also Kovaleski v. Tallahassee Title Co., 363 So. 2d 1156 (Fla. Dist. Ct. App. 1978) (court applied *Audlane* rationale regarding architect's duty to title abstracting company).

§ 9.5 Theory of Strict Liability in Tort

Page 213, add at end of section:

In *Cubito v. Kreisberg,* 419 N.Y.S.2d 582 (App. Div. 1979), the court held that in determining the liability of an architect to third parties for injuries caused by the architect's negligence, the test of patent or latent defect is not to be applied. The question of liability depends rather on whether the architect exercised due care in preparing the plans.

§ 9.6 —Possible Applications of Strict Liability

Page 213, add to note 61:

aff'd, 707 F.2d 671 (2d Cir. 1983).

§ 9.7 Abnormally Dangerous Activity

Page 216, add to note 77:

See also German v. Federal Home Loan Mortgage Corp., 885 F. Supp. 537, 570 (S.D.N.Y. 1995).

Page 217, add to note 87:

aff'd, 565 S.W.2d 223 (Tex. 1978)

§ 9.8 Contractors' Errors

Page 220, add after "See" in note 101:

Block v. Lohan Assocs. Inc., 645 N.E.2d 207 (Ill. App. Ct. 1993) (court held that architect could not be held liable in negligence action arising from subcontractor's fall from ladder when contract limited architect's responsibilities to only design and determination as to design conformance; contract did not extend to worker safety or to acts and omissions of contractors or subcontractors in performing their work); Ivanov v. Process Design Assocs., 642 N.E.2d 711 (Ill. App. Ct. 1993) (engineer/construction manager does not owe contractor's employees a duty to ensure safe jobsite; duty is governed by contract between the parties. Engineer may, however, voluntarily assume the duty to provide a safe workplace by the terms of the contract).

Page 221, add at end of section:

It is often prudent for the designer to rely on an experienced contractor or supplier to design certain components of the work. For example, curtainwalls, elevators, and other components or subsystems are often conceived in detail during the construction process and designed by specialty subcontractors. But delegation of design work has resulted in blurred lines of responsibility, authority, and liability for contractors and design professionals. The 1997 A201 delineates when and how a designer may delegate design functions to a contractor. Under the 1997 A201, a designer may delegate design responsibilities to a contractor by specifying performance and design criteria in the contract. The contractor must then arrange for such work to be performed by a licensed designer that must sign and seal its work product. The owner and architect are thereafter entitled to rely on the adequacy, accuracy, and completeness of the delegated work product. N. Potter, "Design Delegation Provisions of AIA Document A201, 1997 Edition," 18 *Con. Law.* 27 (No. 3, July 1998).

In 1987, AIA A201 provided at subparagraph 3.12.11 that the architect was entitled to rely on the accuracy and completeness of professional certification of performance criteria of materials, systems, or equipment required by the contract. The 1997 version replaced 3.12.11 with an expanded 3.12.10. In general, the 1997 revisions appear to assist designers by clarifying the procedures by which they may delegate design responsibility to the contractor. Potter, at 27–28.

The first portion of new subparagraph 3.12.10 provides that a contractor cannot be required to perform design functions on a construction project unless the contractor needs to provide such services in order to carry out the contractor's responsibilities for construction means and methods. The contractor is not permitted to provide professional design services in any event if it is a violation of applicable law. Potter, at 28.

The second part of AIA A201 1997 subparagraph 3.12.10 requires the owner and architect to specify all performance and design criteria of any contractor-provided design services or certifications. In other words, the design professional may delegate design functions to a contractor, but the contractor is obligated to provide the design only after the design requirement that the contractor must meet has been defined. Potter, at 28.

For properly delegated design services, the third part of the new subparagraph requires the contractor to provide licensed design professionals whose written approval, signature, and seal shall appear on all submitted drawings or certifications. The final part of 3.12.10 entitles the owner and architect to rely on the adequacy, accuracy, and completeness of the contractor-provided design. The architect's review or approval of the contractor-provided design is only for the limited purpose of checking for conformance with information given and the design concept expressed in the contract. Under 3.12.10, the architect, not the contractor, is responsible for the quality of the performance specifications. The contractor need only meet the criteria established by the project designer and is not responsible if those criteria are inappropriate. Potter, at 29.

The project architect must also review, approve, or take other appropriate action on all the design submittals made by the contractor and its design professional. In this way, the architect can check the submittal for conformance with information given and with the design concept expressed in the contract documents. The contractor is not responsible for the adequacy of the performance or design criteria required by the contract documents, and not responsible if those criteria prove to be inappropriate or do not produce the desired result. "The New A201, What's in It for the Contractor? An Overview and Analysis," *Constructor* 12–13 (Aug. 1997).

The design delegation language of the AIA's new B141, appears in subparagraph 2.6.4.3 and allows professional design services or certifications by a design professional related to systems, material, or equipment specifically required of the contractor in the contract. Subparagraph 2.6.4.3 requires the architect to specify appropriate performance and design criteria that such services must satisfy. Shop drawings and other submittals related to the work designed or certified by the design professional retained by the contractor is required to bear such professional's written approval when submitted to the architect. The architect is entitled to rely on the adequacy, accuracy, and completeness of the services, certifications, or approvals performed by the contractor's design professional, "as with previous editions of B141." American Institute of Architects, "Promises, Promises: Forging Healthy Project Relationships," at 13 (1997) (hereafter *Promises, Promises*).

Design delegation raises an important issue for owners, however, since it is imperative to determine whether the trade contractors performing design work, as well as the general contractor, are covered by errors and omissions insurance. P. Cobey, "The New B141: An Owner's Manual," 3 *The Construction Forum News* 2, at 4 (No. 2, Jan. 1998). In addition, AGC's endorsement of the AIA's new design delegation language included language to encourage AIA "to include in all of its owner-architect agreements . . . language clearly calling to the owner's attention any delegation of design responsibilities to the contractor." It should be emphasized that full disclosure of any delegation of design is in the best interest of all parties to the construction project. The owner must know who holds responsibilty for the design of all portions for the project. But the contractual allocation of design responsibilities must be crystal clear to the contactor as well. J. Mock, "Fairer? By Delegating Design," 239 *Enginering News-Record* 61 (Dec. 8, 1997).

Two decisions from the Kansas City Hyatt Regency collapse in 1981 illustrate the importance of the AIA's efforts to clarify the design delegation procedure in the 1997 edition of A201. Potter, at 27, *citing Missouri Bd. of Architects, Prof'l Eng'rs and Land Surveyors v. Daniel M. Duncan,* Case No. AR-84-0239 (Missouri Admin. Hearing Comm'n); *Duncan v. Missouri Bd. of Architects, Prof'l Eng'rs and Land Surveyors,* 744 S.W.2d 524 (Mo. 1988). Both decisions rejected the engineer's argument that delegation of the steel-to-steel connection design to a steel fabricator had effectively transferred all liability for those connections to the fabricator. The court of appeals held that although "the structural engineer on a project may, as a matter of custom, elect to have connections designed by the fabricator . . . [t]he adequacy of the connection design remains the responsibility of the structural engineer" (at 529). The court held that absent a specific disclaimer, an engineer who seals the plans thereby assumes responsibility "for the entire engineering project and all documents connected therewith" (at 536). Under public policy and state statutory law, the engineer was held to have a nondelegable responsibility for projects to which he affixes his seal, and "[c]ustom, practice, or 'bottom-line' necessity cannot alter that responsibility" (at 540). Potter, at 27.

Including design delegation in the contract also confronts whether by delegating design, the architect has increased its responsibility to the owner beyond the reasonable standard of care. By including design delegation under the permitted contractual duties, it is suggested that no additional liability is imposed on the designer for delegating any portion of the design. Another portion of B141 also suggests that the responsibility to the owner may be increased. 1997 B141 includes an agreement that the architect agrees not to engage in any activity or accept any employment, interest, or contribution that would reasonably appear to compromise the architect's judgment. *Promises, Promises,* at 7. However, traditional limits to the architect's liability have also been continued. For example, under the 1997 B141, the design professional agrees to endeavor to guard the owner against defects and deficiencies in the work of the contractor, but is not responsible for construction means, methods, techniques, sequences, or procedures, or for the acts or omissions of the contractor, subcontractors, or for the failure of any of them to carry out the work in accordance with the contract documents. The design professional did agree to exercise reasonable care in advising the owner of defects of which the design professional became aware. As is typical in these agreements, the design professional has only the authority to act to the extent provided in the contract documents.

For years, a design professional's liability has been determined by judging its performance against the standard of care in the industry. Simply stated, a design professional is liable if it fails to exercise the degree of skill exercised by members of the professions in the project's location who have similar training and experience. The design professional is required to act as a prudent professional. These concepts are well settled and well understood not only in the design profession, but in other professions as well. This knowledge facilitates consistent risk allocation because it enables a professional to assess the complexity of the project and set its fee accordingly. R. Staed, "General Counsel Corner," *Construction Forum News* 7 (Jan. 1998).

On the other hand, a fiduciary duty is a significantly higher standard and is unfamiliar to most design professionals. A fiduciary duty connotes a special relationship between the client and the professional that is beyond what is normally expected of the professional. A fiduciary duty is most often recognized when managing funds for another where the person handling the funds is placed in a position of trust and confidence far different from a typical relationship between a design professional and a client. A fiduciary is a trustee who holds assets in trust for the beneficiary and is charged with preserving those assets and investing money wisely. In the typical setting, a design professional simply is not a trustee.

In *Vikell Investors Pacific, Inc. v. Kip Hampden, Ltd., et. al.*, 946 P.2d 589 (Colo. Ct. App. 1997), a Colorado appeals court rejected an allegation that a soil engineer owed a fiduciary duty to a property owner in connection with a downhill excavation. The court denied the allegation that the engineer had a high degree of control over the client's property and that the client had placed a special level of trust and confidence in the engineer above and beyond the normal engineering relationship. The court noted that the engineer was a member of a team of people working for the client that was limited to providing recommendations for review by the other members of the team. The engineer maintained it had no practical control over the project.

State law may also regulate the designer's delegation of design functions. For example, the Florida Administrative Code obligates the engineer-of-record to provide the contractor with written engineering requirements. Potter, at 29, *citing* Fla. Admin. Code Ann. R. 61g.15-30.005. The contractor must determine if conflicts exist between its own documents and specifications from the owner. Each party must also review the other's final design. In contrast, the 1997 revisions to AIA A201 entitled the designer to rely on the contractor-provided design without any specifically required review.

Except where state law imposes supplemental duties on the primary designer, as in Florida, it appears that the new subparagraph 3.12.10 established procedures under which the designer may effectively delegate liability for delegated design work, especially when it involves ancillary parts of the design. Although the primary project designer retains some responsibility to review the delegated work under 3.12.10, that review is only for the limited purpose of checking for conformance with information given and the design concept expressed in the contract. The effectiveness of delegation may depend on the adequacy of the primary designer's performance specifications or design criteria that provide guidelines for the delegated design work. Potter, at 29.

In many cases, the contractor will no longer be able to assume that its design submissions will necessarily be subject to an independent quality review by the project designer or that the design work will fall under a total project design responsibility. Under the new A201, design professionals may be able to avoid the liability that the Kansas City Hyatt decisions held was nondelegable. Furthermore, a contractor's disclaimer of liability for design may not be effective. Potter, at 30.

§ 9.9 Guarding Owners

Page 221, add to note 112:

C.L. Maddox Inc. v. Benham Group, Inc., 88 F.3d 592 (8th Cir. 1996) (designer was not responsible for guarding contractor against defects and deficiencies in designer's work, despite provisions in contractor-designer contract that required designer to keep contractor informed of the progress and quality of the work, and to endeavor to guard contractor against defects and deficiencies in the contractor's work, because contract also included a provision that designer shall not be responsible for construction means, methods, techniques, sequences, or procedures, or for acts or omissions of contractor or its subcontractors. Court found that designer had duty to visit site and make recommendations to contractor, but did not impose duty to guarantee that contractor would not make any errors).

Page 221, add at end of section:

A judge in a state court in Oakland, California, instructed the jury that under the typical American Institute of Architects agreement, the designer was a fiduciary to the building owner, whose duties went beyond informing the client of problems the designer had observed and required the designer to see that the problems were corrected. A fiduciary responsibility goes beyond a professional standard based on how other professionals would act in a similar situation, or a fitness standard under which negligence need not be proved but only that the desired results were not achieved. A fiduciary standard imposes a greater liability on a design professional and changes the traditional relationship between architects, engineers, and clients. "Jury's $7-Million Verdict Based on Designer's 'Fiduciary' Role," 238 *Engineering News-Record* 11 (No. 26, June 30, 1997).

§ 9.12 Claims Related to Licensing

Page 228, add after carryover paragraph:

In *Secretary of Labor v. Foit-Albert Associates, Architects & Engineers,* OSHRC No. 92-654 (Apr. 21, 1997), the commission found that an engineer with a contract to provide construction phase inspection services was not subject to OSHA standards. Foit-Albert was charged with violations of federal regulations governing cast-in-place concrete construction after part of a cast-in-place concrete floor collapsed. Foit-Albert's services during construction included the review of contract drawings, the review and preparation of changes for approval by the owner, and inspection of the work for compliance with design specifications. Its contract provided that Foit-Albert was not responsible for acts or omissions by the architect, contractor, subcontractor, or others who performed the work. Although Foit-Albert had no contractual authority to stop work, reject work, or authorize deviations, it had informed the contractor about deficiencies in the shoring and concrete placement on another part of the floor that collapsed and had refused to accept work that did not conform to the project's specifications. The area that collapsed was shored without Foit-Albert's knowledge, and it had no opportunity to inspect the shoring before the collapse. The commission found that Foit-Albert lacked the degree of control over safety issues required to bring a design professional within the scope of the construction standards. *See* "OSHA Construction Standards May Apply to Design Professionals Who Provide Construction Services,"

XII *Postner & Rubin Construction and the Law* 2–3 (Nos. 2 & 3, Fall-Winter 1997).

In contrast, in *Secretary of Labor v. CH2M Hill Central,* OSHRC No. 89-1712 (Apr. 21, 1997), the commission applied OSHA standards to an engineer who had broad responsibility for construction activities, even though the engineer's contract expressly disclaimed responsibility for safety. CH2M Hill was charged with OSHA violations after a methane gas explosion killed three construction workers. The engineering firm was retained by the Milwaukee Metropolitan Sewage District to provide program management, engineering, construction management, and start-up management services for a water pollution abatement project. Both CH2M Hill's contract with the owner and the owner's contract with the contractor indicated that the contractors were solely responsible for construction means and methods and for safety programs. The commission determined that CH2M Hill possessed "global" project responsibilities extending from the pre-bid through start-up phases. Although CH2M Hill did not have the authority to stop work, its authority to order defective work corrected, authority over scheduling and allocation of resources, and authority to resolve conflicts between contractors were sufficient to make the OSHA standards applicable. The commission also reviewed contract modifications drafted by CH2M Hill relating to a differing site condition, the presence of soil layers that produced methane gas. It concluded that because the primary purpose of the change order was to minimize a safety hazard, CH2M Hill was necessarily involved with and responsible for safety issues. *See* "OSHA Construction Standards," *supra,* at 2–3.

CHAPTER 10

THE DESIGN PROFESSIONAL'S CRIMINAL LIABILITY

§ 10.5 — OSHA Violations

Page 242, add after first full paragraph:

In *Secretary of Labor v. Foit-Albert Associates, Architects & Engineers,* OSHRC No. 92-654 (Apr. 21, 1997), the commission found that an engineer with a contract to provide construction phase inspection services was not subject to OSHA standards. Foit-Albert was charged with violations of federal regulations governing cast-in-place concrete construction after part of a cast-in-place concrete floor collapsed. In contrast, in *Secretary of Labor v. CH2M Hill Central,* OSHRC No. 89-1712 (Apr. 21, 1997), the commission applied OSHA standards to an engineer who had broad responsibility for construction activities, even though the engineer's contract expressly disclaimed responsibility for safety. *See* § **9.12**.

Page 242, add at end of section:

The OSHA Review Commission ruled in 1993 that a design firm that did not exercise substantial supervision over construction was not subject to OSHA construction standards. On appeal, the U.S. Court of Appeals for the First Circuit affirmed the case on the narrow ground that the firm had no employees on the site at the time of the accident. T. Smith, "Site Safety: Rights, Risks and Responsibilities," 68 *Civil Eng'g* 55, at 57 (No. 5, May 1998).

Under OSHA, the Secretary of Labor has introduced specific regulations for the construction industry stating that A/Es deemed to be "engaged in construction work" may be subject to the OSHA standards. OSHA authorizes the secretary of labor to begin enforcement proceedings for violations. The proceedings may result in financial penalties and in some cases may lead to criminal sanctions. Smith, at 56.

More recently, however, the OSHA commission held that an engineering firm was subject to the OSHA construction standards in a case involving a methane gas explosion that killed three employees working on a water pollution abatement project in Milwaukee. Both the engineer and the construction contractor received OSHA citations, but the administrative law judge ruled that the engineering firm did not exercise supervision over the construction and was not subject to OSHA standards. The commission reversed the decision, finding that the engineer's tasks were broad and involved hands-on oversight. The commission noted that the engineering firm had overall managerial or administrative responsibilities under its contract for construction management and planning and had broad contractual and de facto safety authority. On appeal to the Federal Court of Appeals, the case was recently sent back to the commission on a procedural matter. Smith, at 57.

In another recent case, an engineering firm was retained by an architect to inspect for contractor compliance with plans and specifications for a university building in New York. After a shoring collapse injured three employees, OSHA issued a citation to the firm. Affirming the decision of the administrative law judge, the commission ruled that the regulations were not applicable because the firm did not have overall managerial or administrative responsibility for the project. The commission also noted that the engineer had no contractual or actual authority to direct the work of the contractors, although the firm did not notify the contractor of observed safety hazards. The secretary of labor appealed the decision to the U. S. Court of Appeals for the Second Circuit but subsequently withdrew the appeal. Smith, at 57.

§ 10.6 —ADA Violations

Page 242, add at beginning of section:

Since its passage, the Americans with Disabilities Act (ADA) has created a nightmare of compliance issues for designers and their clients. Among them are: Who is responsible for ADA compliance? Who decides how to balance economic and compliance conflicts, the owner or the designer? Issues of wheelchair seating capacity compete with the recently emerged demand that wheelchair spectators be able to see over standing spectators in front of them, which competes with the need to integrate wheelchair spectators with the spectator audience. D. Green, "Corporate Counsel Corner," 17 *Construction Lawyer* 3 (No. 3, July 1997).

Revisions to the accessibility guidelines of the 1992 Americans with Disabilities Act will not be proposed for public comment until September. The line-of-sight issue, central to several court cases involving arenas will be clarified, but the broader question of designer liability will not be included because it was not in the original legislation. The revisions also are expected to bring accessibility requirements into conformance with building codes. Officials say a final rule will not be in place until 1999. The Federal Access Board was expected to release its proposed changes in July. The Department of Justice also has been preparing amendments to ADA. The two plans are expected to be announced together. "Guideline Revision Hit Delays," 240 *Engineering News-Record* 13 (No. 13, March 30, 1998).

For an owner to be liable for the designer's failure to conform to the ADA, the owner must have actual knowledge of the violation and exercised a significant degree of control over the work. For example, In *United States v. Days Inn of America, Inc.*, 1998 U.S. App. LEXIS 18159 (8th Cir. 1998), the court considered whether Days Inn was responsible for the failure to "design and construct" a hotel in compliance with the Americans with Disabilities Act.

Because the ADA does not, the court determined what types of entities are liable for failing to "design and construct" an accessible facility under § 303. The court noted that the Department of Justice (DOJ) had issued a Technical Assistance Manual, which directed that architects and contractors may be liable for failing to design and construct accessible facilities. *See* Americans with Disabilities Act, Department of Justice, Technical Assistance Manual, III-5.1000 (Jan. 1993). The court found that the DOJ directive supported the government's assertion that any party substantially participating in the design and construction of a facility shares the responsibility if the facility violated ADA's standards.

To give effect to the plain language of § 303, as well as deference to the DOJ's interpretation of the statute, the court concluded that to bear responsibility for an inaccessible facility under § 303, a party must possess a significant degree of control over the final design and construction of a facility. Days Inn's mere instruction that its facility comply with the ADA or some other statute would not constitute significant control over the design and construction of the facility.

The court concluded that to be liable, Days Inn must have been responsible for the design and construction of the hotel, but explained that the owner's responsibility must not be tangentially or remotely connected with the project. To give effect to the language of the statute, the owner must possess a significant degree of control over the final design and construction of the facility. Further, the *Days Inn* court ruled that despite a potential significant degree of control, the owner must have actually exercised the control and had actual knowledge that the final plans violated the Act. Without such actual knowledge, the owner would not have failed to design and construct the proposed hotel in compliance with the accessibility requirements of the Americans with Disability Act.

The court noted that although Days Inn reviewed and approved preliminary designs, Days Inn never received or demanded the final plans for the project. Moreover, the architect made final the design plans before receiving Days Inn of America's response to the preliminary design. As a result, Days Inn's review of building plans did not play much, if any, factor in the design and construction of the project. Further, the court could not determine as a matter of law whether the preliminary plans disclosed the ADA violations. An owner with no knowledge that its franchisee has constructed a facility in violation of the ADA should not suffer liability under § 303, regardless of the franchisor's available authority to ensure ADA compliance.

The court remanded the case to the district court to determine whether Days Inn possessed actual knowledge that the final design and construction plans for the hotel violated the ADA. If Days Inn had such knowledge, it would be liable for the violations because it retained ample power to require compliance with the ADA. Without such actual knowledge, however, it would not have "failed to design and construct" the proposed hotel in compliance with the accessibility requirements of the ADA.

Page 243, add at end of section:

The Justice Department sued architect Ellerbe Becket, Inc., in federal district court in Minneapolis for designing six arenas that do not comply with the Americans with Disabilities Act's standards for new facilities. Included in the suit are five completed buildings and one arena under construction: Boston's Fleet Center, Philadelphia's Corestates Center, Portland's Rose Garden, Cleveland's Gund Arena, and Buffalo's Marine Midland Arena are completed; MCI Centre in Washington, D.C., is under construction. The Justice Department claims that the arenas fail to provide spectators who have disabilities with a line of sight to the playing surface that is comparable to that of other spectators. Winston, "Justice Sues Arena Architect," 237 *Engineering News-Record* 11 (No. 17, Oct. 21, 1996).

The Justice Department's lawsuit against Ellerbe Becket was filed after eight months of settlement negotiations broke down. The suit asks for a civil penalty and an order preventing the architect from continuing to design stadiums and arenas that do not provide the proper line of sight. Ellerbe stated that it would not stop any work in progress. *Id.*

In *United States v. Ellerbe Becket, Inc.,* 976 F. Supp. 1262 (D. Minn. 1997), the Department of Justice sought to preclude Ellerbe Becket from designing facilities in the future that do not provide for wheelchair lines of sight over standing patrons. Ellerbe Becket brought a motion to dismiss on the basis that the court lacks subject matter jurisdiction and that the complaint fails to state a claim upon which relief can be granted. D. Green, "Corporate Counsel Corner," 17 *Construction Lawyer* 3 (No. 3, July 1997). The federal district court in Minnesota denied the motion by architect Ellerbe Becket Inc., to dismiss the lawsuit. The Minnesota case will be the flagship case because it focuses solely on the liability of architects. S. Wright, "Disabilities Law Tests Architects," 239 *Engineering News-Record 10 (No. 15, Oct. 13, 1997).*

According to the Justice Department, inclusion of the word *design* in the law indicated Congress's intention to subject those who design buildings to liability. But Ellerbe Becket pointed to language stating that only entities that "design and construct" facilities of public accommodation are liable under the law. That would leave an inexplicable gap in coverage of the statute by excluding "commercial" facilities, asserted the Justice Department. The American Institute of Architects, which filed a brief in support of Ellerbe Becket, acknowledged that architects are liable, but that their legal responsibility is under their contractual obligations with the building owners. *Id.* at 10.

After reviewing conflicting federal court decisions, the court evaluated whether Ellerbe Becket participated in the construction and design of the arenas. The Justice Department had argued that Ellerbe Becket participated in the design and construction of the facilities. The court denied Ellerbe Becket's motion to dismiss and allowed the case to continue. The federal judge concluded that architects are not excluded from liability under the ADA as a matter of law, but noted that there are disputes over interpretations of the relevant provisions of the law. The federal judge found that Congress had clearly intended that commercial facilities be subject to the accessibility standards for new construction, but stopped short of addressing whether a party may be liable under the ADA for designing a noncompliant facility if it had no involvement in constructing the facility. The court said it did not need to decide whether a party may be liable where it only designed a facility and did not participate in its construction since the Justice Department alleged that Ellerbe had participated in both design and construction of the stadiums and arenas.

In *United States v. Ellerbe Becket, Inc.*, 976 F. Supp. 1262 (D. Minn. 1997), a federal district court in Minnesota ruled that architects are not excluded from liability under the new construction provision of the ADA. The court found the ADA covers commercial facilities in addition to public accommodations. Commercial facilities are those intended for nonresidential use whose operations affect commerce. The court refused to limit liability to owners, operators, lessors, or lessees of public accommodations, and as the result would leave no entity liable for violations of new construction accessibility standards for buildings that are only commercial facilities and not public accommodations. In so doing, the court relied on its finding that Congress clearly intended commercial facilities to be subject to the ADA's accessibility standards for new construction.

The *Ellerbe Becket* decision is consistent with an earlier case decided by a federal district court in Florida holding that architects are subject to liability under the ADA. *Johanson v. Huizenga Holdings, Inc.*, 963 F. Supp. 1175 (S.D. Fla. 1997), stated if architects are not liable under the ADA, it is conceivable that no entity would be liable for construction of a new commercial facility that violated the ADA.

The *Ellerbe Becket* litigation was recently settled when the architectural firm agreed to design new stadiums and arenas so spectators in wheelchairs still have a full view when other fans stand up. The agreement settles a lawsuit filed by the Justice Department in October 1996 charging that the Ellerbe Becket firm had violated the Americans with Disabilities Act with its designs of six arenas. The U.S. District Court in Minneapolis approved the agreement. "Federal Complaint on Arena Design Is Settled," *The Kansas City Star* D-8, (April 28, 1998).

The government settled for an agreement by Ellerbe Becket to design future sites along guidelines that the government said would meet the law's requirements. The agreement does not represent an admission of guilt by Ellerbe Becket and no civil penalty was imposed. Ellerbe Becket maintained that the ADA was not clear and was open to interpretation as to precisely what was required.

Ellerbe Becket agreed to take into account the likelihood that some spectators would stand for part of all of events such as basketball games and rock concerts, and to design wheelchair seating so its occupants could still see when others stood. The agreement includes detailed measurements for the average height of standing spectators and the average height of a person in a wheelchair to be used in calculating sight lines for wheelchair users that the Justice Department said would be comparable to those for other spectators. The agreement clarified ADA compliance for the entire design industry.

A recent, but unsuccessful, attempt to expand designer liability to third parties under the Americans with Disabilities Act (ADA) occurred in *Paralyzed Veterans v. Ellerbe Becket Architects & Engineers, P.C.,* Civ. Action No. 96-1354 (TFH) (D.D.C. 1996), wherein the plaintiffs brought an action under the ADA alleging that the designer of the MCI Centre failed to accommodate wheelchair-bound persons attending events at the arena. The Paralyzed Veterans of America sued Ellerbe Becket for ADA violations in the MCI Centre's design. However, a federal district court dismissed Ellerbe as a defendant, asserting that the law places responsibility for ADA compliance with owners and operators, not designers. The plaintiffs asserted that the design for the MCI Centre violated the ADA because most proposed wheelchair locations had obstructed views of the arena. They argued that the ADA requires that those in wheelchair positions have comparable views to those not in wheelchair positions. The judge denied the motion for preliminary injunction on the ground that the ADA specifically makes owners, operators, lessors, and lessees responsible for compliance. The judge noted that the intent of the statutory language appeared to be that those who pay for design services are responsible for ADA compliance. Bell, "Eroding Foundations: Increased Liability of Construction Design Professionals," 32 *Procurement Lawyer* 6 (No. 2, Winter 1997).

The court in *Paralyzed Veterans* felt that with moderate changes, wheelchair spectators' ability to see over standing spectators and the dispersal and integration requirements of the wheelchair locations around the facility could be achieved. The *Paralyzed Veterans* court has now approved the modified plans. The only other case to decide whether the court has jurisdiction over the designer in an ADA dispute concerned the Florida Panthers hockey arena. The plaintiffs alleged that the wheelchair seating did not provide views comparable to those of other patrons. In *Johnson v. Ellerbe Becket, Inc.,* Civ. No. 96-7026 (D. Fla. Jan. 27, 1997, slip. op.), the court kept all parties in the case. Green at 3. The *Johnson* suit was withdrawn after the plaintiffs reviewed project documents with an ADA consultant and determined that the arena was in compliance, according to Ellerbe Becket. There was no settlement. "Plaintiffs Voluntarily Drop ADA Lawsuit Against Ellerbe," 239 *Engineering News-Record* 5 (No. 16, Oct. 20, 1997). Regardless of the *Johnson* settlement, federal courts clearly are split over the issue of an architect's liability under the law. The United States Court of Appeals has not yet ruled on the issue.

Although this attempt failed, there may well be other attempts to establish designer liability to third parties under the ADA. When a designer creats plans and specifications that do not comply with ADA requirements, the owner may be liable to third parties. In that situation, the owner will seek to make the designer a party to any litigation and will attempt to recover any damages the owner must pay from the designer. *Id.*

The owner should be the one to make the final decision on how far to go in resolving the various and mutually exclusive issues. Although the designer can come up with solutions, such solutions may well be economically unrealistic, creating a project that cannot be completed within the owner's budget. Green at 3.

§ 10.12 False Statements

Page 250, add at end of section:

Contracts with the federal government also carry penalties for certified but false claims. The penalties apply to false change orders. The False Claims Act provides, in relevant part, that any person who

> (1) knowingly presents, or causes to be presented, to an officer or employee of the United States government or a member of the armed forces of the United States a false or fraudulent claim for payment or approval;
>
> (2) knowingly makes, uses, or causes to be made or used, a false record or statement to get a false or fraudulent claim paid or approved by the government . . . is liable to the United States Government for a civil penalty of not less than $5,000 and not more than $10,000, plus three times the amount of damages which the government sustains because of the act of that person.

31 U.S.C. § 3729(a).

A *claim* is defined as

> any request or demand, whether under a contract or otherwise, for money or property which is made to a contractor, grantee, or other recipient if the United States Government provides any portion of the money or property which is requested or demanded, or if the Government will reimburse such contractor, grantee, or other recipient for any portion of the money or property which is requested or demanded.

31 U.S.C. § 3729(c).

Actual damages under the False Claims Act are equal to three times the difference between the market value of the products received and the market value of the products requested. In addition, civil penalties may be assessed against the contractor under the False Claims Act even if the government fails to show actual damages. Each separate false claim constitutes a separate violation for the purpose of damage awards under the False Claims Act.

A designer may be liable under the False Claims Act if it

- has actual knowledge of false information
- acts in deliberate ignorance of false information
- acts in reckless disregard of the truth or falsity of the information.

United States v. Advance Tool Co., 902 F. Supp. 1011 (W.D. Mo. 1995).

A designer will not be liable if an inaccurate claim was the result of an innocent mistake or "mere negligence." Further, the government need not prove an intent to deceive or specific intent to defraud, and it is no defense that the government failed to discover the false claim.

The False Claims Act was little used until amendments were made in 1986. The 1986 changes refurbished the law into a powerful tool against fraud in the defense industry. At the time, because of the Reagan military buildup, the industry was flush with federal money—and fraud, such as the infamous $500 toilet seat. P. Reidinger, "Fraud Doctors," 82 *A.B.A.J.* 51, 52 (May 1996). There has been a dramatic increase in government FCA recoveries. Total government civil FCA recoveries rose from $54 million in fiscal year 1986 to $1.09 billion in 1994. As the reach of the civil FCA expands, the sparse law on FCA damages becomes more critical. C. Dees & C. Bouquet, "Beyond 'Diminished Value': New Challenges in the Law of Civil False Claims Act Damages," 25 *Public Contract Law Journal* 597, 598 (No. 4, Summer 1996).

The False Claims Act reaches much further than submission of a falsified invoice to the government; the Supreme Court has held that the False Claims Act extends to all fraudulent attempts to cause the government to pay out sums of money. *United States v. Neifert-White Co.,* 390 U.S. 228, 233 (1968). Its broad scope is especially important because of the many, far-reaching certifications required of designers contracting with the government. *See* R. Cushman & S. Butler, *Construction Change Order Claims* § 4.5A (Cum. Supp. 1997).

CHAPTER 11

OWNERSHIP AND REUSE OF DESIGN PROFESSIONALS' DESIGNS

§ 11.2 Design Ownership

Page 259, add to note 3:

Fred Riley Home Bldg. Corp. v. Cosgrove, 864 F. Supp. 1034 (D. Kan. 1994) (builder who reviewed home design prepared by designer by standing beside designer as various plans were sketched was not coauthor or co-owner of copyright in the altered plans because changes were insubstantial and not original to builder and altered plan was substantially similar to designer's copyrighted plans).

§ 11.6 Statutory Copyright Protection

Page 263, add at end of section:

The Lanham Act (Trademark Act of 1946, Pub. Law. No. 104-118, as amended; as codified at 15 U.S.C. § 1051 *et seq.* (West 1982 & Supp. 1996), protects marks used in commerce that distinguish goods or services. Illicit copiers of construction documents are likely to replace the original architect's mark with their own. "Section 43(1) protects architects from [this type of] false designation of their work. Even one false designation of authorship can be enough to create confusion." *East/West Venture v. Wurmfeld Associates,* 13 U.S.P.Q.2d 1908, 1910 (S.D.N.Y. 1989). Penalties for Lanham Act violations can be substantial, and injunctive relief is available. 15 U.S.C. § 1116. When both copyrights and trademarks are infringed, remedies are presumably not preclusive. D. Roberts, "After the Ball: Subsequent Use of Construction Documents After the Project for Which They Were Originally Prepared: Sketchy Area of the Law," 17 *Construction Lawyer* 35, 39 (No. 2, Apr. 1997).

§ 11.7 —Drawings and Specifications

Page 263, add at end of section:

In *Guillot-Vogt Associates, Inc. v. Holly & Smith,* 848 F. Supp. 682 (E.D. La. 1994), the court determined that engineering drawings were also included within the protection. The court in *CSM Investors, Inc. v. Everest Development Ltd.,* 840 F. Supp. 1304 (D. Minn. 1994), explained that "architectural work" for purposes of copyright protection is a design as embodied in a tangible medium of expression, including architectural plans or drawings, and includes overall form as well as arrangement and composition of spaces, elements, and design, but does not include individual standard features.

In order for the designer to be considered the owner of a copyright and be protected under the Act, the work must be a "work made for hire." A *work made for hire* is statutorily defined to be made by an employee or by written agreement. In *Bryce & Polazzola Architects, Inc. v. A.M.E. Group,* 865 F. Supp. 401 (E.D. Mich. 1994), the court determined that a design prepared at an oral agreement was not a "work made for hire" under the Act.

§ 11.9 —Architectural Works

Page 264, add to note 41:

Ray, *Analysis of the Architectural Works Copyright Protection Act of 1990,* 15 Constr. Law. 23 (No. 2, Apr. 1995) (Architectural Works Copyright Protection Act of 1990 was designed to fill a gap in the American copyright laws that prevented full compliance with the Berne Convention).

Page 265, add to carryover paragraph:

The Architectural Works Copyright Protection Act of 1990 is not clear as to exactly what parts of an architectural work are protected. However, if courts apply a reasonable interpretation of the Act's terms and view "functionally required" narrowly, the Act should achieve the copyright goals of fostering creativity while not unduly restricting the ability to borrow and adapt architectural ideas and concepts. Ray, "Analysis of the Architectural Works Copyright Protection Act of 1990," 15 *Construction Lawyer* 32 (No. 2, Apr. 1995).

§ 11.14 — Contractual Agreements

Page 269, add to note 67:

See also Arthur Rutenberg Homes, Inc. v. Drew Homes Inc., 29 F.3d 1529 (11th Cir. 1994) (certificate of release signed by architect satisfies § 204(a)'s requirement for a writing); Great S. Homes v. Johnson & Thompson Realtors, 797 F. Supp. 609 (M.D. Tenn. 1992) (subsequent writings signed by copyright owner and transferee memorializing their oral transfer agreement related back to agreement and cured any defects in transferee's standing); Imperial Residential Design, Inc. v. Palms Dev. Group, Inc., 70 F.3d 96 (11th Cir. 1995) (oral assignment of design rights is valid to prove ownership in a copyright infringement lawsuit if a written agreement is signed later memorializing the transfer and there is no dispute between parties over ownership of the design).

Page 269, add at end of section:

In *Johnson v. Jones*, 149 F.3d 494, 1998 U.S. App. LEXIS (6th Cir. 1998), an architect sued an owner and both the replacement designer and builder for alteration and use of its architectural drawings without permission in violation of the Copyright Act and the Lanham Act.

The architect had originally submitted a standard American Institute of Architects contract, *Abbreviated Form of Agreement Between Owner and Architect*. The AIA-form contract provided in § 6.1 that the architect shall be deemed author of the documents and other drawings prepared with respect to the project and shall retain all rights to said documents, including copyrights. Section 6.1 further provided that the copyrighted drawings shall not be used by the owner or others on other projects, for additions to the project or for completion of the project by others, unless the architect was adjudged to be in default under the agreement, or the architect agrees in writing with appropriate compensation to the architect.

The owner had not yet purchased the home, but was anxious to get the project moving and asked the architect to recommend a surveyor to do the mortgage and topographical survey of the property. During this time, the architect began working on a design for the house. Subsequently, Johnson delivered the "Design Development Program" that outlined the necessary additions to, and remodel of, the house. The architect expect to obtain a signed contract but learned that the owner's attorney had not completed a contract review. Nevertheless, the owner made it clear that the architect was to continue working, which the architect did under the assumption that the owner would eventually sign the AIA contract.

Later, the owner asked the architect to also serve as the contractor in charge of the renovation. The architect agreed, but said a different contract would have to be used. The architect provided a copy of the AIA's *Standard Form Agreement Between Owner and Design/Builder* that contained a provision similar to § 6.1 that stated the drawings, specifications, and other documents furnished by the design-builder would not become the property of the owner and shall not be used by the owner on other projects, or for the completion of this project except by written agreement.

The owner objected to the AIA's ownership clause and asked the lawyer to draft an alternate clause. The alternate clause permitted the design-builder to retain ownership of the design drawings, but gave the owner the right to retain a set and utilize them for "any purpose she desires." In response to the owner's suggested clause, Johnson responded with more revisions, but made no reference to the revised ownership provision. Johnson later claimed that the omission was a mistake and that he had intended to contest the ownership provision as the owner's alternative provision. The owner did not accept the architect's additional revisions and terminated the architect because of the inability to agree to project terms.

The owner hired another designer and builder and gave them a copy of Johnson's drawings. The new builder noticed that Johnson's plans had copyright notices on them and refused to proceed until the copyright issue was resolved. The owner's attorney called the new builder, "explained everything was fine," and agreed to send a written confirmation. Without the written confirmation, the new builder began construction with Johnson's drawings, including removing Johnson's name and seal and replacing them with the new builder's. A written confirmation of the lawyer's opinion was never sent. Johnson later noticed the similarity of the building under progress with the design he had submitted, investigated, and found that his plans were being used, and initiated the lawsuit.

The court investigated, but found no implied license to use Johnson's drawings. The court found the AIA contracts contained express provisions that retained ownership with the design-builder and that the drawings could not be used to complete the project without a written agreement if the design-builder was not involved. The court also found that the acquisition of Johnson's drawings from the owner, rather than from Johnson, did not suggest an implied license.

The court also found that the new builder had taken the architect's drawings and represented them to be the builder's own. The court found it difficult to imagine how a designation of origin of a product could be more false or more likely to cause confusion or mistake as to the meaning of the trademarks involved as the new designer's use of Johnson's drawings. The court also found that Johnson and the new builder provided the same kind of services and used similar marketing, competing against each other. The appellate court concluded the trial court was correct to find the new builder liable under the Lanham Act for false designation of origin.

The court found no doubt that the new builder intended to pass Johnson's work off as its own. Although the new builder spent no time creating the design, it earned its fee from using Johnson's drawings. In addition, the new builder had submitted Johnson's design to the city for necessary permits in order to save valuable time. The court found that the new builder received a benefit from "countless" subcontractors seeing Johnson's excellent work and thinking that it was actually the new builder's work. Any potential new client would have also seen the project and been led to believe that the new builder, not Johnson, was responsible for the design. The court found that the new builder's actions to deliberately pass off Johnson's work as its own involved actual theft of Johnson's plans. The appellate court found the district court had not abused its discretion in finding that this was an "exceptional case" warranting the award of attorney's fees to Johnson.

See also I.A.E., Inc. v. Shaver, 74 F.3d 768 (7th Cir. 1996) (the existence of an implied license to use the copyright for a particular purpose precludes a finding of infringement); *Silva v. MacLaine,* 697 F. Supp. 1423 (E.D. Mich 1988), *aff'd,* 888 F.2d 1392 (1989) (a nonexclusive license may be granted orally, or may be implied from conduct); *Consumers Union of the United States v. New Regina Corp.,* 664 F. Supp. 753 (S.D.N.Y. 1997) (the necessary elements of a false designation claim under the Lanham Act are an involvement of goods or services, an effect on interstate commerce, and a false designation of origin or false description or representation of the goods or services; a description of origin will be considered false if it creates a likelihood of confusion in the consuming public).

§ 11.16 —Boilerplate Agreements

Page 270, add after carryover sentence:

For example, in *Colton, McMichael, Lester, Auman, Visnovske, Investment v. Mueller,* 896 S.W.2d 741 (Mo. Ct. App. 1995), a Missouri appellate court determined that unauthorized use of an engineer/designer's design to complete a project supported the tort of conversion. In *Colton,* the designer advised that before it would seal its site development drawings, its outstanding fees must be paid. Instead of paying the designer, the owner found another engineering firm to seal the drawings. *Conversion* is the unauthorized assumption of the right of ownership over personal property of another to the exclusion of the owner's rights. Although conversion does not lie for the appropriation of an idea or a debt, where intangible rights are merged in or identified with some document, the court determined that an action alleging conversion may be maintained.

§ 11.17 Authorized Design Use and Reuse

Page 270, add at end of section:

For example, field revisions to copyrighted design drawings are a permitted use. *Fred Riley Home Building Corp. v. Cosgrove,* 864 F. Supp. 1034 (D. Kan. 1994) (builder who reviewed home design prepared by designer by standing beside designer as various plans were sketched was not coauthor or co-owner of copyright in the altered plans because changes were insubstantial and not original to builder and altered plan was substantially similar to designer's copyrighted plans). Similarly, abbreviated and incomplete versions of plans may be used in promotional sales brochures without affecting the validity of the copyright. *Harris Custom Builders, Inc. v. Hoffmeyer,* 874 F. Supp. 899 (N.D. Ill. 1995).

§ 11.18 —"Fair Use" of Design Documents

Page 270, add after numbered list:

For example, in *Lindberg v. County of Kitsap*, 948 P.2d 805 (Wash. 1997), the Supreme Court ruled that copies of engineering documents must be made available to the public under the "fair use" exception of the Copyright Law allowing copies under limited circumstances, such as when they will be used to serve a public interest. Lindberg asked the Kitsap County Department of Community Development for copies of site, drainage, and erosion-control plans for a proposed mobile home park that were submitted to the county between 1987 and 1993 as part of the platting application process. The Lindbergs wanted copies of the documents to prepare presentation for public hearings on the projects and to check the actual site conditions against the drawings on file.

The Community Development Department denied the request, explaining that it had been advised by the Kitsap County prosecuting attorney that all engineering documents stamped by a licensed professional engineer are copyrighted and that copies could not be made without permission of the copyright owners. Lindberg was told he had to get the engineers' permission. The trial court ordered the county to provide copies to the Lindbergs for comment during public hearings only.

Page 271, add at end of section:

The contract may also permit some use of the designer's plans. For example, if the design-builder defaults in its obligations to the owner, Article 3 of AIA Document A191, Standard Form of Agreements Between Owner and Design/Builder, requires the architect to grant a limited license to the owner to use the documents to complete the project. The requirement is conditioned on the owner paying the architect any outstanding monies owned by the design-builder to the architect and executing an agreement that indemnifies the architect against claims arising from the owner's reuse of the documents without the architect's involvement. In the absence of a license given by the architect—the party who holds the copyright and other property interests in the documents—the owner would not have the right under the Part 1 Agreement to continue to use the documents produced by the architect to complete the project. Thus, the license serves as a means to avoid unfairly penalizing the owner in the event of the design-builder's default. McCallum, Ellickson, & Goldberg, "The 1996 Editions of AIA Design/Build Standard Form Agreements," 16 *Construction Lawyer 40 (No. 4, Oct. 1996).*

§ 11.19A —Reuse Statutes (New)

Statutes that permit public agencies to "reuse" design documents are generally based on the notion that clients have purchased the plans and should therefore be free to do what they wish with them. Reuse statutes have been enacted in Florida (prototypical school plans), Fla. Stat. Ann. § 235.211 (West 1991 & Supp. 1997); Tennessee (prototypical correctional facility), 1988 Tenn. Pub. Acts ch. 800, § 2, Tenn. Code Ann. § 12-4-116 (1990 & Supp. 1995); New Mexico, 1984 N.M. Laws, ch. 65, § 96 & § 15, N.M. Stat. Ann. § 13-1-123 (Michie 1992 & Supp. 1996); and Louisiana La. Rev. Stat. Ann. § 38:2317 (West 1988 & Supp. 1996) (reuse of documents for all state projects). Moreover, a recently proposed law would have amended Georgia state law by:

1. Vesting "title" to public school construction documents in the local board or other political subdivision of the state, giving that entity

the right to use the plans, with or without modification, in the construction of other school buildings;

2. Allowing the reusing board or agency to "delete" from the plans and specifications the signature and seal of the architect that originally prepared them;
3. Absolving the original architect of liability;
4. Allowing the supplanting architect to seal the submissions of plans for building permits and certificates of occupancy;
5. Allowing the supplanting architects to attach their signature and seal to public school drawings not prepared by them or under their supervision, transferring "full professional responsibility" for any original plan defects or any modifications thereto to the supplanting architect; and
6. Attaching on the documents the name of the original architect, and allowing mere review by the subsequent architect.

D. Roberts, "After the Ball: Subsequent Use of Construction Documents After the Project for Which They Were Originally Prepared: Sketchy Area of the Law," 17 Construction Lawyer 35, 36 (No. 2, Apr. 1997).

Not all reuse statutes are limited to public agencies. For example, in 1992 California passed legislation providing that in the event of damage to a single-family home that is a result of declared natural disasters and is covered by insurance, the architect must release a copy of the plans to the homeowner's insurer or to the homeowner if the plans will be used only for verifying the fact and amount of damage for insurance purposes. Under this legislation, the homeowner cannot use the plans to rebuild without the prior written consent of the architect. If the architect does not consent, the architect is not liable if the plans are subsequently used by the owner to rebuild all or part of the residence. J. Sweet, *Legal Aspects of Architecture, Engineering and the Construction Process* 231 (5th ed. 1994), *citing* Cal. Bus. & Prof. Code § 5536.3 (Deering's 1999).

There is a danger in reusing plans. An engineer's judgment is applied at every stage of design, from selecting sources of input through inspecting welds in the final structure. This personal judgment can never be fully communicated through printed pages and specifications. Moreover, it is difficult for a single set of drawings to incorporate the numerous changes that design professionals and contractors typically make to correct errors and adapt to site conditions. The person who designed the original details is most likely to understand their underlying assumptions and the likely consequences of changes for the structural system as a whole. The logic of traditional laws that hold architects responsible for public safety argues strongly against legislation that intentionally severs information links among architects, contractors, and owners. Roberts at 36–37.

Design professionals contend that most projects are one of a kind and that in reality design is a trial-and-error process. If another design professional completes the project, the original designer may be denied the opportunity to correct design errors as they surface during construction. Similarly, liability exposure can result if the design is used for an addition to the project or for a new project for which it may not be suitable. Even if the designer is absolved, a long and costly trial may be required. Sweet at 229–30, *citing Karna v. Gyron Reed Syndicate,* 374 F. Supp. 687 (D. Neb. 1974) (designer absolved when project's use unforeseeably changed).

The severance of the designer and the design will combine with the inevitable imperfections of even well-prepared plans to increase financial risk for everyone involved. The foreseeable increase in liability to reuse owners, contractors, and third parties would have to be considered by any architect who competes for a contract to prepare a design that is subject to reuse. Design professionals contend that the extent of use by the owner is an important factor in determining the value of design professionals' services and their fee, a factor recognized by the frequent use of a percentage of construction cost to determine compensation. If a design professional knows that drawings and specifications will be used again, a larger fee may be justified. Sweet at 230, *citing Garcia v. Cosicher,* 504 So. 2d 462 (Fla. Dist. Ct. App. 1987) (contract provided for repeat fees in event of owner reuse).

Contractors would also have to consider the added risks of bidding on jobs that may require more expensive design corrections and delays because the architect has taken over someone else's work product with full knowledge of its antecedents. Reuse statutes provide varying degrees of liability protection to the original architects. *See* N.M. Stat. Ann. § 13-1-123 (Michie 1992 & Supp. 1996); Tenn. Code Ann. § 12-4-116 (Michie 1990 & Supp. 1995); La. Rev. Stat. Ann. § 38:2317 (West 1988 & Supp. 1996). However, they are generally silent as to protecting owners and contractors. Bidders may not even be aware that the bid documents are being reused from an earlier project. There is no recognized formula for pricing contingencies for unpredictable risk when building to plans and specifications that have been reused. Roberts at 37.

Reuse statutes appear to differ widely in the extent to which they insulate an architect from liability for problems on later jobs. Louisiana's reuse statute appears to create a particularly unfair risk exposure. Under that statute, the original architect is absolved from liability on reuse projects only if that architect is not "involved" in the later project. If the architect attempts to help avoid future problems by passing on knowledge of problems incurred during the first construction, such assistance may be characterized as "involvement" and may create liability on a job for which the first architect receives little if any fee. The proposed Georgia statute offers simply that the original architect of the reused plans shall not be responsible for any defect therein. Roberts at 37–38.

If an architect's liability in reuse schemes is uncertain, it logically follows that recovery by owners, contractors, or third parties against the architect is also uncertain. This financial uncertainty is increased for all parties when the original architect's control and direct input are eliminated. Courts have assumed the existence of this direct contact in establishing the current rules governing architect liability to third parties. *Chubb Group Insurance Cos. v. C.F. Murphy & Associates, Inc.,* 656 S.W.2d 766, 780 (Mo. Ct. App. 1983). Open-ended reuse of architectural work product renders professional services more analogous to product manufacturing, where the manufacturer must effectively tender perfect goods to avoid liability after the goods leave the factory. Architect liability could easily slide from the prevailing standard of care to something more closely resembling strict product liability. Roberts at 37.

Federal copyright law complements traditional state regulation of professional services (Roberts at 38, *citing Wamp v. Tennessee State Board of Architectural & Engineering Examiners,* 868 S.W.2d 273, 275 (Tenn. 1994)) by ensuring that the information link between an original architect and reusers of those documents is retained, or at least not inadvertently broken or altered. See **§ 11.6** *et seq.* Valid reuse legislation demands effective assignment of copyrights. Some statutes may vest title to the architectural and engineering plans produced for the structure in the governmental subdivision of the state, although the original architect may be allowed to retain a copy. This language fails to answer the obvious questions of whether *title* means ownership of the physical plans themselves (which the "retained copy" language would indicate), or whether *title* means ownership of the underlying copyrights? In *Cassway v. Chelsea Historic Properties I, Ltd. Partnership,* 26 U.S.P.Q.2d 1791 (E.D. Pa. 1993), architects sued a client-developer for infringement when that client gave the original architect's drawings to new architects who copied and revised them. The plaintiffs originally entered into a written agreement with the developer, which stated that the drawings "are and shall be the property of the owner." *Id.* 1793. The court held that this language did not transfer all copyright interests to the owner, reasoning that transferral of copyright ownership must be explicit to prevent inadvertent loss of copyright. A transfer can be invalid when there is no explicit mention of copyright.

Roberts at 38, *citing Playboy Enterprises, Inc. v. Dumas,* 831 F. Supp. 295, 308 (S.D.N.Y 1993), *aff'd,* 53 F.3d 549 (2d Cir. 1995).

Effective assignment is important because penalties for infringement are severe, and they can potentially be applied to several parties in a judicially invalidated reuse scheme. Roberts, at 38–39, *citing Johnson v. Jones,* 921 F. Supp. 1573, 1586 (E.D. Mich. 1996). If courts deem an assignment ineffective, persons who copy the work, make derivative works based on it, or use unauthorized copies such as nonimmune owners, "downstream" architects, consulting engineers, contractors, subcontractors, suppliers, and employees of all these parties, may be directly or indirectly liable for infringement. *Johnson v. Jones,* 149 F.3d 494, 1998 U.S. App. LEXIS (6th Cir. 1998) (follow-on builder and designer along with owner who used original designer's plans liable for violation of designer's copyright); *Arthur Rutenberg Homes, Inc. v. Maloney,* 891 F. Supp. 1560, 1568 (M.C. Fla. 1995) (homeowner jointly and severally liable with residential builder and drafter for knowing infringement); *Aitken, Hazen, Hollman, Miller, P.C. v. Empire Constr. Co.,* 542 F. Supp. 252, 256 (D. Neb. 1982) (company affiliated with infringer liable for contributory and vicarious liability); *Herman Frankel Organization v. Tegman,* 367 F. Supp. 1051 (E.D. Mich. 1973) (drafter and builder who gave drafter original plan to copy jointly liable for creation of unauthorized derivative work). Roberts, at 38.

The right to copy construction documents pursuant to a state reuse statute was addressed in *Guillot-Vogt Assoc., Inc. v. Holly & Smith*, 848 F. Supp. 682, 689–690 (E.D. La. 1994), the court held that this assignment was not binding on the original engineer who held an independent copyright. The court rejected defendants' arguments that they were acting in good faith and under the ostensible direction of Louisiana law. Roberts, at 38.

Persons who have copied in reliance on an invalid written assignment or under some other subjectively reasonable claim of right may be protected by the legal fiction of an implied license. Courts have implied a nonexclusive license that can be granted orally, or "even implied from conduct." Nimmer § 10.03 [A] at 10-40.1. Though some courts have refused to imply a license for mere payment of fees by owners and delivery of the drawings to that owner by the architect, *Johnson v. Jones,* 921 F. Supp. 1584 (intent of the architect to grant license not found), others have not. Roberts, at 39, *citing I.A.E., Inc. v. Shaver,* 74 F.3d 768 (7th Cir. 1996).

A designer may be hired for only one design phase at a time with no guarantee that the next phase will be awarded to the same designer. Designers may release their license when delivering a completed phase by words that imply that the designers are contributing to the overall project rather than retaining a license in the ideas or concepts expressed in the preliminary phases (for example, "we hope our ideas contribute . . . "). It is highly probable that an implied nonexclusive license could become a common defense. Roberts, at 39.

State reuse statutes authorize the obliteration and deletion of an original architect's seal (§ 12-4-116(b) Tenn. Code Ann. (when correcting facilities); La. Rev. Stat. An. § 38.2317), and replacing it with that of another. A mark holder may expressly "contract away" the right of attribution, *Cleary v. News Corp.,* 30 F.3d 1255, 1259 (9th Cir. 1994) that is protected by the Lanham Act's second goal of avoiding market confusion. *Id.* at 1261. In the context of professional services that can have such impact on public health and safety, the individual's commercial right to waive attribution should yield to the public's right to know the true identity of the persons who perform such services. Roberts, at 39.

In § 501(a) of the Copyright Act, Congress abrogated state sovereign immunity for copyright violations. However, in 1996, the legal consequences of a state's position as a party in reuse schemes were obscured by the United States Supreme Court decision in *Seminole Tribe of Florida v. Florida,* 517 U.S. 44, 116 S. Ct. 1114 (1996). Applying the Eleventh Amendment, the Court held that Congress could not unilaterally abrogate a state's sovereign immunity to citizen suits, and Chief Justice Rehnquist's majority opinion expressly noted its applicability to copyright actions against states. It follows that infringement claims against a state may hinge on whether the applicable reuse statute or some other state law clearly indicates the state's consent to be sued in federal court for actions arising out of a reuse contract. Roberts, at 39.

§ 11.23 —Remedies

Page 274, add at end of section:

In *Johnson v. Jones*, 149 F.3d 494, 1998 U.S. App. LEXIS (6th Cir. 1998), an architect sued an owner and both the replacement designer and builder for alteration and use of its architectural drawings without permission in violation of the Copyright Act and the Lanham Act. The court found that the new builder had taken the architect's drawings and represented them to be the new builder's. *See* § **11.14**.

The court found that the new builder's entire fee, instead of just 15 percent of it, should have been given to Johnson because the new builder had invested no time or expense in the preparation of the drawings. Section 504(b) of the Copyright Act provides that the copyright owner is required only to provide proof of the infringer's gross revenues and then the infringer is required to prove the deductible expenses. Since the new builder had not presented any evidence of deductible expenses, the district court should have awarded the new builder's entire fee to Johnson.

Finally, the appellate court found that Johnson could not recover statutory damages or attorney's fees under the Copyright Act because the new builder's infringement commenced before Johnson had registered the copyright. Under the Copyright Act, statutory damages and attorneys fees are reserved for infringers who had constructive notice that the work was covered under a valid copyright. But since Johnson had not registered the copyright, the new builder could not discover Johnson's copyright by checking the federal register. If the incentive structure of the Copyright Act was to be properly applied, Johnson should not receive the reward of statutory damages, because Johnson had not satisfied the requirement of prompt registration.

§ 11.24 —Attorneys' Fees

Page 274, add to first paragraph:

However, attorneys' fees may not be recovered for violations of copyright before registration in some jurisdictions. *Great Southern Homes v. Johnson & Thompson Realtors,* 797 F. Supp. 609 (M.D. Tenn. 1992).

§ 11.28 —The Berne Convention

Page 276, add to note 120:

There were two benefits to the United States of accepting the Berne Convention. First, the United States gained instant copyright relations with countries with which it did not previously have agreements. Second, it was difficult for the United States to convince nations in which copyright piracy occurred to protect the rights of U.S. copyright owners when the United States itself was not a member of the treaty. The United States had lost billions of dollars from copyright piracy in foreign countries with which it had no bilateral copyright agreements. Ray, *Analysis of the Architectural Works Copyright Protection Act of 1990,* 15 Constr. Law. 26 (No. 2, Apr. 1995).

CHAPTER 12

LIABILITY FOR INNOVATIVE BUT UNPROVEN DESIGNS

§ 12.4 Who May Sue Innovative Professionals?

Page 283, add to note 19:

Edgeworth Constr. v. N.D. Lea & Assoc., [1993] 3 S.C.R. 206, 12 C.L.R. (2d) 161, [1993] 8 W.W.R. 129, 83 B.C.L.R. (2d) 145, 107 D.L.R. (4th) 169 (negligent misrepresentation claims may be brought against designer by contractor if the contractor or subcontractor has reason to believe that the designer's negligent preparation of bid documents caused them financial loss).

Page 284, add at end of section:

The *Fleischer v. Helmut, Obata & Kassabaum, Inc.*, 870 S.W.2d 832 (Mo. Ct. App. 1993), decision does not appear to have been cited by any subsequent related cases. This may reflect the general trend in American law to reject privity of contract between a plaintiff and the design professional defendant as a prerequisite for a professional malpractice suit.

§ 12.5 The Innovative Designer Is Not an Insurer of the Design

Page 286, add at end of section:

Firestone Steel Products Co. v. Brojas, 927 S.W.2d 608, 613 (Tex. 1996), reiterates that strict liability is not a viable cause of action against a designer who provides drawings or a prototype to an owner or contractor for the latter's use in preparing a finished product.

§ 12.8 —Implied Warranty as a Basis for Recovery

Page 290, add at end of section:

The *Taramac Development Co. v. Delamartr, Freud & Associates,* 234 Kan. 618, 675 P.2d 361 (1984) decision, which suggests the viability of an implied warranty theory against a design professional, has still not found favor. Rather, the decision in *R.J. Longo Construction Co. v. Transit America, Inc.,* 921 F. Supp. 1295, 1311 (D.N.J. 1996), rejecting a breach of implied warranty claim against a professional, reflects the position taken by the vast majority of jurisdictions. *Taramac* and the decision in *Tommy L. Griffin Plumbing & Heating Co. v. Jordan,* 463 S.E.2d 85, 89 (S.C. 1995) (reaffirming South Carolina's prior holding allowing a breach of implied warranty claim against a design professional) remain distinctly in the minority.

§ 12.10 —Express Contractual Indemnity

Page 294, add at end of section:

California law has been clarified with respect to the unavailability of "equitable indemnity"—in other words, allowing jointly and severally liable tortfeasors to "share" losses in accordance with their respective degrees of fault, if contractual indemnity rights are secured by agreement.

Maryland Casualty Co. v. Bailey & Sons, Inc., 35 Cal. App. 4th 856, 893, 41 Cal. Rptr. 2d 519 (1995) [*see also Regional Steel Corp. v. Superior Court,* 25 Cal. App. 4th 525, 529, 32 Cal. Rptr. 2d 417 (1994)], holds that, under California law, a party's having bargained for contractual indemnity preempts the availability of implied or equitable indemnity that might otherwise be available in accordance with *American Motorcycle Ass'n v. Superior Court,* 20 Cal. 3d 578, 606, 146 Cal. Rptr. 182 (1978). The rationale of the *Maryland* decision is very simple: presumptively, if the parties have bargained for contractual indemnity, they have done so to the exclusion of any other subset of the law or indemnity.

It may be possible to circumvent the *Maryland* decision by including, contractually, a specific provision affirming the availability of equitable indemnity should the contracted indemnity not be viable in law or in fact. This drafting technique, however, has not been judicially tested. Nevertheless, an indemnitee who desires to obtain maximum indemnity protection may choose to employ the aforesaid provision, which purports to retain, as an alternative to contractual indemnity, the common law right of implied or equitable indemnity.

§ 12.11 Expert Testimony with Respect to Innovative Designs

Page 296, add at end of section:

The question of employing an expert witness, a professional beyond the specific discipline of the defendant design professional, may be significant in innovative design cases. Usually, expert witness qualification statutes (*see, e.g.,* Fed. R. Evid. 702) are silent on the interdisciplinary use of professionals as experts. Because, however, professional training of design professionals *may* overlap the architecture and engineering design disciplines (*see Ponderosa Center Partners v. McClellan/Cruz/Gaylord & Associates,* 45 Cal. App. 4th 913, 915, 53 Cal. Rptr. 2d 64 (1996) (engineer permitted to provide "certificate of merit," pursuant to Cal. Civ. Proc. Code § 411.35, in suit against architect)), it may be possible, under appropriate professional circumstances, for a design professional of one discipline to testify against an innovative designer of a different profession. Although this interdisciplinary approach may seem improper at first blush, there could be very limited circumstances whereby an engineer, because of certain training and expertise, has the ability to address the applicable standard of care for an architect's innovative design. Of course, the admissibility of expert testimony is generally subject to the sound discretion of the trial court. *See Putensen v. Clay Adams, Inc.,* 12 Cal. App. 3d 1062, 1081, 9 Cal. Rptr. 319 (1970).

§ 12.13 Deceit Claims: Informed Consent/Breach of Fiduciary Duty

Page 298, add after note 91:

A judge in a state court in Oakland, California, instructed the jury that under the typical American Institute of Architects agreement, the designer was a fiduciary to the building owner, whose duties went beyond informing the client of problems the designer had observed and required the designer to see that the problems were corrected. A fiduciary responsibility is greater than a professional standard based on how other professionals would act in a similar situation, or a fitness standard under which negligence need not be proved but only that the desired results were not achieved. A fiduciary standard imposes a greater liability on a design professional and changes the traditional relationship between architects, engineers, and clients. "Jury's $7-Million Verdict Based on Designer's 'Fiduciary' Role," 238 *Engineering News-Record* 11 (No. 26, June 30, 1997).

Page 300, add at end of section:

Another possible basis for liability under the category of "deceit" may exist for the innovative design professional who does not supply plans or specifications, but instead provides professional "information." It is entirely possible, for example, that an innovative professional engineer may provide highly specialized seismic calculations to an architect for purposes of the construction of an unique design; these calculations may be submitted to a third party, such as the project owner. In some jurisdictions, the supplier of information may not be charged by that third party, in the purely economic damage setting, with malpractice. Rather, the claim must be based upon either negligent misrepresentation or intentional misrepresentation. *See Bily v. Arthur Young & Co.,* 3 Cal. 4th 370, 410–14, 11 Cal. Rptr. 51 (1992) (no accounting malpractice claim available against CPA firm); *see also Ossining Union Free School District v. Anderson, LaRocca, Anderson,* 73 N.Y.2d 417, 539 N.E.2d 91, 93–96 (1989). The policy rationale underpinning such authorities is that before a nonprivity economic loss claimant may charge the professional with liability, he or she must have been in the nature of an intended beneficiary who justifiably relied on the information. Barring such a special relationship between the nonprivity claimant and the professional defendant, no recovery is possible for nonintentional torts. *Bily,* although its holding focuses upon accountants, was applied to a real estate appraiser's information in *Soderberg v. McKinney,* 44 Cal. App. 4th 1760, 1768, 52 Cal. Rptr. 2d 635 (1996).

§ 12.14 Punitive Damages

Page 301, add at end of section:

United States Supreme Court authority, *BMW of North America v. Gore,* 116 S. Ct. 1589, 1595–99, 134 L. Ed. 2d 804 (1996), demonstrates that punitive damages awards are governed by federal due process standards. Consequently, there are certain strictures on punitive damages awards and the procedures concerning same that must be evaluated, and satisfied, when such damages become an issue in litigation.

CHAPTER 13

THE DESIGN PROFESSIONAL AS CONSTRUCTION MANAGER

§ 13.4 Construction Managers

Page 307, add at end of section:

A growing number of smaller architectural firms are venturing into construction management in response to rising client demand as buildings, systems, regulations, and construction logistics grow more complex. AIA reports that 64 percent of clients believe ability to manage construction is important in selecting designers. B. McKee, "Architects as Construction Managers," *Architecture,* Dec. 1, 1994, at 111. However, some clients may be concerned about conflicts of interest when architects become construction managers. The architect as construction manager may eliminate checks and balances in the process.

Most architectural firms that perform construction management work set up separate entities for liability and tax purposes. This keeps architectural fees separate for purposes of liability insurance premiums related to construction management.

The degree of risk the architect accepts depends whether it acts as a CM agent or a CM at risk. The CM agent role offers lower risk because it provides an arm's-length, mainly advisory role for the owner. The CM at risk often makes a promise on time of completion, maximum project cost, and safety. The AIA's Document B801/CMa, Standard Form of Agreement Between Owner and Construction Manager (1992), was designed for use by architects who practice construction management. In essence, the architect acting as construction manager revives the concept of the "master builder" that dominated construction through the late 1800s.

§ 13.5 General Standard of Care and the Nature of the Duty

Page 309, add after "See" in note 13:

Block v. Lohan Assocs., Inc., 269 Ill. App. 3d 745, 206 Ill. Dec. 202, 645 N.E.2d 207 (1993) (architect not liable when subcontractor's employee fell from ladder; contract limited architect's responsibility to design and determination as to design conformance, and did not extend to worker safety); Ivanov v. Process Design Assocs., 267 Ill. App. 3d 440, 204 Ill. Dec. 810, 642 N.E.2d 711 (1994) (design professional hired to perform usual onsite observation and construction management activities for project that it designed generally does not owe contractor's employees a duty to ensure safe jobsite conditions, but contract may provide otherwise).

Page 309, replace note 15 with:

Carvalho v. Toll Bros. & Developers, 278 N.J. Super. 451, 651 A.2d 492, 498 (App. Div.), *cert. granted,* 140 N.J. 326, 658 A.2d 726 (1995), *aff'd & remanded,* 143 N.J. 565, 675 A.2d 209 (1996) (engineer had legal duty to exercise reasonable care for safety of workers on construction site when engineer had responsibility for progress of work but not for safety conditions yet was aware of working conditions on construction site that created risk of serious injury to workers).

Page 309, add after second sentence in first full paragraph:

In *Business Men's Assurance Co. v. Graham,* 891 S.W.2d 438 (Mo. Ct. App. 1994), the court observed that in addition to the contractual duties arising from the contract between BMA and the designer, the designer had a duty to provide professional architectural services in a manner consistent with the skill and competence of other members of its profession. BMA's general negligence claim was based on the designer's common law duty to provide architectural services in a professional manner.

§ 13.9 —Duties Imposed by Courts

Page 313, add to note 34:

See also Gables CVF, Inc. v. Bahr, Vermeer & Haecker Architect, Ltd., 244 Neb. 346 (architect who agreed to make periodic observations was liable for breach of contractual duty to inform owner of deviations from business plans), *modified,* 244 Neb. 613, 506 N.W.2d 706 (1993).

Page 314, add at end of section:

For example, in *Roberts & Schaefer v. Hardaway*, 1998 U.S. App. LEXIS 21252 (11th Cir. 1998), a court determined that a trade subcontractor had not agreed to accept all risk of loss on lump-sum, fast-track, design-build project. Hardaway signed three lump-sum construction subcontracts with the design-builder, Roberts & Schaefer, for portions of a fast-track, phosphate benification plant prior to completion of the design. Hardaway was subsequently terminated, and, in the litigation that followed, claimed it was due additional performance costs. The designer argued that because the subcontract was awarded on a lump-sum basis, Hardaway should not be able to recover its claims for overtime and overtime inefficiencies. Because Hardaway had not agreed to accept the risk of all loss or damage arising from any of the work through unforeseen or unusual obstructions, difficulties, or delays that may be encountered in the prosecution of the work, the court concluded that the designer remained responsible to Hardaway for its additional costs.

The *Roberts & Schaefer* court reviewed Hardaway's subcontracts and determined that Hardaway did not bargain to accept the risk that the designer's substantial delays might require Hardaway to incur overtime costs beyond such costs anticipated by the contract. The court believed a subsequent agreement between the designer and Hardaway to accelerate the work that included certain overtime costs demonstrated that Hardaway did not bear the risk for incurring overtime and other costs resulting from the designer's significant delays. The court rejected the designer's argument that the lump-sum subcontract precluded Hardaway from recovering damages for overtime and related costs.

Hardaway also demanded additional costs for design errors that caused misalignment of bolt holes. Roberts & Schaefer also argued that the lump-sum subcontract prevented recovery. The designer pointed to portions of the specifications that required Hardaway to straighten and align anchor bolts as required. The court found that the specifications did not require Hardaway to bring faultily holed materials into alignment or accept the financial risk to do so.

The designer also argued that Hardaway should have included costs for poor foundation and design errors in its bid because Hardaway knew the project was being built on a fast-track schedule. The court determined that the lump-sum subcontract did not indicate that Hardaway bargained to take the risk that the design-builder would provide poor foundation or improper designs. Other design errors for which the court permitted recovery of additional performance costs included walkways that were too narrow to allow Hardaway to bring in the machinery it was to install, requiring Hardaway to remove installed structural steel in order to do so.

Similarly, in *Metric Constructors, Inc. v. Hawker Siddeley Power Eng'g, Inc.*, 468 S.2Ed 435 (N.C. Ct. App. 1996), Panda Rosemary Corporation hired Hawker Siddeley Power Engineering to design and build a cogeneration power plant. Hawker subcontracted with Metric Constructors for construction of the plant. Because the project was to be completed on a fast-track, design-build basis, Hawker had not completed all of the design work prior to commencement of construction. Under its contract with Metric, Hawker was responsible for engineering, design drawings, and procurement of major equipment items. Hawker promised to issue drawings at a rate that would allow Metric to finish on time. Metric was to receive a $9,000 bonus per day for early completion.

Hawker failed to deliver the required services and drawings. Its drawings were issued weeks or even months after the dates promised to Metric. Other drawings were issued, then revised, forcing Metric to demolish its work and start over. Metric was forced into substantial expenditures to complete the project on schedule. Hawker refused to pay Metric for the cost overruns and extra work. Metric filed a lien on the plant and foreclosed the lien. Metric also sued Hawker for breach of contract. The jury awarded Metric more than $6.6 million, which was affirmed on appeal. (The appeal dealt only with whether Metric had the right to include in its claim the damages incurred by a sub-subcontractor, and the propriety of certain jury instructions.)

§ 13.11 Claims by Owners

Page 317, add after "See also" in note 50:

Gables CVF, Inc. v. Bahr, Vermeer & Haecker Architect, Ltd., 244 Neb. 346 (architect who agreed to make periodic observations was liable for breach of contractual duty to inform owner of deviations from building plans), *modified,* 244 Neb. 613, 506 N.W.2d 706 (1993);

§ 13.12 Claims by Third Parties

Page 318, add to note 55:

J.E. McDonald, *Common Law Liability of Architects and Engineers for Negligence to Non-Contractual Parties,* 9 Constr. Law. No. 2, at 5 (Apr. 1989).

Page 319, add after "See also" in note 56:

Yocum v. City of Minden, 649 So. 2d 129 (La. Ct. App. 1995) (contractor's employee injured in excavation sued designer for failure to exercise due care to prevent dangerous condition. Contractor and its insurers were liable for designer's expenses incurred in defending employee suit under indemnity provision in owner-contractor contract requiring contractor to indemnify owner and designer from claims, including attorney fees, arising out of contractor's work).

Page 319, in note 56, add before Chiarelli citation:

Ivanov v. Process Design Assocs., 267 Ill. App. 3d 440, 204 Ill. Dec. 810, 642 N.E.2d 711 (1994) (site construction manager/engineering firm that agreed to act as agent or representative of owner and be responsible for continuously inspecting or supervising contractor's work had authority coexistent with owner to require that contractors comply with safety requirements; thus, it was responsible for safety conditions. Language in contract could be found to mean that firm had assumed duty to provide safe workplace for contractors' employees).

Page 319, add to note 57:

Block v. Lohan Assocs., Inc., 269 Ill. App. 3d 745, 206 Ill. Dec. 202, 645 N.E.2d 207 (1993) (architect not liable when subcontractor's employee fell from ladder; contract documents limited architect's responsibility to design and determination as to design conformance, and did not extend to worker safety); Ivanov v. Process Design Assocs., 267 Ill. App. 3d 440, 204 Ill. Dec. 810, 642 N.E.2d 711 (1994) (design professional hired to perform usual onsite observation and construction management activities for project that it designed generally does not owe contractor's employees a duty to ensure safe jobsite conditions, but contract may provide otherwise); Yocum v. City of Minden, 649 So. 2d 129 (La. Ct. App. 1995) (contractor's employee injured in excavation sued designer for failure to exercise due care to prevent dangerous condition; court found that designer had moral duty to warn employee if designer knew of unreasonably dangerous condition, despite absence of legal duty under contract clause that prohibited designer from advising on safety precautions and programs in connection with construction).

Page 319, add after third sentence in first full paragraph:

However, one court found a safety duty implied from other specific duties the contract required the designer to perform. The New Jersey Supreme Court, in *Carvalho v. Toll Bros. & Developers,* 278 N.J. Super. 451, 651 A.2d 492 (App. Div.), *cert. granted,* 140 N.J. 326, 658 A.2d 726 (1995), *aff'd & remanded,* 143 N.J. 565, 675 A.2d 209 (1996), ruled that a project engineer had a legal duty to exercise reasonable care for the safety of construction workers. It so held even though the contract made the contractor solely responsible for means and methods of construction, stated that the project engineers shall not have control over the construction means and methods or the contractor's safety precautions, and stated that the contractor "alone" shall be responsible for the safety and adequacy of equipment and methods, including OSHA compliance.

The New Jersey Supreme Court found designer responsibility for safety on the jobsite because of an overlap between work progress and work safety. The court found that matters of construction safety bore directly on the engineer's contractual responsibility for supervising the progress of the work. The court reasoned that if safety conditions could affect work progress, the engineer had the authority and control to take or require corrective measures to address safety concerns. The court imposed a legal duty to exercise reasonable care for the safety of workers on a construction site when the engineer has a responsibility for the progress of the work but not for safety conditions, yet is aware of working conditions on the site that create a risk of serious injury to workers.

The New Jersey Supreme Court also found that the indemnity clause in the construction contract was not sufficiently broad to cover the engineer. Furthermore, the contractor had not added the engineer as an "additional insured" to the contractor's CGL policy as required by the contract. Although the court required the contractor to compensate the engineer to the extent the engineer would have been protected as an additional insured under the contractor's policy, because the contractor's insurer was insolvent, the engineer's insurance became the primary coverage.

To protect designers, if the contractor is to be responsible for safety, contracts should require the general contractor to indemnify, defend, and obtain liability insurance insuring the owner and design professionals against safety-related claims. However, naming the designer as an additional insured to the contractor's commercial general liability (CGL) insurance policy gives the designer little, if any, protection, as liability for a design error or omission is usually excluded from most CGL policies. The party named as additional insured gets only the coverage provided in the policy. The kind of liability insurance the contractor must provide must be defined in the specifications. If there had been contractual liability insurance by the contractor in *Carvalho,* the engineer would probably have been protected. See § **16.3**.

The contract documents should make clear that the contractor's obligation to indemnify is independent of and in addition to any obligation of the contractor to obtain insurance for its benefit or the benefit of the owner and design professionals. "In addition, the contract documents should make clear that any insurance obtained by the contractor for the benefit of the owner and the design professional is 'primary' to any other insurance purchased by the owner and design professionals so that the insurance purchased by the contractor will be called upon first to defend and indemnify the owner and design professional." Richard A. Mandel & David M. Kupfer, " 'Dead Man Walking' New Jersey Supreme Court 'Pulls Switch' on Project Engineer in Carvalho v. Toll Brothers," *Construct!,* Summer 1996, at 5, 7. "Design professionals will have to be ever vigilant, not only with regard to fulfilling their new duty concerning site-safety, but also with regard to the careful drafting of [the insurance requirements included in] contract documents, prequalification and selection of competent and financially stable contractors and insurers, and securing proof (such as certificates of insurance) that the required insurance has in fact been obtained." *Id.*

Page 319, add to first full paragraph:

For example, in *Peck v. Horrocks Engineering,* 106 F.3d 949 (10th Cir. 1997), despite limited support in other states, a federal court determined that Utah would not impose a duty on an engineer for site safety on the basis of knowledge of the unsafe condition and inaction, when the engineer contractually declined to accept responsibility for work safety and did not in fact exercise control over worker safety at the jobsite.

Page 320, add to note 61:

The Illinois Structural Work Act was repealed in 1995.

Page 321, add to note 64:

See also Jim's Excavating Serv. v. HKM Assocs., 265 Mont. 494, 878 P.2d 248 (1994) (contractor may recover purely economic loss against engineer when engineer knew or should have foreseen that contractor was at risk in relying on information engineer supplied).

Page 321, add after "See" in note 71:

Thomson v. Espey Huston & Assocs., Inc., 899 S.W.2d 415 (Tex. Ct. App. 1995) (any negligence by engineering consulting firm in performing inspection contract caused no injury beyond economic loss to subject of contract itself, which pursuant to the economic loss rule, did not give rise to tort cause of action);

CHAPTER 14

RISK MANAGEMENT

§ 14.4 Risks to Live With/Risks to Protect Against

Page 334, add at end of section:

How should designers respond to potential liability if the economic loss rule is not enforced? Try even harder to do the designer's job well. Next, look carefully at any commission that a client offers. Not all commissions are or should be accepted. In 1996, engineers surveyed by the American Consulting Engineers Council rejected $80 million worth of work that they considered too risky, up from $51.3 million in 1995, according to the ACEC's 18th annual liability survey. Krizan, "Costs Decline for Engineers," 238 *Engineering News-Record* 22, 23 (No. 9, Mar. 3, 1997). Some of the many things that may be considered when evaluating a commission are the contractor's claims history and how much less the low bid on the job was than the second low bid. Is the contractor doing work that it has never done before? Does this project push the state of the art? J. Sweet, "A View from the Tower," 17 *Construction Lawyer* 47 (No. 2, Apr. 1997). Finally, make sure professional liability insurance coverage is available, but watch the deductibles and defense cost provisions.

For a geotechnical engineer, if the owner wants to put the risk of unexpected subsurface conditions on the contractor (and maybe even if the owner intends to take that risk itself through a differing site conditions clause), persuade the owner to include an exculpatory provision in the prime contract, for the engineer's protection. Also try to get an indemnity clause from the owner in the contract. A designer performing the usual site services should worry if there is a "no damage" or "no pay for delay" clause in the prime contract. If the contractors cannot sue the owner, there is a good chance they will come after the designer. If there is such a clause, try to get exculpation in the prime contract or indemnification in the design contract with the owner. Sweet at 47.

§ 14.5 Professional Liability Risk

Page 336, add after carryover paragraph:

Architects who design condominiums are among the design professionals most likely to be sued for errors and omissions, according to a study of more than 8,600 closed claim files by Design Professional Insurance Corporation (DPIC), a professional liability insurer. The study showed that condos accounted for only 1 percent of the architects' fees, but more than 7 percent of closed claims and 14 percent of the total architect claims paid by DPIC. Structural engineers also are more likely to experience claims, but their claims trend has been improving, according to the DPIC survey. Structural engineers working on condominium projects are also at particular risk. Structural claims overall are divided among walls (12 percent), roofs (11 percent), beams and joists (10 percent) and foundations and footings (9 percent). "Architects and Condos Don't Mix," 237 *Engineering News-Record 21 (No. 8, Aug. 19, 1996).*

During the 1980s, many developers built cheaply, sold the units, dissolved their corporations, and left architects and engineers holding the bag. Most of the claims against architects were for economic loss relating to roof and wall problems.

Condominium projects are repetitive and residential, two characteristics that account for a relatively low fee as a percentage of construction cost. In addition, the architect's client is usually a residential real estate developer, whose two primary incentives are to keep construction costs as low as possible and to build as quickly as possible. The low initial cost imperative results in the developer buying the minimum services from the designer and often eliminating from the construction drawings the details of construction essential to weatherproof integrity in the envelope. Such details include flashing details at critical locations in the weather envelope. Services that are typically excluded from an architect's condominium work include contract administration and construction inspection or observation.

All of these influences combine to virtually ensure defect claims against a design professional arising out of a condominium project. A design professional can pass these projects by, or can establish prudent business arrangements for them that include the measures necessary to provide some degree of protection from this common exposure. But in no case should a design professional simply contract for condominium services as though it were business as usual.

§ 14.6 Loss Precipitators and Catalysts

Page 337, add after first paragraph:

When dealing with an old client with insufficient assets or new clients with unknown credit, an appropriate retainer should be required. Stop work when payment is 10 days overdue. Decline assignments that cannot provide an appropriate fee. A. O'Leary, "Architects: How to Attract a Professional Liability Lawsuit," 38 *Design Cost & Data* No. 3, at 24 (July–Sept. 1994).

*Page 337, add after "**Miscommunication**" subheading:*

Regular communications are of prime importance to client understanding and good will. Written minutes should be issued to report on all meetings with the client, contractors, and others, and to confirm understandings and decisions. A written report of each site visit during construction and copies of all correspondence promote awareness of behind-the-scenes activities. Answer letters immediately and return all telephone calls to avoid creating doubts.

Do not avoid decisions. Procrastination only allows complaints to accumulate and proliferate. When decisions are not made promptly, uncertainty results that tends to stimulate other complaints and escalate existing ones. A. O'Leary, "Architects: How to Attract a Professional Liability Lawsuit," 38 *Design Cost & Data* No. 3, at 24 (July–Sept. 1994). In *MKK Technologies, Inc./Northstar Construction v. Scott,* 63 F.3d 402 (5th Cir. 1995), the contractor on a prison project sued the Texas Department of Criminal Justice, alleging that the department interfered with the progress of the project, caused substantial delays and cost overruns, and took possession of the completed facility without paying for the cost overruns. The contractor submitted its claim to the owner's designated representative, pursuant to the contract's dispute resolution clause. Six months later the contractor brought a § 1983 suit in federal district court against the department and its director, contending that the department had instructed the designated representative to refrain from deciding the claim in an effort to deprive the contractor of its right to payment under the contract.

The district court dismissed the complaint for failure to state a § 1983 claim and the contractor appealed. Before the circuit court heard the case, the owner's designated representative rendered its decision, awarding the contractor a maximum of $2.1 million.

The owner often goes into a project thinking the architect is its champion, its knight. That is true only up to a point. Architects and construction lawyers agree that while shoddy or even dangerous design mars some projects, most conflicts stem from crossed signals between the owner and designer. Owners don't appreciate design and structural issues at the core of the architect's profession. Architects don't fathom how deeply personal the experience of building a home can be for clients. Fatsis, "House Plans Can Be Blueprints for Conflict," *Wall Street Journal,* Friday, Nov. 3, 1995, at B8.

Page 339, add to carryover paragraph:

See also § **11.19A**.

Page 339, add after first full paragraph:

Property owners often think they are buying an architect's drawings, but under the architect institute's standard contract, the drawings belong to the architect. In high-end homes, part of the market value is in the design. Owners of luxury homes should negotiate the architect's rights to reuse elements of a particular design. An owner who wants a house to remain unique may need to buy the ownership rights to the documents and the intellectual copyright to the drawings and designs. See § **11.14**. Fatsis, "House Plans Can Be Blueprints for Conflict," *The Wall Street Journal,* Friday, Nov. 3, 1995, at B8.

Page 339, add after fourth full paragraph:

The U.S. Army Construction Engineering Research Laboratories (CERL) have developed a new computer system called Reviewer's Assistant that captures comments from past design and specification reviews for future use. Reviewer's Assistant was developed to support the Corps' design-review process. "New Program May Be Design Reviewer's Best Friend," 32 *Civil Engineering* No. 2 at 23 (Feb. 1995).

The Reviewer's Assistant program lets the user tag comments for specific components, systems, or categories of projects. When these elements occur in another project, past experiences can be tapped to see how they were addressed. The program can be customized by any firm that does design reviews. The program provides a set of "starter" comments, representing about 500 of the most common design-related review comments.

The software is distributed at no cost on the Internet, CivilNet, and CompuServe. More than 500 architecture/engineering firms have expressed interest in using the software. With such free software available, can even the smallest design firm avoid a design review? The Corps' Reviewer's Assistant may have been developed to prevent design errors, but it can also be used to evaluate malpractice claims.

§ 14.6 LOSS PRECIPITATORS

Even without contract language, the law may impose an obligation on the parties to exercise a degree of care and skill performing the tasks they undertake that may protect the designer. For example, the appellate court in *American and Foreign Insurance Co. v. Bolt*, 1997 U.S. App. LEXIS 2376 (6th Cir. 1997) *reh'g denied*, 1997 U.S. App. LEXIS 6343 (6th Cir. 1997), concluded that a general contractor can be liable for negligence even where it followed the owner's drawings.

In *American and Foreign Insurance Co.*, the design required a higher roof line for a new building that likely would cause heavier ice and snow accumulation on the lower roof of an existing, connected building. The designer had added a note on the plans that the contractor must reinforce the existing roof where the new roof adjoined with additional purlins between existing purlins to support the extra snow load. The contractor added the additonal purlins according to the notation on the drawings and bolted them to the existing frame rather than on the roof deck as was required for the original purlins. The designer, and owner's expert, acknowledged that the contractor had added the new purlins in compliance with the notation on the drawings. However, the contractor had admitted at trial that when the purlins were installed, the contractor knew that the instructions dictated an improper method for installing the purlins. Because of the collapse of the lower roof, the owner experienced property damages over $200,000. The court concluded that a contractor could be liable for negligence so long as it breached some duty independent from its established contractual duties. The court explained that the law imposed an obligation on parties to exercise a degree of care and skill performing whatever task they undertake. The court stated that neither the owner nor the contractor bothered to determine how to properly install the purlins. The contractor also knew that the manner in which it was installing the additional purlins was not correct. Yet, the contractor chose to continue installing the purlins. Because the contractor chose to continue to install the purlins knowing that the installation method used was not correct, and because the contractor recognized the resulting peril to those persons working in the warehouse, the appellate court held the general contractor liable for the damages from the roof collapse.

Page 339, add at end of section:

Construction Manager. A study by David Haviland, professor of architecture at Rensselaer Polytechnic Institute, of designers in the CNA Architects and Engineers Professional Liability Program found designers with a high number of claims against them are more likely to work on projects that have a separate construction manager. D. Haviland, "Firms

Reduce Liability Claims Through Careful Planning," *Engineering Times,* Oct. 1994, at 4.

Method of Designer Selection. Professor Haviland also found that designers with the lowest number of claims are most likely to be selected based on their qualifications rather than price. Cost-selected firms were also less likely to show a profit. Haviland, "Firms Reduce Liability Claims Through Careful Planning," at 4.

Site Selection. Haviland's study also indicated that claims are higher when sites are not approved before professional services begin. *Id.*

Liability Insurance No Guarantee. Designers create unrealistically high expectations in the minds of their prospective clients. They suggest that their professional liability insurance is a guarantee of perfection, even though the insurance does not cover errors that are not negligent. A. O'Leary, "Architects: How to Attract a Professional Liability Lawsuit," 38 *Design Cost & Data* No. 3, at 24 (July–Sept. 1994).

Client Consideration. Designers can reduce claims from their clients if the clients are better treated. The most common types of thoughtlessness and imprudent actions provide motivation to clients for assertion of claims. Many times the professional liability claim is simply striking back at the designer for not treating the client with the proper degree of consideration and respect. Id.

The firms participating in the *A/E Management Practices Study* were asked to provide their opinions on 138 factors that acted as claims preventers or starters, or both. Respondents were asked to rate the importance of each factor on a scale of zero (not important) to five (very important). Looking at the Top 20 lists, eight of the preventers and four of the starters are related in some way to experience:

- the experience of the key actors providing services, with the project type, and working together;
- the experience as a factor in selecting the firm in the first place; and
- the experience gained by the firm's staff in working continuously rather than intermittently on projects in the office.

While experience cannot be manufactured, it can be developed and nurtured. New clients and projects can be selected to build on an existing experience base. Experienced designers can mentor newer firm members. The firm may recruit—or form a strategic alliance—to develop a specific area of expertise. D. Haviland, "In Managing Projects, Claims Factors Include Past Experience, Firm Stability, Client Roles," 20 *Engineering Times* 22 (No. 1, Jan./Feb. 1998).

A dimension of experience lies in a firm's stability. Two of the Top 20 claim preventers and one of the Top 20 starters involve firm stability. One approach to firm stability lies in focusing on clients. Acquiring clients—not just projects—challenges design firms to form stronger relationships, provide consistently high levels of service, and build capabilities that continue to meet needs over the long run, all increasing firm stability. *Id.,* at 23.

A look at the Top 20 lists suggests that the client is a very important ingredient in project success. The client's experience, clarity, and flexibility in establishing project parameters, approach to making decisions and resolving differences, and willingness to compensate design professionals for the risks they are asked to assume are all factors in preventing or starting claims. *Id.*

Another key to assessing and managing project risks is the clarity, coordination, and consistency among key project parameters. Sometimes they may be inconsistent with each other, perhaps as a result of the many twists and turns some projects take as their owners finally gain the financial and regulatory approvals needed to proceed. It is the design professional's task to evaluate consistency and advise the owner when the project parameters are unclear, incomplete, or inconsistent. *Id.*

Respondents placed special attention on design investigation and documentation on the one hand, and carry-through into construction on the other. The latter includes the design professional's involvement in construction contract administration, careful coordination of project agreements during the construction phase, and effective site observation and management. *Id.*

None of the 138 factors was seen exclusively as a claims starter or preventer. Clearly a given factor (for example, fast-track projects) can be seen either way, depending on the circumstances. Even though fast-tracking ended up on the Top 20 starters list, 34 of the 72 engineers and architects participating in the study suggested it could also be a claims preventer, however weak. *Id.*

§ 14.7 Tools for Managing Risk

Page 340, add after sixth paragraph:

The American Consulting Engineers Counsel's Organizational Peer Review Program, endorsed by NSPE/PEPP, may be used by designers to identify how successfully the designer has implemented these suggestions and how its organization may influence its business risk.

Under the Peer Review Program, a team of practitioner colleagues looks into a firm's operations and their effect on quality. Peer Review topics are general management, professional development, project management, business development, financial management, and human resources management. Company management gets a confidential, sometimes brutally honest, report specifying potential pitfalls and opportunities. The review sets a baseline for additional initiatives, such as TQM and ISO 9000.

The designer decides when to have the review, whom to have on the team, and what to emphasize. The review team evaluates the company against its own standards, not others. CEOs have said that a Peer Review is better than a management study costing 20 times as much. Several liability insurers offer incentives to firms using the process. Information on Peer Review is available from PEPP at (703) 684-2861. Pierce, "Organizational Peer Review: Road to Quality, Satisfaction," 35 *Private Practice News* No. 5, at 2 (National Society of Professional Engineers June 1995).

Designers with the lowest professional liability loss and the lowest insurance premiums are the ones that employ a combination of total quality management, partnering, and alternative dispute resolution, according to a study of 200 of the top 500 design firms. "Risk Management Study of Large Design Firms," conducted by Johnson & Higgins Construction Group, aided by Arthur Andersen consultants. Those designers with total quality management programs have 31 percent lower professional liability losses than those that do not. Those using ADR have 19 percent lower losses than those that do not. Designers that do formal partnering have 10 percent lower losses than those that do not. Interestingly, only 5 percent of the responding firms use all three risk management methods. Schriener, "Partnering, TQM, ADR Lower Insurance Costs," 236 *Engineering News-Record* 16 (No.2, Jan. 15, 1996).

Half of the claims resolved in 1996 were done through negotiation: 23 percent by litigation settled before trial, 16 percent by mediation, 8 percent by litigation settled in court, 2 percent arbitration, and 1 percent by other methods of alternate dispute resolution. The average cost of defending against a claim for engineering firms in 1996 fell to $15,649 from $22,955 in 1995. For insurers, the cost dropped to $2,818 from $7,163. Krizan,

"Costs Decline for Engineers," 238 *Engineering News-Record* 22, 23 (No. 9, Mar. 3, 1997).

More than 50 percent of professional malpractice claims against designers are *not settled by the parties,* if you combine the reported results of the use of arbitration and litigation (they are both resolution by third-party decision). Why? It may be because it is relatively inexpensive (as far as litigation goes, that is) to gamble with a third party's decision for a malpractice dispute. The 1996 American Consulting Engineers Council (ACEC) survey indicated that the engineer's average cost to defend a claim was only $15,649. The insurance company spent even less to defend: $2,818. What professional would not spend $15,000 on the chance that a judge or an arbitrator would decide the engineer had not erred? This $15,000 figure is not much when compared to the cost of professional liability insurance at 2 to 4 percent of annual billings. Because the 1996 ACEC survey showed that more than half of the malpractice claims were resolved *without any payment to the claimant,* it seems like a good bet to refuse to settle and risk a decision from a judge or arbitrator.

One may also wonder why defending an engineer in a malpractice action is so inexpensive. Is it because the dispute involves only judgement, rather than schedules, daily reports, notice, and all the other documents involved in a typical contractor's claim that make construction litigation so expensive?

The malpractice claims that were settled also tell a story about how willing engineers may be either to compromise or to accept the resolution suggestions of a neutral party. Of malpractice claims that were settled, 31 percent were settled by the parties themselves before or during trial. Only 17 percent were settled with some sort of alternate dispute resolution technique: 16 percent by mediation and 1 percent by another ADR method. Despite the impact of ADR in construction, mediation does not seem to have migrated to design-related disputes—at least for engineers. The ACEC's report suggests that engineers are reluctant to accept suggestions from outsiders.

Other actions that reduce losses include in-house legal and risk management. Firms that have their own risk management and legal staff reported 23 percent lower losses than those with no in-house staff.

Designers for general buildings have the highest average losses as a percentage of revenue, due to heavy competition and little negotiating clout. Designers also reported that they pay 112 percent of the settlement amounts as defense costs.

Owners and others that select designers should read the Johnson & Higgins survey. If they did, only designers using all the three risk management techniques would be considered for new projects. This study should also accelerate designers' attempts to convince owners to select designers based on qualifications rather than costs. See Devaney, "The Qualifications Based Selection of Architects for Public Owners: A Solution for the Short and the Long Term," *Missouri Municipal Review* 26 (June 1995). These three programs may add overhead cost, but will substantially reduce the errors that cause claims.

Page 342, add after first sentence in first paragraph:

Hold harmless agreements are agreements in which the design firm agrees to assume the legal liability of its client. Those who have not been asked to sign one yet probably will be soon.

There are three general types of hold harmless agreements. The limited form means the design firm assumes liability for any act or omission due to its own negligence. The intermediate form means it assumes all liability arising from an act or omission, except that due to the sole negligence of its client. The broad form stipulates the firm assumes all liability arising from an act or omission, including the negligence of its client. Insurance Services Professional Program, 6 *E & O Program News* No. 2, at 1, (Fall 1994).

Signing a hold harmless agreement will not change the coverage provided by E&O insurance. Most professional liability carriers will not accept liability for another's negligence but will accept the liability in a limited or intermediate hold harmless agreement. This means the E&O coverage will not protect the design firm from all the liability imposed by a broad form hold harmless agreement.

Hold harmless agreements often also contain conditions like approval of defense counsel or consent to settle that cannot be transferred to another without prior approval from the firm's insurance carrier.

Page 342, add to seventh paragraph:

For example, in *Valhal Corp. v. Sullivan Associates, Inc.,* 1995 WL 2621 (3d Cir. Jan 3, 1995), the court of appeals explained that although limitation of liability clauses are not favored and must meet stringent conditions to be enforceable, limitation of liability clauses are enforced and a part of businesses and commercial life. Because the $50,000 liability cap was seven times greater than the designer's fee, the limitation of liability clause did not immunize the designer from the consequences of its own actions, and was not against public policy as expressed under Pennsylvania statute. Because the limitation of liability clause was reasonable and enforceable, the appellate court reversed the $1 million jury verdict to the developer for the designer's breach of contract.

§ 14.8 Focus on Architects' and Engineers' Malpractice Insurance

Page 347, add after fifth sentence in sixth paragraph:

Design professionals' failure to renew their claims-made policies, even when confronting potential claims, can deny coverage for the designers' malpractice. In *Graman v. Continental Casualty Co.,* 87 Ill. App. 3d 896, 409 N.E.2d 387 (1980), the school district notified the architect of problems with a roof in 1973. Four years later, unable to fix the problems, the school district sued the architect, alleging defective design. The court held that there was no coverage because the designer had allowed the policy to lapse in 1974, while the school district had not made its claim until 1977. Chemers & Knox, "When Designs Don't Work: Professional Liability Coverage of Architects and Engineers," 15 *Construction Lawyer* No. 1, at 17 (Jan. 1995).

Page 348, add to third full paragraph:

If a prior acts exclusion is in place, claims timely made but based on an occurrence that predates the policy period will not be covered. The prior acts exclusion can be removed by endorsement for an additional premium, if the designer is unaware of any facts that could suggest a claim may be brought against it. Chemers & Knox, "When Designs Don't Work: Professional Liability Coverage of Architects and Engineers," 15 *Construction Lawyer* No. 1, at 17 (Jan. 1995).

CHAPTER 15

INJURIES RESULTING IN DAMAGE CLAIMS

§ 15.1 Introduction

Page 356, add after "See, e.g.," in note 1:

Thomson v. Espey Huston & Assocs., Inc., 899 S.W.2d 415 (Tex. Ct. App. 1995) (any negligence by engineering consulting firm in performing inspection contract caused no injury beyond economic loss to subject of contract itself, which, pursuant to the economic loss rule, did not give rise to tort cause of action).

§ 15.4 Adjacent Property Owners

Page 364, add to carryover paragraph:

See § **7.15**.

In *Johnson v. Board of County Commissioners,* 21 Kan. App. 2d 76, 897 P.2d 169 (1995), the Board of County Commissioners of Pratt County hired Mid-Continent Engineers to design a bridge to replace an old wooden bridge over the river that ran through the Johnsons' property. Shortly after completion of the new bridge, the river flooded and damaged the Johnsons' property. The Johnsons argued that the new bridge caused the flood damage, because it prevented water from diverting into the flood plain and kept more water in the channel where it could erode the north bank of the river on the Johnsons' property.

The court of appeals determined that one who undertakes to render services to another, which he should recognize as necessary for the protection of a third person is subject to liability to the third person for physical harm resulting from a failure to exercise reasonable care if (1) the failure to exercise reasonable care increases the risk of harm to the third person, or (2) he has undertaken to perform a duty owed by the other party to the contract to the third person, or (3) the harm is suffered because of reliance of the other contracting party or the third person upon the work.

The court of appeals applied these tests and stressed expert testimony to the effect that a fundamental part of bridge design is the consideration that the bridge could cause possible damage to the property of landowners on the river. The court held that Mid-Continent should have recognized that its engineering services for the design of the bridge were necessary for the protection of those landowners, and that by failing to foresee or advise the county of the effect of the bridge on the landowners' property, Mid-Continent Engineers increased the risk of harm to those landowners. The court of appeals concluded that Mid-Continent Engineers owed a duty and could be found liable in negligence to the landowners.

§ 15.7 Damages for Delay

Page 369, add to note 61:

Crewdson, *Recovering Delay Damages Against an Architect: An Owner's Approach,* 9 Constr. Law. No. 1, at 24 (Jan. 1989).

§ 15.8 Damages for Personal Injuries

Page 371, add after carryover paragraph:

The New Jersey Supreme Court in *Carvalho v. Toll Bros. & Developers,* 278 N.J. Super. 451, 651 A.2d 492 (App. Div.), *certification granted,* 140 N.J. 326, 658 A.2d 726 (1995), *aff'd & remanded,* 143 N.J. 565, 675 A.2d 209 (1996), ruled that a project engineer had a legal duty to exercise reasonable care for the safety of construction workers. It so held even though the contract made the contractor solely responsible for means and methods of construction, stated that the project engineers shall not have control over the construction means and methods or the contractor's safety precautions, and stated that the contractor "alone" shall be responsible for the safety and adequacy of equipment and methods, including OSHA compliance.

The court found designer responsibility for safety on the jobsite because of an overlap between work progress and work safety. The court found that matters of construction safety bore directly on the engineer's contractual responsibility for supervising the progress of the work. The court reasoned that if safety conditions could affect work progress, the engineer had the authority and control to take or require corrective measures to address safety concerns. The court imposed a legal duty to exercise reasonable care for the safety of workers on a construction site when the engineer has a responsibility for the progress of the work but not for safety conditions, yet is aware of working conditions on the site that create a risk of serious injury to workers.

Page 371, add to note 70:

Amazon v. British Am. Dev. Corp., 628 N.Y.S.2d 204 (1995) (provisions of the contract between the owner and architect that provided that the architect would supervise the contractor's work did not provide basis for designer responsibility for personal injury to third party caused by contractor's broom finish and slope of traffic island).

Page 371, add after first full paragraph:

In *Peck v. Horrocks Engineering,* 106 F.3d 949 (10th Cir. 1997), on the day of a trench collapse, a Horrocks employee helped decide what to do about a steel culvert that crossed the path of the pipeline being laid. The decision was to dig the pipeline trench deeper, to go under the culvert. Peck, an employee of the contractor, was working in a 7-foot trench about 20 feet from the culvert when the trench collapsed. In violation of OSHA regulations, the trench in which Peck was killed had been neither sloped nor shored. The fact that Horrocks was consulted about the trench that collapsed was not, in itself, sufficient to obligate the engineering firm to ensure safety, the court said.

In *Peck,* the engineering agreement between Horrocks and the water district explicitly disavowed any responsibility for maintaining worker safety on site. In addition, the construction contract specified that the contractor would be responsible for all safety precautions and required the contractor to carry appropriate insurance.

The court noted that there is a split of authority regarding whether an engineer who contractually assumes a responsibility to the owner for general supervision of a construction project thereby assumes a duty of care to the employees of the general contractor to supervise the safety of their working conditions. The minority rule imposes a standard of care, whereas the majority rule denies contractual liability. The federal court determined that Utah follows the majority rule. The court also found that the disavowal provision agreed to by Horrocks was added to the standard engineering form by the American Institute of Architects specifically to avoid liability under the minority rule. The court concluded that Utah would not impose a duty on an engineer on the basis of knowledge and inaction alone, when the engineer contractually declined to accept responsibility for worker safety and did not exercise control over worker safety at the jobsite.

Page 372, add at end of section:

Designers may not use the accepted work doctrine to protect themselves against personal injury claims. *Pierce v. ALSC Architects, P.S.,* 890 P.2d 1254 (Mont. 1995) (accepted work doctrine inconsistent with principles of modern tort law and should no longer be followed; architect assumed a nondelegatable duty to ensure that the project was completed in a safe manner, and accepted work doctrine could not apply because it would permit delegation of that duty); *L.H. Bell & Associates, Inc. v. Granger,* 112 Ariz. 440, 543 P.2d 428 (1975).

CHAPTER 16

REDUCING DAMAGES

§ 16.2 Contributory and Comparative Negligence

Page 381, add at beginning of note 5:

APAC Carolina, Inc. v. Town of Allendale, 863 F. Supp. 815 (D.S.C.), *aff'd,* 41 F.3d 157 (4th Cir. 1994) (contractor may impliedly warrant the adequacy of the plans and also be held responsible for a subcontractor's loss caused by design defects if the contractor has waived its rights to recover for the design defects against the owner).

Page 382, add at end of section:

In *CRS Sirrine, Inc. v. Dravo Corp.,* 219 Ga. App. 301, 445 S.E.2d 782 (Ga. Ct. App. 1994); upheld explanation for award 464 S.E.2d 897 (Ga. Ct. App. 1995), Dravo, a construction company, agreed to jointly pursue a United States Navy contract to construct a large, technically complex power plant at the Norfolk Navy Shipyard in Virginia with Sirrine, a engineering firm. Sirrine prepared the technical proposal, including quantity estimates, and Dravo prepared the bid based on Sirrine's proposal and quantities. The Sirrine-Dravo Joint Venture was awarded the contract.

The power plant was a design-build project. The design-builder's bid was submitted on the basis of preliminary design and engineering done by the bidders. The detailed design and engineering work was to be done after award of the contract on a fast-track basis as the project was constructed.

Construction cost $30 million more than anticipated. Numerous changes in the project had to be made as the result of problems with Sirrine's design that delayed completion of the project and increased the cost of the work. Dravo sued Sirrine for $12.5 million for breach of contract and fiduciary duties, including material overruns that far exceeded the quantities in the technical proposal.

The trial court found that Sirrine had breached its contractual and fiduciary duties by failing to provide sufficient, accurate information on which to base the bid; failing to make reasonable efforts to design the project within budgeted quantities; failing to track quantities in its own design; and failing to promptly notify its partners that budgeted quantities would be exceeded. The trial court also found, however, that Sirrine had not caused all of Dravo's damages.

After the trial court awarded Dravo $5,518,000, Sirrine twice appealed the judgment's calculation. Sirrine challenged the manner in which the amount of the award was determined, claiming that the award should have been limited to specific increases in costs that could be attributed solely to specific breaches of Sirrine, because the trial court had found that some of the cost overruns were caused by Dravo. The appellate court ruled that Dravo had shown the damages with a reasonable degree of certainty and had satisfactorily demonstrated the portion attributable to Sirrine.

§ 16.3 Indemnity

Page 382, add after first sentence in first paragraph:

There is no requirement that the architect indemnify the owner against claims arising out of professional errors and omissions. P. Cobey, "The New B141: An Owner's Manual," 3 *The Construction Forum News* 2, at 4 (No. 2, Jan. 1998).

Page 383, add after carryover paragraph:

Construction and engineering firms must incorporate environmental risk management into every facet of their business strategy. The most common risk for street, road, and highway construction projects are related to the excavation of soils with preexisting contamination. Designers should include terms in their contracts that absolve them of liability for preexisting contamination. Often this protection is in the indemnity section of the contract, though it can be inserted as a stand-alone "preexisting contamination" clause. J. Slivka, "Environmental Exposure," 68 *Civil Engineering* 53, at 55 (No. 9, Sept. 1998).

Page 383, add after third full paragraph:

For example, in *Katzner v. Kelleher Construction Corp.,* 545 N.W.2d 378 (Minn. 1996), contractors hired by a design-build firm had no duty to indemnify the design-builder against claims caused by the design-builder's own negligence; in fact, a state law prohibited such indemnification agreements. In *Katzner,* Ellerbe Becket Construction Services, Inc., was the designer-builder of a project in Shoreview, Minnesota. It hired Spancrete Midwest Company to install all precast, prestressed concrete. Kelleher Construction Corporation was hired to perform concrete and masonry work, and it subcontracted some of that work to Gresser Inc. Katzner, an employee of Gresser, fell and suffered serious injuries. Katzner sued Kelleher and Ellerbe Becket, charging them with negligence in maintaining an unsafe workplace. Kelleher and Ellerbe Becket brought Spancrete into the litigation.

Ellerbe Becket claimed that Kelleher's and Spancrete's contract required them to defend and indemnify Ellerbe from all claims arising out of or resulting from performance of the work. On appeal, the Supreme Court of Minnesota ruled that Ellerbe Becket had no claim against its contractors because a contract requiring another to indemnify a firm for its own negligence is unenforceable under a 1984 Minnesota law. The court also noted that an insurance provision in the contracts was intended only to protect Ellerbe Becket from claims arising out of the activities of downstream companies, not its own negligence. *See also National Hydro Systems v. M.A. Mortensen,* 529 N.W.2d 690 (Minn. 1995) (indemnification clause in engineer's agreement is not favored and must be clearly expressed; because clause was equivocal as to whether it applied to claims occasioned by indemnitee's own negligence, subcontractor claim against engineer for negligent preparation of equipment specifications was not covered by indemnity).

§ 16.6 Betterment

Page 385, add after first full paragraph:

The principle is expressed as the doctrine of *betterment* or the doctrine of added value—the loss caused by the failure of the professional should not compensate for more than the actual damage. *Black's Law Dictionary* defines *betterment* as:

> An improvement put upon a property which enhances its value more than mere replacement, maintenance, or repairs. The improvement may be either temporary or permanent. Also applied to denote the additional value which a property acquires in consequence of some public improvement, as laying out or widening a street.

For example, assume that a design firm fails to include return air grilles in its plans and specifications. Under the betterment concept, the design firm is liable for the additional cost of installing the missing air grilles. However, the owner is responsible for their actual cost, because the owner would have been obliged to pay for the air grilles had they been properly stipulated in the original plans and specifications and thereby been a part of the construction bids.

If the omission had been discovered before the bids were opened, an addendum would have been issued and the cost of the missing items would have been added to the original bid price. Under this basic principle, if the defect is one that can be corrected or cured without additional cost to the owner, there has been no actual damage to the owner. If the correction requires additional construction costs to achieve the proper result as originally intended, the design firm is responsible for those additional costs. "Betterment and Added Value," 36 *Private Practice News* 3 (No.1, Jan. 1996).

Page 386, add at end of section:

However, if the designer's contract requires performance for a lump sum, the concept of betterment may not apply. For example, in *Alex Bhatti v. McCabe*, 1997 Ark. App. LEXIS 547 (1997), the chancellor awarded McCabe "repair or replace" damages of $17,781 for defects in the construction of a house under a lump-sum contract, which was offset by the amount of the contract price that McCabe still owed to Bhatti. According to Bhatti, the chancellor erred in awarding McCabe damages for three items: (1) the cost of clearing that part of McCabe's lot in which the septic tank was placed; (2) the cost of landscaping this area after the septic tank had been put in place; and (3) the cost of constructing a driveway. Bhatti characterized these items as "betterments" that were not part of the contract with McCabe. The court agreed that the cost to McCabe of clearing the part of the lot where the septic tank was placed, the subsequent cost of landscaping this area, and the cost of pouring a driveway were required to repair defects and are not payments for betterments that were outside the scope of the contract.

§ 16.9 Other Insurance Coverage

Page 390, add to note 20:

The Illinois Structural Work Act was repealed in 1995.

Page 390, add after carryover paragraph:

However, professional liability exclusions were not effective against an additional insured or with regard to professional service-related claims. In *Priso Serena Sturm Architects, Ltd. v. Liberty Mutual Insurance Co.*, 1995 U.S. Dist. LEXIS 18202 (N.D. Ill. 1995), the general contractor for a new school was required in its contract to provide insurance for the school's architect, Priso Serena Strum. In accordance with its contract, the general contractor purchased two policies from Liberty Mutual Insurance Company (LMIC), including one Commercial General Liability policy.

Claiming defective work, the owner sued the general contractor, the contractor's surety, and the architect after the project was over. The owner also claimed that the architect had breached its contract with the owner by failing to determine that the quality and execution of the work were below the required standards; by failing to guard the owner against defects and deficiencies in the work; and by failing to properly prepare the design and construction documents. The general contractor's surety also complained that the architect had contributed to property damage on the project by negligently misrepresenting the quality and progress of the work.

The architect requested that LMIC defend and indemnify the architect against both the owner's and surety's suits. The insurance company refused.

The insurance policy's endorsement provided coverage for anyone whom the named insured was obligated by an agreement to provide insurance; also, the construction contract terms required the general contractor to procure insurance with the architect named as an additional insured. Thus, the United States District Court for the Northern District of Illinois concluded that the architect was an additional insured under the policy.

Even though the architect was covered by the insurance policy, LMIC still claimed that it was not obliged to defend the architect, because the professional liability exclusion in the policy excluded any liability for professional services. The court concluded that the professional liability exclusion did not preclude the architect from maintaining its claims, because the general contractor was required to obtain the insurance by the construction contract and the terms of that contract did not exclude coverage. Further, the court noted that although one of the policy endorsements did contain a professional liability exclusion, each of the policy endorsements also contained language specifically providing coverage for persons for whom the general contractor was obligated by agreement to provide insurance.

The *Priso* case demonstrates the need for greater quality control in the writing of additional insured endorsements on the part of the carrier and the agent. In effect, purchasing professional liability insurance under a CGL policy paid for by another is a very good deal for designers. The costs and deductibles are much less than for professional liability insurance. Owners must be wary, though, under such an arrangement, for if coverage is thrown out their designers may not be insured.

§ 16.9 OTHER COVERAGE

In *Hurst-Roche Engineers, Inc. v. Commercial Union Insurance Co.,* 51 F.3d 1336 (7th Cir. 1995), Quality Granite sued Hurst-Roche, an engineering firm engaged to design and administrate the construction of a 22-building apartment complex, alleging that a letter written by an engineer contained defamatory statements imputing a lack of ability to perform its trade or business. At the time, Hurst-Roche had two commercial liability policies. The engineer tendered the defense of the action to the insurers. The insurers disclaimed coverage and refused to provide a defense. Hurst-Roche paid for the defense of the libel suit brought by Quality Granite and commenced an action against the insurers. Quality Granite recovered $430,000 in compensatory damages and $100,000 in punitive damages at trial of the libel suit.

Both of Hurst-Roche's commercial liability policies covered *personal injuries,* which was defined to include libel and slander. However, the policies also contained a professional liability exclusion clause. Although the language was different in each policy, both clauses excluded from coverage claims arising from the rendering or failure to render professional engineering services.

The court in *Hurst-Roche* determined that the letter was written by the general manager as part of the professional services provided to the owner and therefore was not covered by the commercial liability policies. The court concluded that the insurers were correct to deny coverage.

Page 390, add after fourth full paragraph:

Reinsurance is a special form of insurance obtained by insurance companies to help spread the risk of loss. Liability insurers and sureties rarely carry the entire policy limit without reinsurance. Also, title insurance and professional liability insurance in addition to financial guarantees that back up the project will likely have reinsurance. The existence of reinsurance is not apparent from the primary insurance policy. Rudnik, "Reinsurance as a Source of Recovery for Insured Losses," 15 *Construction Lawyer* No. 1, at 31 (Jan. 1995).

Reinsurance most often is the funding source after the primary insurance company becomes insolvent. Since 1989, 152 insurance companies have been declared insolvent. Even when the primary carrier is insolvent, however, the reinsurer usually will pay its proportionate share of the loss only to the receiver appointed to administer the primary insurer's insolvency. To avoid either a delay in recovery from a reinsurer or a reduction in the value of the reinsurance that the receivership may impose, direct collection from the reinsurer is desirable.

If concerned about the financial stability of the primary carrier, policy holders can avoid the consequences of insolvency by an endorsement called a cut-through endorsement. Cut-through endorsements create a direct contract between the reinsurer and the holder of the policy. Cut-through endorsement may be only in a reinsurance policy rather than in the primary policy. The conduct of the reinsurer and primary insurer may also establish the existence of a cut-through endorsement.

Without special circumstances, like a cut-through endorsement, there is no contractual privity between the insured and the reinsurer. Attempting to collect directly from a reinsurer will likely not succeed. *Id.* at 34.

§ 16.10 Releases

Page 392, add at end of section:

Designers do not have to be a party to a release in order to be protected by it. For example, in *APAC Carolina, Inc. v. Town of Allendale, 863 F. Supp. 815 (D.S.C.), aff'd,* 41 F.3d 157 (4th Cir. 1994), APAC Carolina contracted to build a sewage treatment facility for two South Carolina towns. In preparing its bid, APAC relied on plans prepared by CRS Sirrine, Inc., the designer. The plans were later determined so defective and inaccurate that the project could not have been built as designed.

APAC subcontracted with Welco Construction & Utilities Company. Welco used the same inaccurate plans to arrive at its bid. Welco claimed over $500,000 in additional costs against APAC because of the defective plans. APAC attempted to collect Welco's additional costs from the towns, but the towns denied responsibility. Welco sued APAC, and APAC in turn sued the towns.

The trial court awarded Welco $500,000 but denied APAC's claim against the towns because APAC had waived any claims to additional compensation. APAC appealed and argued that because it had not prepared the plans or held itself out as a designer, it could not have impliedly warranted the adequacy of the plans. The appellate court concluded that although APAC may not have held itself out as a designer, that did not negate APAC's implied warranty of the adequacy of the plans to Welco. The appellate court upheld Welco's $500,000 award against APAC.

CHAPTER 17

CONTRACTUAL DEFENSES

§ 17.2 Contractual Indemnification Provisions

Page 403, add to note 3 after Chesapeake citation:

Yocum v. City of Minden, 649 So. 2d 129 (La. Ct. App. 1995) (contractor's employee injured in excavation sued designer for failure to exercise due care to prevent dangerous condition. Contractor and its insurers were liable for designer's expenses incurred in defending employee suit under indemnity provision similar to AIA A-201, 3.18.1, in owner-contractor contract, requiring contractor to indemnify owner and designer from claims, including attorney fees, arising out of contractor's work).

Page 404, add to note 3 before last paragraph:

But see Katzner v. Kelleher Constr. Corp., 545 N.W.2d 378 (Minn. 1996) (court ruled that designer had no claim against its contractors because a contract requiring another to indemnify a firm for its own negligence is unenforceable under a 1984 Minnesota law. Court also noted that an insurance provision in the contracts was intended only to protect designer from claims arising out of activities of downstream companies, not its own negligence).

Page 404, add to carryover paragraph:

The 1997 revisions to A201 Paragraph 3.18.1 modified the indemnification provision to exclude loss of use and to clarify that the indemnification is only for losses for which the contractor is responsible. Loss of use is a consequential damage waived in the 1997 revisions to Paragraph 4.3.10. The exclusion of loss of use and the comparative fault clarification significantly reduce the contractor's indemnity obligations.

Page 405, add after first paragraph:

When termination is an issue, the design professional should consider its right to indemnity. The design professional may request indemnity from the owner for any claims arising from the termination. The precise language of the indemnity clause must be negotiated between the parties. It is typical, however, that the indemnity clause will be limited to those situations in which the design professional is not negligent or otherwise liable to the contractor. The design professional may also wish to include an indemnity provision that addresses termination in its original contract. Heley & Bloomquist, "The Design Professional's Role in Termination of the Contractor," 17 *Construction Lawyer* 3, 11 (No. 2, Apr. 1997).

Page 406, add to note 19:

National Hydro Sys. v. M.A. Mortensen, 529 N.W.2d 690 (Minn. 1995) (indemnification clause in engineer's agreement is not favored and must be clearly expressed; because clause was equivocal as to whether it applied to claims occasioned by indemnitee's own negligence, subcontractor claim against engineer for negligent preparation of equipment specifications was not covered by indemnity).

Page 407, add to carryover paragraph:

In Minnesota, an indemnification clause in an engineer's contract was equivocal as to whether it was intended to cover the engineer's own negligence, resulting in the court holding that a subcontractor's claim against the engineer was not covered by the indemnity provision. *National Hydro Systems v. M.A. Mortensen Co.,* 529 N.W.2d 690 (Minn. 1995).

Page 407, add after second full paragraph:

The 1997 revisions to A201 Paragraph 3.18.1 modified the indemnification provision to exclude loss of use and to clarify that the indemnification is only for losses for which the contractor is responsible. Loss of use is a consequential damage waived in the 1997 revisions to Paragraph 4.3.10. The exclusion of loss of use and the comparative fault clarification significantly reduce the contractor's indemnity obligations.

§ 17.5 —No Damages for Delay Clauses

Page 412, add after "See, e.g.," in last line of note 49:

Jim's Excavating Serv. v. HKM Assocs., 878 P.2d 248 (Mont. 1994) (contractor may recover purely economic loss against an engineer when the design professional knew or should have foreseen that the contractor was at risk in relying on the information the designer supplied);

Page 413, add after "cf." in note 49:

Thomson v. Espey Huston & Assocs., Inc., 899 S.W.2d 415 (Tex. Ct. App. 1995) (any negligence by engineering consulting firm in performing inspection contract caused no injury beyond economic loss to subject of contract itself, which, pursuant to the economic loss rule, did not give rise to tort cause of action).

§ 17.6 —No Consequential Damages Clauses

Page 416, add at end of section:

A waiver of consequential damages appears in B141 (1997) in paragraph 1.3.6. Probably no other provision in the new document more clearly demonstrates the general absence of owner representatives.

§ 17.8 —Limitation of Liability to Specific Sum

Page 418, add after second sentence of section:

A limitation of liability clause, unlike a release, waiver, or liquidated damages clause, does not exculpate the architect from any liability to the owner, but instead apportions the risk or exposure between the parties. The purpose of a limitation clause is to permit the owner and the architect to agree to a predetermined amount or type of damage to which the owner is entitled if the architect does not properly perform under its agreement. Harris, "Limitation of Liability Clauses: Allocating Risky Business," 13 *Construction Lawyer* 18 (No. 4, Oct. 1993).

Limitation of liability clauses typically involve one or more of the following limitations: (1) the architect's fee, (2) a stipulated sum, (3) the architect's insurance coverage (sometimes in conjunction with a provision granting the owner, at its expense, the option to purchase additional coverage), and (4) no consequential or incidental damages. The most widely used clause limits the architect's liability to the owner to a fixed dollar amount or the amount of the architect's fee, whichever is greater:

> In recognition of the relative risks of the owner and architect on the project, owner agrees, to the extent permitted by law, that architect's liability to owner for any errors, acts, omissions, negligence, or breaches of the Agreement, shall be limited to $_____ or architect's fee, whichever is greater.

Harris, "Limitation of Liability Clauses: Allocating Risky Business," 13 *Construction Lawyer* 18 (No. 4, Oct. 1993).

It is not certain, however, that the law will enforce a limitation of liability provision. In many jurisdictions, the enforceability of these provisions in construction and design contracts is in question. *See also* Fox & Wolff, "Enforcing Limitation of Liability Provisions in Owner/Architect/Engineer Contracts," 62 *Defense Counsel Journal* 407 (1995).

Only four states have directly addressed limitation of liability provisions by statute: Wisconsin (Wis. Stat. § 895.49 (1994)), Texas (Tex. Civ. Prac. & Rem. Code Ann. § 120.004 (West 1986)), Virginia (Va. Code Ann. § 54.1-411 (Michie 1994)), and California (Cal. Civ. Code § 2782.5 (Deering 1986)). The Wisconsin statute expressly prohibits any provision that limits or eliminates tort liability in construction contracts. Limitation of liability agreements are enforceable under the California and Texas statutes, but prohibited for architects or engineers under the Virginia statute. Claiborne & Potter, "Legislative and Judicial Responses to Limitation of Liability Provisions," 16 *Construction Lawyer* 61 (No. 4, Oct. 1996). Despite questions and limited statutory recognition, the trend has been to enforce limitation clauses entered into by parties of equal bargaining power and sophistication.

Page 418, add at end of first paragraph:

Similarly, in *Valhal Corp. v. Sullivan Associates, Inc.,* 1995 WL 2621 (3d Cir. Jan. 3, 1995), the court of appeals explained that although limitation of liability clauses are not favored and must meet stringent conditions to be enforceable, limitation of liability clauses are enforced and are a part of businesses and commercial life. Because the $50,000 liability cap was seven times greater than the designer's fee, the limitation of liability clause did not immunize the designer from the consequences of its own actions and was not against public policy as expressed under Pennsylvania statute. Because the limitation of liability clause was reasonable and enforceable, the appellate court reversed the $1 million jury verdict of the developer for the designer's breach of contract. *See also Marbro, Inc. v. Borough of Tinton Falls,* 297 N.J. Super. 411, 688 A.2d 159 (1996) (limitation of liability clause did not act as disincentive for design professional to perform its contract properly and was enforceable).

The California Supreme Court decertified an appellate court ruling in *Viner v. Brockway* that threw out a limitation of liability clause in engineering contracts. The order to decertify the opinion by the supreme court means the opinion cannot be cited as precedent in California—at least in disputes that involve engineers' contracts with homeowners. "California Court Decertifies Engineers' Limit of Liability Case," 35 *Private Practice News* No. 6, at 1, (National Society of Professional Engineers July 1995).

Where no state statute exists, some courts have looked to the law pertaining to indemnity provisions and exculpatory clauses and to the anti-indemnity statutes that prohibit them. More than 40 states have enacted anti-indemnity statutes. *See Claiborne & Smith,* "Legislative Division Update," *12 Construction Lawyer* 30 (No. 2, Apr. 1992). In *Dillingham v. CH2M Hill Northwest,* 873 P.2d 1271 (Alaska 1994), the parties' contract limited the engineer's liability to $50,000 or the engineer's total compensation, whichever was greater. The City of Dillingham contended that Alaska's anti-indemnity statute, which prohibits indemnity provisions in construction contracts, applies to limitation of liability clauses as well as to indemnity provisions. The Alaska court rejected the proposition that the term *indemnity* should govern whether a limitation of liability clause in an engineering clause is enforceable, but held the limitation of liability clause void under Alaska's anti-indemnity statute because the law's intent was to prevent a party from bargaining away liability for negligent acts. Claiborne & Potter, "Legislative and Judicial Responses to Limitation of Liability Provisions," 16 *Construction Lawyer* 63 (No. 4, Oct. 1996). Similarly, in *Marbro, Inc. v. Borough of Tinton Falls,* 297 N.J. Super. 411, 688 A.2d 159 (1996), the court rejected the argument that the limitation of liability clause was unenforceable under New Jersey's anti-indemnification statute and found that the anti-indemnification statute did not apply to limitation of liability clauses.

Several courts, in determining the enforceability of the limitation clauses at issue, have focused specifically on whether the owner's claims against the architect were brought in tort or contract. For example, in *Graham, Inc. v. City of Cave City,* 289 Ark. 105, 709 S.W.2d 94 (1986), the Supreme Court of Arkansas ruled that a limitation of liability clause was unenforceable only because the owner was suing the engineer for breach of contract. The limitation clause at issue put a cap on liability for professional negligent acts, errors, or omissions. The court ruled that because the clause did not mention a limitation of liability for breach of contract such a limitation would not read into the contract. Harris, "Limitation of Liability Clauses: Allocating Risky Business," 13 *Construction Lawyer* 19 (No. 4, Oct. 1993).

In *Long Island Lighting Co. (Lilco) v. Imo Delaval, Inc.,* 668 F. Supp. 237 (S.D.N.Y 1987), the court distinguished a claim by the owner against the engineer seeking economic losses in contract, as opposed to a claim in tort for personal injury or property damage. The *Lilco* court held that a limitation clause was not rendered unenforceable by New York's anti-indemnification statute because the owner was a sophisticated party and was seeking economic losses as a result of the engineer's breach of contract. Harris, "Limitation of Liability Clauses: Allocating Risky Business," 13 *Construction Lawyer* 19–20 (No. 4, Oct. 1993).

Page 419, add before first sentence:

Other courts have looked to public policy outside of the statutory context when determining the enforceability of limitation of liability clauses.

Page 419, add to note 81:

Potter-Shackelford Constr. Co. v. Law Eng'g, Inc., 1996 U.S. App. LEXIS 33368 (4th Cir. Dec. 6, 1996) (written proposal for testing and recommendations, which included limitation of liability clause, applied to both testing and recommendations because one invoice was sent for both testing and recommendations and other circumstances relating to contract demonstrated that both services were part of a single contract to which limitation of liability provision applied).

Page 419, add after third full paragraph:

In *Estey v. MacKenzie,* 902 P.2d 1220 (Or. Ct. App. 1995), the parties' agreement limited the liability of the engineering firm to the $200 contract amount for inspection of a home. The owner demanded $340,000. The court found that only an overpowering public policy will justify interference with parties' freedom to contract. The court enforced the limitation of liability clause because the court found that no such policy existed in the context of an engineering firm's performance of a residential inspection. The court also noted that limitation of liability clauses may not be enforced if they are not bargained for or conspicuous. Claiborne & Potter, "Legislative and Judicial Responses to Limitation of Liability Provisions," 16 *Construction Lawyer* 63–64 (No. 4, Oct. 1996).

The Supreme Court of Kansas held that a contract limiting a home inspector's liability to the cost of the inspection was valid and enforceable. In *Moler v. Melzer,* 24 Kan. App. 2d 76, 942 P.2d 643 (1997), the court held that a home buyer's damages for a faulty inspection were limited to the cost of the inspection and did not include the cost of repairing structural defects discovered after the inspection was completed, upholding the limitation of liability clause. The court pointed out that Kansas has never required additional consideration to support a contractual limit on liability. It further noted that the Kansas Consumer Protection Act applies only to consumer transactions in property and not to services such as home inspection. Finally, the court held that the limitation of liability clause was not deceptive because it was clearly evident in the contract, being accompanied by a box to be checked by the home buyer after reading the provision.

In *Gibbes, Inc., II v. Law Engineering, Inc.,* 1992 U.S. App. LEXIS 7602 (4th Cir. 1992), the Fourth Circuit Court ruled that, under Georgia law, a limitation clause limiting the engineer's liability and disclaiming implied warranties was enforceable. The Fourth Circuit Court of Appeals relied upon Georgia common law in holding that the limitation clause was enforceable and did not contravene public policy. The *Gibbes* court held that because the owner was a sophisticated businessman, he would be held to his bargain.

In contrast, a New York court, in *Ricciardi v. Frank,* 620 N.Y.S.2d 918 (1994), refused to enforce a clause that limited an engineer's liability to the inspection fee for a residence. The purchasers had not negotiated the limitation of liability clause before retaining the engineer and the court felt that the protection of homeowners outweighed the policy of freedom of contract. Claiborne & Potter, "Legislative and Judicial Responses to Limitation of Liability Provisions," 16 *Construction Lawyer* 64 (No. 4, Oct. 1996).

Similarly, in *Schaffer v. Property Evaluations, Inc.*, 854 S.W.2d 493 (Mo. Ct. App. 1993), the court refused to enforce the limitation of liability clause in a home inspection dispute. The buyer obtained an inspection report that certified that the concrete foundations walls were in overall satisfactory structural condition. The contract with the buyer limited the inspection firm's liability to the cost of the report. After purchasing the home, the buyer experienced water leakage in the basement. The buyers had the foundation inspected by an engineer to determine the cause of the water leaks. The engineer concluded that the foundation walls were unstable and should be replaced. The engineer estimated that the cost would be between $20,000 and $25,000. The jury returned a verdict in favor of the buyer for $15,000. The property inspection firm appealed because the jury had not been instructed to return a verdict for $153, the inspection fee. The Court of Appeals ruled against the inspection firm on the grounds that there was no evidence that any of the terms of the inspection contract had been negotiated. Also, no separate consideration existed at the time the buyers executed the contract containing the limitation.

Page 420 , add to note 85:

Valhal Corp. v. Sullivan Assocs., Inc., 44 F.3d 195 (3d Cir. 1995); Marbro, Inc. v. Borough of Tinton Falls, 297 N.J. Super. 411, 688 A.2d 159 (1996) (limitation of liability clause did not act as disincentive for design professional to perform its contract properly and was enforceable).

Page 420, add at end of section:

However, the appellate court reversed the $1 million jury verdict to the developer for the designer's breach of contract and stated that the limitation of liability clause was reasonable and enforceable. *Valhal Corp. v. Sullivan Associates, Inc.,* 1995 WL 2621 (3d Cir. Jan. 3, 1995). The court of appeals explained that although limitation of liability clauses are not favored and must meet stringent conditions to be enforceable, they are enforced and are a part of businesses and commercial life. Because the $50,000 liability cap was seven times greater than the designer's fee, the limitation of liability clause did not immunize the designer from the consequences of its own actions and was not against public policy as expressed under Pennsylvania statute.

Engineers who wish to enforce limitation of liability clauses should make sure the limitation of a liability clause is the result of real bargaining. In addition, require that the client initial the limitation of liability clause separately; offer the client an alternative to limiting liability in writing such as a higher contract price to cover the cost of additional liability insurance; and disclose the risks if the engineering design fails. National Society of Professional Engineers "California Court Decertifies Engineers' Limit of Liability Case," 35 *Private Practice News* No. 6, at 1 (July 1995).

Even if enforceable, limitation of liability clauses are strictly construed. Ambiguities may provide a court reason to avoid enforcing the clause. In *CRS Sirrine, Inc. v. Dravo Corp.,* 219 Ga. App. 301, 445 S.E.2d 782 (Ga. Ct. App. 1994); upheld explanation of award 464 S.E. 2d 897 (Ga. Ct. App. 1995), Dravo, a construction company, agreed to jointly pursue a United States Navy contract to construct a large, technically complex power plant at the Norfolk Navy Shipyard in Virginia with Sirrine, an engineering firm. Sirrine prepared the technical proposal, including quantity estimates, and Dravo prepared the bid based on Sirrine's proposal and quantities. The Sirrine-Dravo Joint Venture was awarded the contract.

The power plant was a design-build project. The design-builder's bid was submitted on the basis of preliminary design and engineering done by the bidders. The detailed design and engineering work was to be done after the award of the contract on a fast-track basis as the project was constructed.

Construction cost $30 million more than anticipated. Numerous changes in the project had to be made as the result of problems with Sirrine's design that delayed completion of the project and increased the cost of the work.

Dravo sued Sirrine for $12.5 million for breach of contract and fiduciary duties, including material overruns that far exceeded the quantities in the technical proposal.

The trial court found that Sirrine had breached its contractual and fiduciary duties by failing to provide sufficient, accurate information on which to base the bid; failing to make reasonable efforts to design the project within budgeted quantities; failing to track quantities in its own design; and failing to promptly notify its partners that budgeted quantities would be exceeded.

Sirrine believed that, under § 9.3 of the joint venture agreement, it was not responsible for any damage resulting from increases in material quantities. Section 9.3 stated:

> Notwithstanding any of the foregoing, Sirrine shall have no risk, liability, or accumulation will occur of error and omission charges for construction material quantity variations if the actual quantities are different from those in the bid to the Navy. W/L will provide Sirrine with budget quantities for all functional areas of Project and Sirrine's detail design will make every reasonable effort to stay within these quantities within the requirements of the Prime Contract. W/L will be notified promptly if Sirrine believes quantities will be exceeded.

The court of appeals found the first sentence of § 9.3 ambiguous on its face. That provision did not shield Sirrine from all responsibility from increases in construction material quantities, even if such increase were caused by errors or omissions in its prebid or postbid design and engineering work.

Strictly construing limitation of liability clauses does not always mean that they will not be enforced. For example, in *Pratt Central Park Ltd. v. Dames & Moore,* 60 F.3d 350 (7th Cir. 1995), the court strictly construed a designer's limitation of liability clause that imposed a liability limitation of $5,000, despite protests from an owner. In *Pratt,* Dames & Moore had performed 14 environmental inspections for the same client. The first four inspections were performed under a signed contract that set Dames & Moore's limitation of liability at $100,000. The fifth assignment, along with three others, was performed with a $5,000 limit. Three other assignments were performed without signed contracts. On one of the projects that had no signed contracts, the parties had a dispute that required the court to decide what, if any, limitation of liability was to be applied.

For the disputed project, Dames & Moore had submitted a contract form that provided for separate negotiation of limits of liability and added, "client authorization to proceed without execution of this section indicates acceptance of standard terms and conditions described above in 2.0." Section 2.3

contained a $5,000 presumptive limit, and section 2.5 stated, "increased liability limits may be negotiated upon client's written request, prior to commencement of services, and agreement to pay an additional fee." The court concluded that Dames & Moore had made a concrete proposal laying out the terms on which it did business, with a $5,000 liability limit unless the parties provided otherwise. Because the parties *had* provided otherwise on other occasions, when the limit had been increased to $100,000, the court concluded that the client, rather than Dames & Moore, bore the risk of loss over $5,000.

Proponents of limitation of liability clauses argue that such clauses do not completely relieve a contracting party from liability, but simply allow the level of liability to become one of the bargained-for elements of the contract. Claiborne & Potter, "Legislative and Judicial Responses to Limitation of Liability Provisions," 16 *Construction Lawyer* 61 (No. 4, Oct. 1996).

§ 17.9 —Exculpatory Clauses

Page 420, add after first sentence in first paragraph:

For example, the 1997 edition of AIA B141 permits the parties to limit the services the designer may provide. Article 2.8.1 invites the parties to limit on reviews of each submittal; visits to the site during construction administration; punch list inspections; and final completion inspections. Further, article 2.6.1.5 provides that the architect will review "properly prepared, timely" requests for information from the contractor, implying that RFIs that are not "properly prepared" or "timely" will be reviewed only at an additional charge. Many owners will refuse to agree to specific limits and insist that the word "reasonable" be inserted instead. P. Cobey, "The New B141: An Owner's Manual," 3 *The Construction Forum News* 2, at 4 (No. 2, Jan. 1998).

Page 422, add at beginning of note 98:

Gables CVF, Inc. v. Bahr, Vermeer & Haecker Architect, Ltd., 506 N.W.2d 706 (Neb. 1993) (AIA Doc. B141 para. 1.5.5 (1977) does not absolve the architect from liability for a breach of the architect's contractual duty, if one exists, to inform the owner of deviations from the building plans when the architect has agreed to make periodic observations, if the architect had a duty to report deviations from the architect's plans. Deletion of paragraph 1.5 from contract except for subparagraph 1.5.5 and substitution of fee for "observation of construction" did not define the precise nature of such duties, and factual question existed regarding contractual obligation that architect understood to observe construction of condominium units).

§ 17.12 Change Orders

Page 428, add to carryover paragraph:

In its 1997 revisions to A201, the AIA modified Paragraph 8.3.1 to permit time extensions for delays in the commencement or progress of the work. Delays prior to the start of the work, in addition to delays in work in progress, justify time extensions.

§ 17.13 Design/Build Liability

Page 430, add after first paragraph:

Another critical distinction that should be recognized by a designer involved in the design/build process is that the contractor may not rely upon an implied warranty of the plans from the owner. The general contractor must look to either its designer/employee or designer/partner for relief in the case of design error. Asselin & Stout, "Legal Exposure of the Design/Build Participants: The View of the General Contractor," 15 *The Construction Lawyer* No. 3, at 8 (Aug. 1995).

Page 431, add at end of section:

See *Kaplan v. Tabb Associates, Inc.,* 657 N.E.2d 1065 (Ill. App. 1995) (court held corporation's failure to obtain license to provide architectural services voided its contract with an owner, including the arbitration clause, even though the corporation's sole owner who was in charge of the work was a licensed architect).

Combining the design and build functions creates a conflict for the designer. In design/build, the designer must, in effect, serve two masters. In addition to its professional and ethical responsibilities to the owner, it has an obligation to the contractor whereby the designer may have some financial stake in the project overruns. Asselin & Stout, "Legal Exposure of the Design/Build Participants: The View of the General Contractor," 15 *Construction Lawyer* No. 3, at 8 (Aug. 1995). When the designer is a partner or subcontractor to the general contractor performing design/build, the designer must satisfy its professional duty to the owner from an ethical standpoint without violating its commercial and contractual obligation to the contractor. The manner in which the designer views and exercises its professional duty to the owner may cause the design/builder to act in a manner different from that which the general contractor would have expected from a party primarily responsible for the construction of the project.

CHAPTER 18

IMMUNITY DEFENSES

§ 18.2 Sovereign Immunity

Page 434, add after second sentence in second paragraph:

Department of Transportation v. APAC Ga., 217 Ga. App. 103, 456 S.E.2d 668 (1995) (contractor claim for design errors and omissions was not barred by sovereign immunity, because breach was negligence of duties waived by Georgia constitution "for breach of any written contract").

Page 436, add to note 13:

Estate of Bernaldes v. United States, 877 F. Supp. 301 (W.D. Va. 1995) (mine safety inspectors' compliance determinations involved exercise of discretion in carrying out policy-driven duties and thus fell within discretionary function exception to Federal Tort Claims Act).

Page 436, add after second full paragraph:

Waiver of sovereign immunity may also be determined by the laws of the state in which the action is brought. In *St. Denis v. Department of Housing & Urban Development,* 900 F. Supp. 1194 (D. Alaska 1995), the court ruled that a purchaser of a duplex could not bring a negligent nondisclosure suit against the United States as a vendor, alleging a failure to disclose defects in the roof, even though negligent nondisclosure claims are expressly excluded from coverage under the Federal Tort Claims Act, because Alaska law does not recognize an independent tort action against a vendor for pure economic loss.

Under the mistakability doctrine, the government's sovereign power is presumed to remain intact unless surrendered or contracted away in unmistakable terms. The unmistakability doctrine traditionally has been applied where the government is subject to claims that its contract involved the surrender of sovereign power or the government is subject to claims that, if recognized, would require exempting the private party from the exercise of a particular sovereign power. In other words, the unmistakability defense applies when enforcement of the government's contractual obligation would block the exercise of its sovereign authority. K. Mullen, "*Winstar*

Decision Narrows the Government's Defenses for Contract Breach," 32 *Procurement Lawyer* 15, 16 (No. 2, Winter 1997).

In *United States v. Winstar Corp.,* 116 S. Ct. 2432 (1996), the United States Supreme Court limited the applicability of the unmistakability doctrine. First, the *Winstar* Court noted that the unmistakability doctrine is not available to the government in the vast majority of contractor claims for contract breach, because enforcement of the government's contractual obligations does not impede the government's sovereign power. Second, in cases in which contract performance requires the exercise of a power peculiar to the government, the Court made clear that if the contract includes a risk-shifting provision that may be enforced without effectively barring the exercise of that governmental power, the unmistakability defense is unavailable to the government. Mullen at 17.

Page 437, add after first full paragraph:

In *Scott v. City of Seymour,* 659 N.E.2d 585 (Ind. Ct. App. 1995), a pedestrian sued the City of Seymour after tripping in a hole in the street. At the time of the injury, necessary maintenance and resurfacing of the street had been delayed until the end of a downtown redevelopment project. Under Indiana law, a governmental entity is immune from liability when the alleged negligence causing the harm arises from decisions that are made at the policy-making, discretionary level as opposed to the operational level.

Despite the fact that the city's engineer and public works director had decided to allocate the city's resources so as to delay the resurfacing of the street, the court found that the Board of Public Works of the town had not formally voted on or adopted the plan. Without a board vote, the court concluded that the city had not exercised official judgment or engaged in the necessary policy-oriented decision-making process required for sovereign immunity. The court held that the decision to delay the resurfacing of the streets was not the result of a policy-making, discretionary process, and thus was not entitled to sovereign immunity.

Page 437, add after second full paragraph:

In *County of Brevard v. Miorelli Engineering, Inc.*, 703 So. 2d 1049, 1997 Fla. LEXIS 1811 (1997), the Florida Supreme Court also upheld a public agency's soveriegn immunity defense. Miorelli Engineering Inc. agreed with Brevard County to design and build a spring training facility for the Florida Marlins. After the designer began developing the design, a dispute arose between the County and the designer. The County terminated the design-build contract and withheld payments due under the contract.

Miorelli Engineering sued the County, asserting a variety of claims including breach of contract and seeking extra work that had been performed without a written change order as required under the contract. In a motion for partial summary judgment, the County argued that the extra work claim was barred by sovereign immunity because the extra work was outside the terms of the express contract and no written change orders had been issued authorizing the extra work. The trial court denied the County's motion as to the extra work claims. The Fifth District Court of Appeal affirmed that portion of the order that denied the motion for summary judgment on the claim for damages for extra work.

On appeal, the Florida Supreme Court stated that sovereign immunity precluded the designer's claims for recovery of the cost of extra work beyond that described in contract without a written change order from the County. Miorelli Engineering however had asserted that the County had waived the written change order requirement by directing work changes without following the formalities in the contract. The Florida Supreme Court ruled that the doctrine of waiver and estoppel cannot be used to defeat the express terms of the contract and that the County did not waive the written change order requirement by directing work changes without following its own change order formalities.

Page 438, add to note 21:

In Browning v. Vecellio & Grogan, Inc., 945 F. Supp. 930 (W.D. Va. 1996), the federal district court refused to dismiss a suit against a contractor for gross and willful negligence pursuant to a contract between the contractor and a state agency on the ground that the suit was barred by the doctrine of sovereign immunity. The plaintiff sought recovery from the contractor, alleging that its injuries were sustained as a result of the contractor's negligent failure to cover a ditch near the plaintiff's property while working on a contract with a state agency. Under West Virginia law, state employees may share the commonwealth's sovereign immunity when simple negligence is involved. Independent contractors may also share in the immunity if the acts complained of were indivisible with the exercise of the commonwealth's legitimate authority. The court denied the contractor's motion to dismiss because the acts complained of were not necessarily inseparable from the exercise of state power.

Page 439, add to note 25:

Uptergrove v. Housing Auth., No. 52098 (Mo. Ct. App. Oct. 15, 1995) (accumulation of snow and ice not an intrinsic defect of property so as to waive sovereign immunity; housing authority's duty to maintain premises in a safe condition arose out of contract between it and decedent).

Page 439, add after first full paragraph:

In *Federal Sign v. Texas Southern University,* 951 S.W.2d 401 (Tex. 1997), the Texas Supreme Court evaluated whether a university, as an agency of the state, could avoid liability solely on the basis of sovereign immunity. The Texas Supreme Court stated that sovereign immunity encompasses two types of immunity: immunity from suit and immunity from liability. The court concluded that when the state contracts, it waives immunity from liability. The court also concluded that the act of contracting does not waive immunity from suit, absent a special resolution by the legislature waiving immunity.

Page 439, add at end of section:

In *St. Louis Air Cargo Services, Inc. v. City of St. Louis,* 929 S.W.2d 821 (Mo. Ct. App. 1996), officials of Lambert International Airport, part of the City of St. Louis, represented to St. Louis Air Cargo Services, Inc. (SLACS) that if SLACS would finance, build, and operate an adequate facility, the city would centralize and consolidate all of the air cargo activities at Lambert into the new facility. SLACS completed a $15 million facility in September, 1989. The City did not consolidate the air cargo traffic as represented and allowed other tenants to compete with SLACS.

SLACS sued the city, alleging that SLACS had built the facility in reliance on the city's representations and had also calculated its costs, return on investment and ability to service the required debt relying on the city's representations. The city argued that the SLACS claim was in tort and thus barred by sovereign immunity.

The court of appeals held that when a governmental entity makes a positive representation, on which the contractor relies, which turns out to be false, the contractor is in the position of one who undertakes one contract but is confronted with performance of another. However, the governmental entity gets the benefit of another contract. As a result, sovereign immunity did not bar SLACS' claim.

§ 18.3 Statutory Immunity

Page 443, add to end of section:

Sovereign immunity has also been limited by federal case law. The United States Supreme Court, in *United States v. Winstar Corp.,* 116 S. Ct. 2432 (1996), narrowed the applicability of the sovereign acts defense by eliminating cases in which the governmental act is made in obvious self-interest or the contracting parties clearly anticipated the governmental act and the government agreed to bear the risk of its occurrence. As a result of the *Winstar* decision, the government's ability to successfully exert the sovereign acts defense has been curtailed, and contractors now can rely on provisions that shift to the government the risk of future legislative or executive acts to provide compensation in the event of the government's resulting failure to perform the contract. K. Mullen, "*Winstar* Decision Narrows the Government's Defenses for Contract Breach," 32 *Procurement Lawyer* 15, 18 (No. 2, Winter 1997).

§ 18.4 Public Officers' Immunity

Page 445, add to note 47:

Brown v. Tate, 888 S.W.2d 413 (Mo. Ct. App. 1994) (to bring a public official or a public employee within the protection of the public duty doctrine, it is not sufficient that the public employee be acting within the scope of this employment; the public employee must be engaged in some particular duty of the office or employment that calls for professional expertise and judgment).

Page 445, add after carryover quotation:

In *Sinning v. Clark,* 459 S.E.2d 71 (N.C. 1995), homeowners sued two building inspectors and the City of New Bern for negligence that caused structural defects in the construction of their new home. Citing the public duty doctrine, the city contended that because it owed no legally enforceable duty specifically to the homeowners, it could not be held liable for negligence. The court held that the North Carolina General Statutes and the state building code do not create a special duty over and above the duty owed to the general public, and that plaintiffs were not entitled to relief for negligence. Further, the public duty doctrine also bars claims of gross negligence.

In *Moore Engineering, Inc. v. West Fargo,* 42 F.3d 452 (8th Cir. 1994), purchasers of townhomes built in the early 1980s sued the developers, architect, contractors, mortgage lenders, real estate agents, and the City of West Fargo for construction defects. In its claim against West Fargo, the purchasers alleged that the city had negligently failed to enforce city building codes in both the permitting and inspection processes.

The court in *Moore Engineering* held that the city could be held liable for negligence only if it had breached a special relationship or duty owned specifically to the purchasers. The court held that the city's issuance of building permits and building inspections did not provide the purchasers any specific guarantee. The court refused to hear the purchaser's claims against the city and granted the city's motion for summary judgment, because the purchasers could show no privity, direct contact, or any other special relationship upon which to base any duty over and above that which the city owed to the public at large.

Page 445, add after first full text paragraph:

In *Finley v. Lehman,* 463 S.E.2d 709 (Ga. Ct. App. 1995), a city engineer was held not liable for failing to inspect a sewer ditch to assure that it was shored in accordance with OSHA standards adopted by the city. In *Finley,* the city engineer was on the jobsite for purposes other than to inspect the site. The plaintiff presented evidence that the excavation violated both OSHA standards and a city requirement that all sewer construction be performed according to OSHA standards. The engineer's presence at the jobsite at the time of the accident and at numerous other times could not be the basis for liability for failing to inspect the ditch, even though the engineer had observed that the ditch was incompletely shored, because the engineer's purpose for being at the jobsite was not to inspect the ditch and the engineer had not created reliance in anyone by voluntarily undertaking any inspection of the ditch.

Page 445, add to note 49:

See also Hudson v. Town of E. Montpelier, 638 A.2d 561 (Vt. 1993) (Vermont Supreme Court declined to adopt "public duty doctrine" and its "special relationship" exception, which protects governmental units or employees from liability unless the person seeking recovery can show that duty that was allegedly breached was duty owed to that person in particular, rather than to public at large).

§ 18.6 Witness Immunity

Page 449, add after first sentence in first paragraph:

DeBenedictis, "Off-Target Opinions," 80 *A.B.A. J.* 76 (Nov. 1994).

Page 451, add to note 72:

See also Mattco Forge Inc. v. Arthur Young & Co., 5 Cal. App. 4th 392, 6 Cal. Rptr. 2d 781 (1992) (privilege does not protect an expert hired by a litigant against a malpractice suit by the expert's own client).

Page 452, add to note 75:

See also Moore v. Conliffe, 871 P.2d 204, 29 Cal. Rptr. 2d 152 (Cal. 1994) (expert witness who testified falsely in a deposition prior to testimony in arbitration was not liable to opponents in tort for negligence, misrepresentation, or other torts that may result from the false deposition testimony, just as testimony in a judicial proceeding is protected).

Page 452, add after third full paragraph:

Design and construction groups have prepared Recommended Practices for designers who testify as experts. *See* "Courtroom Hired Guns," *Structural Engineering Forum,* Aug. 1994, at 36. In an effort to impose investigation of local standards of care on testifying experts, 30 regional, national, and international organizations that are believed to represent a majority of the architects and engineers in the United States have endorsed the Recommended Practices for Design Professionals Engaged as Experts in the Resolution of Construction Industry Disputes. Among other suggestions, the Recommended Practices suggest that expert witnesses should identify standards of care independent of their own preferences and should not apply present standards to past events.

Page 452, add to note 79:

cert. denied, 642 N.E.2d 1302 (Ill.1994).

CHAPTER 19

STATUTES OF LIMITATION AND STATUTES OF REPOSE

§ 19.2 General Scope of Statutes

Page 458, add at end of section:

For example, under Mo. Rev. Stat. § 516.097, actions must be filed within ten years, but the statute does not apply if the designers or contractors conceal any defect or deficiency and if the defect or deficiency directly results in the defective or unsafe condition for which the lawsuit is brought. In *Butler v. Mitchell-Hugeback, Inc.,* 895 S.W.2d 15 (Mo. 1995), the Supreme Court of Missouri held that parties seeking to avoid the ten year statute of limitations by showing that the designer or contractors concealed the defective condition must prove that the contractors or designers intended to conceal the defects. In this case, because the owner's lack of diligence caused the failure to discover the visible defect in the trusses, the court found that the contractors did not intend to conceal defects. The court also found that whether the contractor intentionally concealed the insufficient use of reinforcing rods was a question of fact.

§ 19.4 Causes of Action

Page 463, add to note 30:

Butler v. Mitchell-Hugeback, Inc., 895 S.W.2d 15 (Mo. 1995) (party seeking to avoid the ten-year statute of limitation by showing that designer or contractors concealed the defective condition, under Mo. Rev. Stat. § 516.097, must prove that contractors or designers intended to conceal the defects).

§ 19.4 CAUSES OF ACTION

Page 463, add after first full paragraph:

The attempt to avoid statutes of repose or limitation may also include characterizing contract actions as torts. The New York Court of Appeals dismissed a lawsuit brought by a public library against a general contractor, an architect, and an engineer, for damage from a burst pipe occurring 15 years after construction of the building, as time-barred by the six-year statute of limitations for breach of contract actions. *City School District v. Hugh Stubbins & Associates, Inc.*, 85 N.Y.2d 535 (1995). Recognizing the potential statute of limitations problem, the library owner based the lawsuit on negligence rather than breach of contract, contending that because it was not the party that had contracted with the contractor and the designers, the applicable statute of limitations should not start to run until the date the pipe burst and should be governed by the three-year statute of limitations for negligence. The court disagreed and dismissed the lawsuit because, although the library owner was not the contracting party, the relationship was the "functional equivalent" of a contractual relationship; the library owner was the intended beneficiary of the contract.

Page 464, add at end of section:

Statutes limiting the time within which suit may be brought do not apply to claims brought by agencies of state and local government entities. However, courts construing statutes of repose have distinguished them as substantively different from statutes of limitation. Given this distinction, contractors and engineers have argued that statutes of repose should also limit a state government's claims for latent defects in design and construction. Courts generally have rejected this argument. Martorelli, "State Statutes of Repose and Government Claims for Latent Defects in Design and Construction," 25 *Public Contracts Law Journal* 199 (No. 2, Winter 1996).

Statutes of limitations are held not to apply to the state unless the language of the statute clearly indicates a contrary intention. For example, the Illinois statute includes within its definition of persons covered by the statute "any body politic," a term construed as subjecting the State of Illinois to the statutory bar. However, the majority of statutes are silent on applicability to state claims. Martorelli at 199. If the government is to be subjected to the operation of relapse statutes to the same extent as private parties, such a result will have to come from the state legislatures, which alone possess the power to address the competing policy issues and amend the existing statues. *Id.*

§ 19.5 Commencement of Action

Page 466, add after first full paragraph:

In *Russo Farms v. Vineland Board of Education,* 280 N.J. Super. 320, 655 A.2d 447 (App. Div. 1995), an adjacent landowner sued the architect, contractor, and school board for damage to its property that construction of a school had caused. The landowner filed its suit July 18, 1990. A certificate of occupancy had been issued for the school building on September 5, 1979, when the project was determined to be substantially complete and opened for classes. The architect had indicated that all of the punchlist items were completed by April 11, 1980, in a certificate of payment to the owner. However, according to the secretary for the contractor, punchlist items were not completed until February 11, 1981. On February 20, 1981, the architect reported to the owner that the last of the punchlist items had been completed and so approved the release of the remaining retainage.

The construction contract provided that final payment shall be made when the "Work has been completed, the Contract fully performed, and a final Certificate for Payment has been issued by the Architect." The trial court determined that the work of the supervising architect was not complete until a final certificate for payment had been issued.

The New Jersey appellate court, in considering the New Jersey statute language that limited actions ten years "after the performance or furnishing of such services and construction," determined that the repose period should not begin to run from the date of substantial completion. Rather, the court found that the intent of the statute was that the period of repose should commence when the contractor had fully performed all its contractual obligations, completely furnished all of its agreed services, and entirely completed the construction project. The appellate court found the filing of the complaint to be timely for purposes of the statute of repose.

Among the reasons the appellate court indicated supported the selection of the final, rather than substantial completion date, was that there is normally some documentation that will serve as evidence of the last date on which work was performed. Further, the court felt that the final completion date is more likely to be documented than is the date of substantial completion.

Page 468, add after "See also" in note 56:

Thomson v. Espey Huston & Assocs., Inc., 899 S.W.2d 415 (Tex. Ct. App. 1995) (action for negligence in performance of engineering services qualifies for application of discovery rule regarding statute of limitations under which limitations period runs from date plaintiff discovers or should, in exercise of reasonable care and diligence, have discovered nature of injury; having engaged engineer to remedy contractor's own lack of expertise, general contractor cannot be expected to assess competence of engineer's work before there is opportunity to test final product).

Page 468, add to note 56:

O'Reilly v. Dock, 929 S.W.2d 297 (Mo. Ct. App. 1996) (In Missouri, the time within which an action for breach of contract may be brought begins when "the damage resulting . . . is sustained and is capable of ascertainment." Ascertainment of some damage or injury is all that is required to commence the running of the statute of limitations. Ascertainment occurs when a person has some awareness that either an injury has been suffered or another person has committed a legal wrong that may result in harm. Simple knowledge of some damage is sufficient to start the statute running. When the breach is not known and there is delayed manifestation of damage resulting from the breach that cannot reasonably be discovered by a lay person, "capable of ascertainment" applies. If some knowledge of the damage was gained five years before the suit was filed, even though the specific breach of contract was not known, a lawsuit that seeks recovery of any resulting damage may be precluded. However, if the manifestation of the defect is not known or reasonably ascertainable by a layperson, damage may be recovered as long as a lawsuit is initiated within five years); Republic Contracting Corp. v. S.C. Dept. of Highways and Pub. Transp., 332 S.C. 197, 503 S.E.2d 761, 1998 S.C. App. LEXIS 88 (1998) (contractor sued owner, DOT, and engineer for damages from defective design for construction of a bridge. Because the discovery rule applied, the cause of action accrued when contractor encountered construction and installation problems in the field. The claim against the owner did not accrue until Republic had exhausted its remedies under the contract or Republic was denied payment under the contract on final completion. Even though the claims arose from the same set of operative facts, the claims against the engineer were time-barred, while the claim against the owner remained viable).

Page 468, add after carryover paragraph:

Similarly, Georgia's Supreme Court ruled that the contractor's right to sue did not accrue until the alleged delay damages began. *Hardaway v. Parsons, Brinkerhoff, Quade & Douglas, Inc.*, 479 S.E.2d 727 (Ga. 1997). Hardaway was the contractor selected to reconstruct State Highway 19, which Parsons designed for the Georgia Department of Transportation. In October 1988, Hardaway asked the DOT to verify the workability of a detailed erector system planned by Parsons for a number of 50-ton bridge girders. In March 1989, Parsons revised its computer analysis of the erector system. Hardaway was informed in June that the system would not operate properly. In April 1993, Hardaway sued the designer, asserting that its negligent design of the erector system and negligent misrepresentation of the system's integrity caused Hardaway to lose money due to extra work and delays.

Parsons claimed that the lawsuit was barred by a four-year statute of limitations that began to run when Hardaway signed its contract. Hardaway argued that the limitations period began in June 1989, when its work began to be delayed and it began to suffer losses.

The Georgia Supreme Court decided that in claims for economic injury sustained due to reliance upon false information negligently provided by a designer, the statute of limitations begins to run when the contractor suffers pecuniary loss with certainty, and not as a matter of pure speculation. The court found that Hardaway's losses did not begin until June 1989.

§ 19.9 Summary of State Statutes

Page 477, add to Arizona:

Fry's Food Stores v. Mather & Assoc., Inc., 183 Ariz. 89, 900 P.2d 1225 (1995) (statute applies only if action arises out of contract or is generated by contractual relationship and is based on a written contract).

Page 483, add to Kentucky:

Ky. Rev. Stat. § 413.245 provides a one-year period to bring an action for "any act or omission in rendering, or failing to render, professional services for others." The statue begins to run at discovery of the injury. In *Old Mason's Home of Kentucky, Inc. v. Mitchell,* 304 S.W.2d 304 (Ky. Ct. App. 1995), the court held that the rendering of architectural services fell within the statute, and barred an action by an owner who had known about the leaking water more than one year prior to filing the action. In addition, although the designer had completed its services in 1983, the action was not filed until 1991.

§ 19.9 SUMMARY OF STATE STATUTES

Page 487, add to Missouri:

Missouri's statute of limitations, Mo. Rev. Stat. § 516.100, begins the time in which an action for breach of contract may be brought when "the damage resulting . . . is sustained and is capable of ascertainment." In *O'Reilly v. Dock,* 929 S.W.2d 297 (Mo. Ct. App. 1996), the court of appeals noted that ascertainment of some damage or injury is all that is required to commence the running of the statute of limitations. Ascertainment occurs when a person has some awareness that either an injury has been suffered or another person has committed a legal wrong that may result in harm. Simple knowledge of some damage is sufficient to start the statute running. However, when the breach is not known and there is delayed manifestation of damage resulting from the breach that cannot reasonably be discovered by lay person, "capable of ascertainment" applies. If some knowledge of the damage was gained five years before the suit was filed, even though the specific breach of contract was not known, the Missouri statute of limitations may preclude a lawsuit that seeks recovery of any resulting damage. However, if the manifestation of the defect is not known or reasonably ascertainable by a layperson, damage may be recovered as long as a lawsuit is initiated within five years.

Page 494, add to South Carolina:

Republic Contracting Corp. v. S.C. Dept. of Highways and Pub. Transp., 332 S.C. 197, 503 S.E.2d 761, 1998 S.C. App. LEXIS 88 (1998), *see* **§ 5.8** and **§ 19.5**.

CHAPTER 20

DEFENDING AGAINST A CLAIM: AN OVERVIEW

§ 20.14 Experts

Page 521, add to note 13:

City of York v. Turner-Murphy Co., 452 S.E.2d 615 (S.C. Ct. App. 1994) (court found that expert testimony was necessary for jury to decide whether engineer violated duty to test concrete walls); Annen v. Trump, 913 S.W.2d 16 (Mo. Ct. App. 1995) (expert testimony is necessary to establish extent of engineering company's duty to supervise construction project and compliance with plans and specifications, because subject is outside of common knowledge and experience of laypersons).

Page 521, add after second full paragraph:

The testimony of two foundation repair experts was found sufficient to establish the applicable standard of care for a professional engineer in *Yantzi v. Norton,* 927 S.W.2d 427 (Mo. Ct. App. 1996). These experts' testimony was sufficient because the homeowners' claim of negligence was based on the standard of care of a foundation specialist, not an engineer.

In the spring of 1988, the homeowners began to notice cracks in the basement walls and the ceiling of their home. They consulted three foundation repair companies that recommended the installation of steel piers in the basement. The homeowners also contacted an engineer who claimed to be an expert in foundation evaluation and repair. The engineer told the homeowners that steel piers would be "useless" and recommended other repair methods. The engineer's repair direction failed, however, and the basement problems became worse. Krueger, "Homeowners' Foundation Experts Can Rebut Professional Engineer," *Missouri Lawyers Weekly,* June 24, 1996, at 2.

The homeowners later installed steel piers as recommended by the foundation experts. The steel piers corrected the problem, but 34 piers were required instead of 15 estimated before the engineer's repair methods were attempted.

§ 20.14 EXPERTS

The court determined that the standard of care to be applied to the engineer was not the standard of professional engineers, but the standard of a foundation evaluator and repair specialist. Although the engineer's training qualified him to engage in foundation inspection and evaluation, the foundation repairmen were also qualified to engage in the same line of work.

CHAPTER 21

PREPARING FOR TRIAL

§ 21.6 —Investigation

Page 531, add at beginning of section:

Investigation of the claim is important not only to adequately prepare for presentation, but also to meet statutory requirements to protect designers and their insurers against frivolous claims. In a limited number of jurisdictions, a person purportedly damaged by the professional negligence of a design professional must obtain independent review of the merits of the claim before pursuing a civil action against the design professional. The statutory mandates vary in methodology. Some statutes require the plaintiff to attach to the complaint a certificate declaring that the attorney has consulted with a qualified individual and that the attorney or qualified individual has concluded that there is reasonable cause for filing the action. Other statutes require the claim to be presented to an independent panel for an advisory, nonbinding opinion, Currently, only a handful of states have enacted such legislation. Davis, "Certificates of Merit and Review Panels: Conditions Precedent to Civil Actions Against Design Professionals," 15 *Construction Lawyer* 88 (No. 2, Apr. 1995).

Indications are that courts broadly construe the types of claims within the scope of statutes requiring certificates of merits or review panels. The plaintiff's characterization of the claims will not avoid the requirements. In *Martinez v. Badis,* 842 P.2d 245 (Colo. 1992), the language in the Colorado statute was determined to be sufficiently broad to include every claim that required proof of professional negligence as a predicate to recovery, whatever the formal designation of that claim might be. Davis, "Certificates of Merit and Review Panels: Conditions Precedent to Civil Actions Against Design Professionals," 15 *Construction Lawyer* 88 (No. 2, Apr. 1995). In *Ponderosa Center Partners v. McClelan/Cruz/Gaylord & Associates,* 45 Cal. App. 4th 913, 915, 53 Cal. Rptr. 2d 64 (1996), an engineer was permitted to provide a certificate of merit, pursuant to Cal. Civ. Proc. Code § 411.35, in a suit against an architect.

States that have enacted the certificate of merit review system specify the contents of the document to be filed, who must file it, and when it must be filed. The review panel system is comparable to nonbinding arbitration.

Compliance with this type of tort reform legislation entails significantly greater effort by claimants than compliance with the certificate of merit statutes. Following receipt of the design professional's response to the claim, a panel is convened for an informal hearing during which the panel reviews the claims, prepares findings, and issues an advisory opinion. A panel is formed for each claim filed. The panel may receive oral or documentary evidence; question the parties, witnesses, and consultants; and subpoena the appearance and testimony of witnesses and the production of documentary evidence. In its written advisory decision, the panel decides the issue of liability; if liability is found and if evidence has been presented regarding damages, the panel determines the amount of damages, if any, that should be awarded. The statute of limitations is tolled during the pendency of the panel review process. The statute will also remain tolled for a specified period following service of the panel's decision upon the parties. Davis at 89.

Often more important than the panel's decision itself is the effect the decision may have on any subsequent civil litigation between the parties. The panel's decision is not binding on any party. Following rejection of the panel's decision by either party, the plaintiff may proceed with a civil action against the design professional. The Kansas statute, for example, expressly provides that the panel's written report shall be admissible in any subsequent litigation. Davis at 89.

In May 1997, Minnesota enacted a new certificate of merit law. Despite the new legislation in Minnesota, there remains strong opposition to certificate of merit laws. Most recently, legislatures in Louisiana, Maryland, Massachusetts, Missouri, and Nevada considered and rejected legislation requiring certificates of merit. Missouri's 1997 attempt to enact a certificate of merit bill was the most successful to date—it passed the Senate but died in the House Judiciary Committee. The outcome was much the same in Maryland, with a certificate of merit bill passing the House but dying in the Senate Judicial Proceedings Committee. Maryland's bill was backed by the state Chamber of Commerce and the Maryland Council of Design Professions, including the Maryland Society of Professional Engineers.

A proposed Nevada certificate of merit bill was amended in an attempt to reach a compromise with trial lawyers. The amendment would have required a plaintiff who did not file a certificate of merit and then lost the case to pay the defendant's legal fees. The trial lawyers still opposed the bill, however, arguing that it would limit the plaintiff's right to be heard in court. The Nevada bill died in subcommittee in July. D. Siegel, "Engineers Find Curbing Frivolous Suits Can Be Trying," 19 *Engineering Times* 11 (No. 8, Aug. 1997).

Even in the states that have certificate of merit laws (Arizona, California, Colorado, Georgia, Hawaii, Kansas, and New Jersey), challenges have not necessarily disappeared, and court rulings can affect how well the laws actually work. For example, Arizona's law requires plaintiffs who sue design professionals and contractors for negligence to file an affidavit from a member of the defendant's profession stating the acts or omissions on which the claim is based. Some lower Arizona court judges have ruled that this requirement is unconstitutional. As a result, the Arizona Court of Appeals is currently considering the constitutionality of the law in a petition for special action. The Arizona Society of Professional Engineers and other design and construction groups filed a "friend of the court" brief, which argued that the law does not impair a plaintiff's right to sue and that the state legislature had a rational basis for requiring certificates of merit. Siegel at 11.

In New Jersey, an affidavit of merit law was enacted in 1995, and since then the courts have been interpreting the law. In July, the New Jersey Supreme Court issued a decision favorable to the design professions. The ruling establishes a clear deadline as to when the affidavit of merit must be submitted. The court's decision could result in the dismissal of many pending cases. The New Jersey Supreme Court also clarified that an expert who files an affidavit must not have a financial interest in the case and that the affidavit must include the expert's qualifications. Siegel at 11.

Despite enactment in only a small number of states, legislation requiring certificates of merit or review panels is an important aspect of design professional liability reform. In 1996, the National Society of Professional Engineers adopted a professional policy urging its state societies to seek enactment of certificate of merit laws. Siegel at 11. It is likely to become even more important as more states enact similar legislation. These statutes may be viewed as erecting impediments to the resolution of professional negligence claims and creating additional procedures to be followed prior to or in conjunction with the filing of a civil action. Nevertheless, these statutes may be viewed, more positively, as a valid and rational means to reduce the number of frivolous actions filed against licensed professionals. It is important to be aware of these statutes. Although statutes requiring certificates of merit or review panels do not ultimately determine whether a claim can be brought, failure to comply is grounds for dismissal of a claim. Davis at 89.

CHAPTER 22

EXPERT CONSULTANTS AND WITNESSES

§ 22.2 The Legal Necessity for Expert Testimony

Page 540, add to note 1:

Walker v. Bluffs Apartments, 477 S.E.2d 472, 473 (S.C. Ct. App. 1996) (plaintiff's expert, who was licensed residential builder and licensed building inspector who taught building codes, was not qualified to render opinion as to architect's standard of care; therefore, summary judgment was properly entered in favor of architect sued by resident of apartment complex for injuries sustained when resident slipped and fell on a sidewalk that was allegedly icy due to improper drainage); *but see* Edgewater Apartments v. Flynn Consulting Eng'rs, 216 A.D.2d 53, 627 N.Y.S.2d 385 (1995) (architect was competent to testify as expert in building owners' negligence action against consulting engineers because architect was familiar with leakage problems and had stopped water seepage that defendants had failed to halt); Yantzi v. Norton, 927 S.W.2d 427 (Mo. Ct. App. 1996) (testimony of two foundation repair experts was found sufficient to establish applicable standard of care for professional engineer, because homeowners' claim of negligence was based on standard of care of a foundation specialist, not an engineer; foundation repair experts were qualified to engage in same line of work and had corrected problem).

Page 540, add before last paragraph:

Some plaintiffs who have failed to obtain the appropriate expert may argue that they can establish the applicable standard of care and breach of the standard through admissions elicited from the defendant architect or engineer. It is not clear whether a defendant's testimony can be used in lieu of the testimony from an independent expert, so a plaintiff may still face problems with this approach. To illustrate, the Wyoming Supreme Court, in *Garaman, Inc. v. Williams,* 912 P.2d 1121 (Wyo. 1996), found that the trial court properly granted a directed verdict in favor of an architect on an owner's counterclaim against the architect for professional negligence in the design of a motel complex, because the owner failed to present an expert to establish the standard of care. *Id.* at 1124. The owner argued that the architect had established the standard of care and the breach of that standard by the architect's testimony at trial. The owner pointed out that the architect had acknowledged a duty to know the applicable codes when designing a building and that, in a few instances, the completed building in question did not comply with those requirements. *Id.* Nevertheless, the court concluded that the architect's testimony was not sufficient to establish the applicable standard of care, under the facts of that case, because the testimony was too general to be considered. *Id.* The court noted that the owner had failed to question the architect in detail about the standard of care that applies when architects are faced with specific problems associated with interpreting and complying with building code requirements. *Id.* The court further rejected the owner's argument that the architect's performance was so deficient that a lay person could discern the negligence, because a lay person would not have sufficient experience to understand architectural concepts such as the interpretation of building codes without being aided by expert testimony.

§ 22.3 Cases Holding Expert Testimony Required

Page 542, add at beginning of second full paragraph:

For instance, in an action brought against an engineer alleging the negligent design of a septic system, the trial court set aside a verdict in favor of the plaintiff because the plaintiff failed to present expert testimony to prove a breach of the standard of care of the engineer. *Matyas v. Minck,* 37 Conn. App. 321, 655 A.2d 1155, 1158 (1995).

Page 542, add after fourth paragraph:

In *City of York v. Turner-Murphy Co.,* 452 S.E.2d 615 (S.C. Ct. App. 1994), the City of York, South Carolina, hired the engineering firm of Mayes, Sudderth and Etheredge, Inc., for design of a wastewater treatment plant. The engineer agreed to provide detailed inspection of the construction work for general compliance with contract documents.

During construction, the engineer's inspector noticed leaks in a concrete wall in the filter structure. After forms were stripped, honeycombing was discovered. The contractor repaired the wall, and the city accepted the plant. A year later, a hole developed in the wall. Another engineer hired by the city took core samples and found extensive voids. The second engineer recommended replacement of the wall.

The city sued Mayes, Sudderth for negligence. At trial, the city presented expert testimony that established that Mayes had a duty to notify the city of defective work during construction. However, the city's expert did not testify that Mayes had violated its duty to notify the city of the contractor's defective work.

The court of appeals ruled that the jury was not equipped to decide whether Mayes violated its duty to notify the city of defective work because the voids in the concrete could not be discovered except through destructive testing. Expert testimony was needed to prove whether Mayes violated its duty to destructively test the concrete walls.

The designer's decision to destructively test for hidden defects requires evaluation of many subjective factors. These factors include past conformance of the contractor's completed work to the contract requirements; the importance of the portion that is suspected to be defective; the cost of the destructive test; and the stage of construction of the project. These factors are better evaluated by experts familiar with design and construction.

In *Annen v. Trump,* 913 S.W.2d 16 (Mo. Ct. App. 1995), an owner sued an engineering company for failing to properly supervise a subcontractor's work. The subcontractor did not place a protective coating on the roof of a new restaurant. The questions of extent of the supervisory duties of an engineer and whether there was compliance with the plans and specifications were determined to be outside the common knowledge and experience of laypersons and thus required expert testimony. Because the owner did not offer any, the owner's judgment against the engineering company was reversed.

CHAPTER 23

ALTERNATE DISPUTE RESOLUTION: THE PROS AND CONS

§ 23.2 Defining ADR

Page 560, add to note 1:

Modifications to AIA A201 in the 1997 revisions now require all claims, other than those relating to aesthetic effect, to be mediated as a condition precedent to arbitration or litigation.

§ 23.3 Arbitration

Page 562, add at end of section:

The presence of an arbitration clause may not guarantee that all disputes related to the performance of the contract may be arbitrated. In *Hazelton Area School District v. Dosak,* 671 A.2d 277 (Pa. Commw. Ct. 1996), the court found that the arbitration provisions of a standard AIA owner-architect contract did not apply to a claim charging the architect with professional negligence. The school district alleged a claim in tort for professional negligence, which did not concern the agreements or their breach; as a result, the claim was not governed by the contract's arbitration provisions.

The court based its analysis on the distinction between tort claims and contract claims, emphasizing the different policy considerations underlying tort law and contract law. The school district began occupying the completed high school in September 1993. In January 1994, the roof of the new school collapsed under the weight of snow. The court determined that the school district expected it would pay $13 million for the construction of a new high school, but the agreements did not indicate that the parties contemplated the possibility that the school district would have to pay more than $2.5 million to repair the new high school's roof after it collapsed.

§ 23.5 —Joinder of Parties

Page 563, replace first paragraph with:

There are three ways in which the consolidation of multiparty arbitrations may be enforced. First, the parties may provide for consolidation in their contracts. A general contractor may often provide for the consolidated arbitration with their subcontracts. Standard form contracts from the AIA and EJCDC do not include consolidation in their arbitration clause as is common in most other design contracts. *See, e.g.,* AIA Doc. B141, para. 7.3 (1987).

Second, state statutes may provide that courts may consolidate arbitrations with common parties, facts, or disputes. For example, both California (Cal. Civ. Proc. Code § 1281.3) and Massachusetts (Mass. Ann. Laws ch. 251, § 2A) permit their courts to order consolidation in appropriate circumstances. *Slaught v. Bencomo Roofing Co.,* 25 Cal. App. 4th 744, 30 Cal. Rptr. 2d 618 (1994) (where subcontract adopted the provisions of the general construction contract that contained an arbitration clause, the courts have compelled joinder of the contracting parties in one arbitration); *New England Energy Inc. v. Keystone Shipping Co.,* 855 F.2d 1 (1st Cir. 1988), *cert. denied,* 489 U.S. 1077, 109 S. Ct. 1527, 103 L. Ed. 2d 832 (1989) (consolidation of two arbitrations was proper, despite silence of arbitration agreements on issue of consolidation, where Massachusetts statute specifically provided for consolidation).

Some state provisions have now been superseded by state enactments of the UNCITRAL Model Law for purposes of international arbitration. To the extent that these provide for court assistance in consolidating arbitrations, they do so only when the parties have so agreed. Hoellering, "Consolidated Arbitration," 52 *Dispute Resolution Journal* 41, 46 (No. 1, Jan. 1997).

The new English Arbitration Act permits parties to agree on the consolidation of related arbitrations or concurrent hearings but specifies that unless the parties confer such power on the arbitral tribunal it cannot order consolidation. Article 35, English Arbitration Act. Canadian enactments provide that on application of all the parties to two or more arbitral proceedings, the court may order consolidation on the terms it considers just. Hoellering at 48.

Third, even without permission to consolidate from either contract or statute, courts may order consolidation. However, the courts in the United States that have considered whether multiparty construction claims should be joined or consolidated have come to different conclusions. In the absence of specific contractual permission, courts of New York, Iowa, Nevada,

South Carolina, Minnesota, New Jersey, and Maryland are liberal in granting consolidation for disputes with common issues. Other state courts, such as Washington, Michigan, Alaska, Louisiana, and Hawaii, deny consolidation and favor separate arbitrations when separate contracts are involved. Callahan, Bramble & Lurie, *Arbitration of Construction Disputes* 23 (1990) (citing 10 *AAA Lawyers' Arbitration Letter* 1 (Mar. 1986); *Maxum Foundations, Inc. v. Salus Corp.*, 817 F.2d 1086 (4th Cir. 1987); *Dierson v. Joe Keim Builders, Inc.*, 216 N.J. Super. 618, 524 A.2d 841 (App. Div.), *cert. denied,* 107 N.J. 148, 526 A.2d 209 (1987)). *See also Bateman Construction, Inc. v. Haitsuka Bros.*, 77 Haw. 481, 889 P.2d 58 (1995) (court had no jurisdiction to consolidate arbitrations when the arbitration agreements were silent as to consolidation).

Federal courts also seem to be divided. Some circuits hold that parties may not be joined to an arbitration unless they have expressly agreed to such a joinder. *In re Arbitration Between Coastal Shipping Ltd. & Southern Petroleum Tankers, Ltd.*, 812 F. Supp. 396 (S.D.N.Y 1993); *Active Glass v. Architect & Ornamental Iron Workers # 580,* 875 F. Supp. 245 (S.D.N.Y. 1995) (courts will not force parties into arbitration when it was clearly not their intention to place given matter under provision of an arbitration agreement) (carpenters' and glaziers' union could not be compelled to engage in multiparty arbitration, absent agreement for multiparty or consolidated arbitration in their collective bargaining agreements). *See also Arbitration and the Law 1993–1994* 141 (American Arbitration Ass'n 1994); *Painewebber Inc. v. Fowler,* 791 F. Supp. 821 (D. Kan. 1992)).

In *United Kingdom v. Boeing Co.*, 998 F.2d 68 (2d Cir. 1993), the Second Circuit Court of Appeals prohibited consolidated arbitrations absent the consent of the parties. In *Boeing,* the court concluded that under the Federal Arbitration Act, private arbitration agreements are to be treated as other contracts negotiated between private parties, and that district courts should be concerned with enforcing the parties' agreement as written, regardless of potential inefficiencies created by such enforcement. The *Boeing* court followed earlier decisions in the Fifth (*Del E. Webb Construction v. Richardson Hospital Authority,* 823 F.2d 145 (5th Cir. 1987)), Sixth (*American Centennial Insurance v. National Casualty Co.,* 951 F.2d 107 (6th Cir. 1991)), Eighth (*Baesler v. Continental Grain Co.,* 900 F.2d 1193 (8th Cir. 1990)), Ninth (*Weyerhaeuser Co. v. Western Seas Shipping Co.,* 743 F.2d 635 (9th Cir. 1984), *cert. denied,* 469 U.S. 1061 (1984)), and Eleventh Circuits (Protective Life Insurance Co. v. Lincoln National Life Insurance Corp., 873 F.2d 281 (11th Cir. 1989). Hoellering at 45.

Other circuits have ordered the consolidation of separate arbitrations when it has been determined that there are common questions to be resolved.

Hoover Group Inc. v. Probala & Associates, 710 F. Supp. 677 (N.D. Ohio 1989) (consolidation of pending arbitrations was proper, although neither contract provided for consolidated arbitration, when one party was common to both agreements, both agreements were basically identical, both arbitrations presented common questions of law and fact, and separate arbitrations presented a danger of conflicting findings and awards); *Sociedad Anonima de Navegacion Petrolera v. CIA. de Petroleos de Chile S.A.,* 634 F. Supp. 805 (S.D.N.Y. 1986) (consolidation of arbitrations between time charterer of vessel and vessel owner and between time charterer and subcharterer was proper given the common questions of law or fact, the possibility of conflicting awards, and risk of substantial prejudice to the party resisting consolidation); *P/R Clipper Gas v. PPG Industries Inc.,* 804 F. Supp. 570 (S.D.N.Y. 1992) (consolidation is appropriately ordered where the objecting party fails to show that it would be significantly prejudiced by the proposed consolidation). *See also* Callahan, Bramble & Lurie, *Arbitration of Construction Disputes* 22 *et seq.* (1990).

In *North River Insurance Co. v. Philadelphia Reinsurance Corp.,* 63 F.3d 160 (2d Cir. 1995), the Second Circuit Court of Appeals was again confronted with the issue of the validity of consolidation of claims into a single arbitration proceeding. In this case, however, the circuit court reversed the district court's decision vacating the award and upheld the decision to consolidate, despite the lack of consent by all of the parties. North River commenced two separate arbitration proceedings against two separate reinsurers. After North River chose the same arbitrator for the two proceedings, and each of the insurers chose the same arbitrator for their individual arbitration proceedings, the two arbitrators could not agree on a third; North River then petitioned the court under the Federal Arbitration Act for an order consolidating the two proceedings. Although the insurers objected, no appeal followed from the district court's decision ordering the consolidation. The court held that equitable principles allow confirmation of an award in a consolidated proceeding, especially when the parties do not appeal from the order of consolidation. Perhaps, on a theory of implied consent to joinder, another shift in the judicial attitude toward consolidation is now beginning. Hoellering at 45.

In determining whether to consolidate arbitrations, courts engage in a two-step process. First, the court must find that the parties have agreed to arbitrate. This is often accomplished by recourse to general principles of contract and agency law. For example, in *Stallings & Sons, Inc. v. Sherlock, Smith & Adams,* 670 So. 2d 861 (Ala. 1995), the Alabama Supreme Court held that an arbitration clause in a general contract did not require a general contractor and its subcontractors to arbitrate their claims against an architect with whom they had no contract. The architect in *Stallings* claimed that the arbitration clause in AIA Doc. A201 obligated the general contractor to submit its claims against the architect to arbitration, because the contractor's claims arose out of the performance of the contract that did require arbitration, even though the architect was not a party to the construction contract. The court rejected the architect's argument because the contract limited the parties compelled to arbitrate their claims to those who expressed their consent in writing signed by the architect, owner, and contractor. Because the architect, owner, and contractor had not signed a written consent, the contract specifically prohibited arbitration of the contractor's claims against the architect. The court would not require a party to submit its claims to arbitration unless it had previously agreed to do so. Then the court must determine whether the agreement encompasses an agreement to consolidate arbitration claims either directly or by implication. An agreement to consolidate may be implied by the language of the arbitration clause; the amendments or addenda to the agreement; the course of dealings between the parties; and incorporation of an administering agency's rules that permit consolidation. Wilner, *Domke on Commercial Arbitration* § 27:02 (Rev. ed.) (1995 Cum. Supp.).

There appears to be a consensus that in the appropriate case, where common issues of law and fact exist, for reasons of economy and consistency of result, the dispute resolution process will benefit from the consolidation of arbitration proceedings. It has been noted that the policies in favor of consolidated arbitration proceedings generally outweigh competing concerns, and that consolidation should be permitted in appropriate circumstances. It can promote efficiency, economy, and expedience by resolving related disputes in one proceeding rather than two or more. Moreover, one uniform award may be more equitable than subjecting parties to the risk of inconsistent or even contradictory awards in multiple proceedings. Hoellering at 44.

In 1996, the American Institute of Architects (AIA) revised its AIA Document A191, Standard Form of Agreements Between Owner and Design/Builder. Article 6, now entitled "Dispute Resolution—Mediation and Arbitration," was revised to require in Paragraph 6.2 that the contracting parties attempt to resolve disputes through mediation before proceeding to arbitration. Another significant change was made in Paragraph 6.4. The restriction on joinder found in the 1985 edition of A191 has been eliminated. In the 1996 edition, an arbitration between the owner and the design-builder may be joined with an arbitration between the design-builder and another party under contract to the design-builder, such as the architect or contractor, if the dispute involves common issues of law or fact. This provision may provide a testing ground to determine whether multi-party arbitrations involving both design and construction issues can be successful, or whether the concerns expressed about joinder and consolidation—frustration of the benefits of speed and cost of arbitration—are legitimate. McCallum, Ellickson, & Goldberg, "The 1996 Editions of AIA Design/Build Standard Form Agreements," 16 *Construction Lawyer* 40 (No. 4, Oct. 1996).

Page 564, add at end of section:

Because most arbitration clauses are drafted on the basis that there are only two parties to a dispute, the complexities of multi-party arbitration, if permitted, are often not considered. In addition, most agency rules (such as those developed by the American Arbitration Association) do not consider procedures for multi-party arbitrations. There are three principal considerations when drafting an arbitration clause for a multi-party contract: how arbitrators are appointed; what procedures the arbitrators should follow; and the position of parties to the contract who may not be involved in the dispute. The best solution is to have the arbitrators for a multi-party contract dispute selected by an independent tribunal. Aitken & Spragge, "Arbitration Clauses in Multi-Party Contracts," *McKenna Law Letter,* Winter 1994/95, at 16.

All parties to the contract must be permitted to participate in the arbitration, even if not part of the dispute, because the resolution will affect the way the contract will be performed in the future. The contract should also recognize that a decision of the arbitrators binds all contracting parties, whether they are parties to the arbitration or not. Courts may also be considered as an alternate to arbitration in multi-party contracts if satisfactory terms cannot be agreed upon for the arbitration clause.

TABLE OF CASES

Active Glass v. Architect & Ornamental Iron Workers #580, 875 F. Supp. 245 (S.D.N.Y. 1995)	§ 23.5
Aetna Ins. Co. v. Hellmuth, Obata & Kassabaum, Inc., 392 F.2d 472 (8th Cir. 1968)	§ 7.10
Aitken, Hazen, Hollman, Miller, P.C. v. Empire Constr. Co., 542 F. Supp. 252, 256 (D. Neb. 1982)	§ 11.19A
Alex Bhatti v. McCabe, 1997 Ark. App. LEXIS 547 (1997)	§ 16.6
Alfred A. Altimont, Inc. v. Chatelain, Samperton & Nolan, 374 A.2d 284 (D.C. 1977)	§ 6.15
Amazon v. British Am. Dev. Corp., 628 N.Y.S.2d 204 (1995)	§ 15.8
American and Foreign Insurance Co. v. Bolt, 1997 U.S. App. LEXIS 2376 (6th Cir. 1997)	§ 14.6
American Centennial Ins. v. National Casualty Co., 951 F.2d 107 (6th Cir. 1991)	§ 23.5
American Motorcycle Ass'n v. Superior Court, 20 Cal. 3d 578, 146 Cal. Rptr. 182 (1978)	§ 12.10
Annen v. Trump, 913 S.W.2d 16 (Mo. Ct. App. 1995)	§§ 20.14, 22.3
APAC Carolina, Inc. v. Town of Allendale, 863 F. Supp. 815 (D.S.C.), *aff'd,* 41 F.3d 157 (4th Cir. 1994)	§§ 16.2, 16.10
Arbitration Between Coastal Shipping Ltd. & S. Petroleum Tankers, Ltd., *In re,* 812 F. Supp. 396 (S.D.N.Y. 1993)	§ 23.5
Arthur Rutenberg Homes, Inc. v. Drew Homes Inc., 29 F.3d 1529 (11th Cir. 1994)	§ 11.14
Arthur Rutenberg Homes, Inc. v. Maloney, 891 F. Supp. 1560, 1568 (M.C. Fla. 1995)	§ 11.19A
Ashco International, Inc. v. Westmore Shopping Center Associates, 42 Va. Cir. 427, 1997 Va. Cir. LEXIS 158 (1997), 97-8-235	§ 6.15
Atlantic Mut. Ins. Co. v. Merton Eng'g & Constr. Co., 83 F.3d 897 (7th Cir. 1996)	§ 5.4
Baesler v. Continental Grain Co., 900 F.2d 1193 (8th Cir. 1990)	§ 23.5
Ballou v. Basic Construction Co., 407 F.2d 1137 (4th Cir. 1967)	§ 6.15
Bateman Constr., Inc. v. Haitsuka Bros., 77 Haw. 481, 889 P.2d 58 (1995)	§ 23.5
Bell Lavalin Inc. v. Simcoe & Erie Gen. Ins. Co., 61 F.3d 742 (9th Cir. 1995)	§ 4.2
Bernaldes, Estate of v. United States, 877 F. Supp. 301 (W.D. Va. 1995)	§ 18.2
Bily v. Arthur Young & Co., 3 Cal. 4th 370, 11 Cal. Rptr. 51 (1992)	§ 12.13
Block v. Lohan Assocs., Inc., 269 Ill. App. 3d 745, 645 N.E.2d 207 (1993)	§§ 9.8, 13.5, 13.12

TABLE OF CASES

Block v. Lohan Assocs., Inc., 159 Ill. 2d 583, 645 N.E.2d 207 (1993)	§§ 2.14, 5.4, 6.12
BMW of N. Am. v. Gore, 116 S. Ct. 1589, 134 L. Ed. 2d 804 (1996)	§ 12.14
Boston Inv. Property #1 State v. Burman, 658 A.2d 515 (R.I. 1995)	§§ 6.10, 7.10
Brown v. Tate, 888 S.W.2d 413 (Mo. Ct. App. 1994)	§ 18.4
Brown Daltas & Assocs., Inc. v. General Accident Ins. Co., 48 F.3d 30 (1st Cir. 1995)	§ 4.3
Browning v. Vecellio & Grogan, Inc., 945 F. Supp. 930 (W.D. Va. 1996)	§ 18.2
Bryant v. Murray-Jones-Murray, Inc., 653 F. Supp. 1015 (E.D. Mo. 1985)	§ 7.10
Bryce & Polazzola Architects, Inc. v. A.M.E. Group, 865 F. Supp. 401 (E.D. Mich. 1994)	§ 11.7
Business Men's Assurance Co. v. Graham, 891 S.W.2d 438 (Mo. Ct. App. 1994)	§ 13.5
Butler v. Mitchell-Hugeback, Inc., 895 S.W.2d 15 (Mo. 1995)	§§ 19.2, 19.4
Call v. Prudential (unreported) (docket number available)	§ 7.20A
Calocerinos & Spina Consulting Eng'rs, PC v. Prudential Reinsurance Co., 856 F. Supp. 775 (W.D.N.Y. 1994)	§ 3.4
Carvalho v. Toll Bros. & Developers, 278 N.J. Super. 451, 651 A.2d 492 (App. Div.), *cert. granted,* 140 N.J. 326, 658 A.2d 726 (1995), *aff'd & remanded,* 143 N.J. 565, 675 A.2d 209 (1996)	§§ 6.12, 7.13, 13.5, 13.12, 15.8
Cassway v. Chelsea Historic Properties I, Ltd. Partnership, 26 U.S.P.Q.2d 1791 (E.D. Pa. 1993)	§ 11.19A
Certified Mechanical Contractors, Inc. v. Wight & Co., 515 N.E.2d 1047 (Ill. App. Ct. 1987)	§ 6.15
Chesapeake Paper Prods. Co. v. Stone & Webster Eng'g Corp., 51 F.3d 1229 (4th Cir. 1995)	§§ 1.5, 5.4
Chubb Group of Ins. Cos. v. C.F. Murphy, 656 S.W.2d 766 (Mo. Ct. App. 1983)	§§ 7.20A, 11.19A
City Sch. Dist. v. Hugh Stubbins & Assocs., Inc., 85 N.Y.2d 535 (1995)	§§ 5.8, 19.4
Cleary v. News Corp., 30 F.3d 1255, 1259 (9th Cir. 1994)	§ 11.19A
C.L. Maddox Inc. v. Benham Group, Inc., 88 F.3d 592 (8th Cir. 1996)	§§ 5.12, 5.19, 5.20, 6.14, 9.9
Colton, McMichael, Lester, Auman, Visnovske, Inv. v. Mueller, 896 S.W.2d 741 (Mo. Ct. App. 1995)	§§ 11.16, 11.20
Consumers Union of the United States v. New Regina Corp., 664 F. Supp. 753, 764 (S.D.N.Y. 1997)	§ 11.14
County of Brevard v. Miorelli Engineering, Inc., 703 So. 2d 1049, 1997 Fla. LEXIS 1811 (1997)	§ 18.2
CRS Sirrine, Inc. v. Dravo Corp., 445 S.E.2d 782 (Ga. Ct. App. 1994), 464 S.E.2d 897 (Ga. Ct. App. 1995)	§§ 5.17, 16.2, 17.8

CSM Investors, Inc. v. Everest Dev. Ltd., 840 F. Supp. 1304 (D. Minn. 1994) § 11.7
Cubito v. Kreisberg, 419 N.Y.S.2d 582 (App. Div. 1979) § 9.5

Darell Thacker v. Menards, Inc., 105 F.3d 382 (7th Cir. 1997) § 7.8
Dehnert v. Arrow Sprinklers, Inc., 705 P.2d 846 (Wyo. 1985) § 6.14
Del E. Webb Constr. v. Richardson Hosp. Auth., 823 F.2d 145 (5th Cir. 1987) § 23.5
DIC Commercial Construction Corp. v. Broward County, 668 So. 2d 697, 1996 Fla. App. LEXIS 1619 (1996) §§ 5.7, 6.14
Department of Transp. v. APAC Ga., 217 Ga. App. 103, 456 S.E.2d 668 (1995) § 18.2
Dierson v. Joe Keim Builders, Inc., 216 N.J. Super. 618, 524 A.2d 841 (App. Div.), *cert. denied,* 107 N.J. 148, 526 A.2d 209 (1987) § 23.5
Dillingham v. CH2M Hill N.W., 873 P.2d 1271 (Alaska 1994) § 17.8
Duncan v. Missouri Bd. of Architects, Prof'l Eng'rs and Land Surveyors, 744 S.W.2d 524 Mo.1988) § 9.8
Dunn Constr. Co. v. Sugar Beach Condominium Ass'n, Inc., 760 F. Supp. 1479 (S.D. Ala. 1991) § 5.8

East River S.S. Corp. v. Transamerica Delaval, Inc., 476 U.S. 858 (1986) § 7.10
East/West Venture v. Wurmfield Assocs., 13 U.S.P.Q.2d 1908 (S.D.N.Y. 1989) § 11.6
Edgewater Apartments v. Flynn Consulting Eng'rs, 216 A.D.2d 53, 627 N.Y.S.2d 385 (1995) §§ 7.5, 22.2
Edgeworth Construction v. N.D. Lea & Assoc., [1993] 3 S.C.R. 206, 12 B.C.L.R. (2d) 161, [1993] 8 W.W.R. 129, 83 B.C.R. (2d) 145, 107 D.L.R. (4th) 169 §§ 6.10, 7.10, 12.4
Edward M Crough, Inc. v. Department of Gen. Servs., 572 A.2d 457 (D.C. 1990) § 7.17
Estey v. MacKenzie, 902 P.2d 1220 (Or. Ct. App. 1995) § 17.8
Evanston Ins. Co. v. Treister, 794 F. Supp. 560 (D.V.I. 1992) § 7.20A

Federal Mogul Corp. v. Universal Constr. Co., 376 So. 2d 725 (Ala. Ct. App. 1979) § 9.2
Federal Sign v. Texas S. Univ., 40 Tex. Sup. Ct. J. 676 (June 20, 1997) § 18.2
Finley v. Lehman, 463 S.E.2d 709 (Ga. Ct. App. 1995) § 18.4
Fireman's Fund Ins. Co. v. SEC Donohue, Inc., 176 Ill. 2d 160, 679 N.E.2d 1197 (1997) §§ 5.7, 7.10
Firestone Steel Prods. Co. v. Brojas, 927 S.W.2d 608 (Tex. 1996) § 12.5
Fleischer v. Helmut, Obata & Kassabaum, Inc., 870 S.W.2d 832 (Mo. Ct. App. 1993) §§ 7.10, 12.4
Fred Riley Home Bldg. Corp. v. Cosgrove, 864 F. Supp. 1034 (D. Kan. 1994) §§ 11.2, 11.17
Fry's Food Stores v. Mather & Assoc., Inc., 183 Ariz. 89, 900 P.2d 1225 (1995) § 11.9

Gables CVF, Inc. v. Bahr, Vermeer & Haecker Architects, Ltd., 244 Neb. 346, *modified,* 244 Neb. 613, 506 N.W.2d 706 (1993) §§ 5.19, 13.9, 13.11, 17.9
Garaman, Inc. v. Williams, 912 P.2d 1121 (Wyo. 1996) § 22.2
Garcia v. Cosicher, 504 So. 2d 462 (Fla. Dist. Ct. App. 1987) § 11.19A
Gateway W. Ry. v. Morrison Metalweld Process Corp., 46 F.3d 860 (8th Cir. 1995) § 6.6
George A. Fuller Co. v. Chicago College of Osteopathic Medicine, 719 F.2d 1326 (7th Cir. 1983) § 6.15
Georgetown Steel Corp. v. Union Carbide Corp., 806 F. Supp. 74 (D.S.C. 1992), 7 F.3d 223 (4th Cir. 1993) § 9.2
German v. Federal Home Loan Mortgage Corp., 885 F. Supp. 537 (S.D.N.Y. 1995) § 9.7
Gibbes, Inc., II v. Law Eng'g, Inc., 1992 U.S. App. LEXIS 7602 (4th Cir. 1992) § 17.8
Government of United Kingdom of Gr. Brit. Through United Kingdom Procurement Office, Ministry of Defense v. Boeing Co., 998 F.2d 68 (2d Cir. 1993) § 23.5
Graham, Inc. v. City of Cave City, 289 Ark. 105, 709 S.W.2d 94 (1986) § 17.8
Graman v. Continental Casualty Co., 87 Ill. App. 3d 896, 409 N.E.2d 387 (1980) § 14.8
Great S. Homes v. Johnson & Thompson Realtors, 797 F. Supp. 609 (M.D. Tenn. 1992) §§ 11.14, 11.24
Griffin Plumbing & Heating Co. v. Jordan, Jones & Goulding, 463 S.E.2d 85 (S.C. 1995) § 6.10
Guillot-Vogt Assoc., Inc. v. Holly & Smith, 848 F. Supp. 682 (E.D. La. 1994) §§ 11.7, 11.19A

Halstead v. United States, 535 F. Supp. 782 (D. Conn. 1982), *aff'd,* 707 F.2d 671 (2d Cir. 1983) § 9.6
Hardaway v. Parsons, Brinkerhoff, Quade & Douglas, Inc., 479 S.E.2d 727 (Ga. 1997) § 19.5
Harris Custom Builders, Inc. v. Hoffmeyer, 874 F. Supp. 899 (N.D. Ill. 1995) § 11.17
Hazelton Area Sch. Dist. v. Dosak, 671 A.2d 277 (Pa. Commw. Ct. 1996) § 23.3
Herman Frankel Organization v. Tegman, 367 F. Supp. 1051 (E.D. Mich. 1973) § 11.19A
Hoover Group Inc. v. Probala & Assocs., 710 F. Supp. 677 (N.D. Ohio 1989) § 23.5
Housing Vt. v. Goldsmith & Morris, 685 A.2d 1086 (Vt. 1996) § 7.17
Hudson v. Town of E. Montpelier, 638 A.2d 561 (Vt. 1993) § 18.4
Hughes Masonry Co. v. Greater Clark County Sch. Bldg. Corp., 659 F.2d 836 (7th Cir. 1981) § 5.8
Hurst-Roche Eng'rs, Inc. v. Commercial Union Ins. Co., 51 F.3d 1336 (7th Cir. 1995) § 16.9

I.A.E., Inc. v. Shaver, 74 F.3d 768 (7th Cir. 1996) § 11.14
Imperial Residential Design, Inc. v. Palms Dev. Group, Inc., 70 F.3d 96 (11th Cir. 1995) § 11.14

Ivanov v. Process Design Assocs., 267 Ill. App. 3d 440, 642 N.E.2d 711 (1994) §§ 6.12, 9.8, 13.5, 13.12

Jim's Excavating Serv. v. HKM Assocs., 265 Mont. 494, 878 P.2d 248 (1994) §§ 5.7, 7.10, 7.11, 13.12, 17.5
Joba Construction Co. v. Burns & Roe, Inc., 329 N.W.2d 760 (Mich. Ct. App. 1982) § 6.15
Johanson v. Huizenga Holdings, Inc., 963 F. Supp. 1175 (S.D. Fla. 1997) § 10.6
Johnson v. Board of County Comm'rs, 21 Kan. App. 2d 76, 897 P.2d 169 (1995) §§ 7.15, 15.3
Johnson v. Ellerbe Becket, Inc., Civ. No. 96-7026 (D. Fla. Jan. 27, 1997) (slip op.) § 10.6
Johnson v. Jones, 149 F.3d 494, 1998 U.S. App. LEXIS (6th Cir. 1998) §§ 11.14, 11.19A, 11.23
Johnson v. Jones, 921 F. Supp. 1584 § 11.19A
Jones v. James Reeves Contractors, Inc., 701 So. 2d 774 (Miss. 1997) §§ 2.12, 7.20

Kaplan v. Tabb Assocs., Inc., 657 N.E.2d 1065 (Ill. App. 1995) § 17.13
Karna v. Gyron Reed Syndicate, 374 F. Supp. 687 (D. Neb. 1974) § 11.19A
Katzner v. Kelleher Constr. Corp., 545 N.W.2d 378 (Minn. 1996) §§ 16.3, 17.2
Kecko Piping Co. v. Town of Monroe, 172 Conn. 197, 374 A.2d 179 (1977) § 6.15
Kerr Construction and Paving Co. v. Khazin, et al., 961 S.W.2d 75, 1997 Mo. App. LEXIS 2079 (Mo. Ct. App. 1997) § 6.15
Kovaleski v. Tallahassee Title Co., 363 So. 2d 1156 (Fla. Dist. Ct. App. 1978) § 9.3

Langford v. Kraft, 551 S.W.2d 392 (Tex. Civ. App. 1977), *aff'd*, 565 S.W.2d 223 (Tex. 1978) § 9.7
L.H. Bell & Assocs., Inc. v. Granger, 112 Ariz. 440, 543 P.2d 428 (1975) § 15.8
Lindberg v. County of Kitsap, 948 P.2d 805 (Wash. 1997) § 11.18
Lippy v. Society Nat'l Bank, 100 Ohio App. 3d 37, 651 N.E.2d 1364 (1995) §§ 6.10, 7.10
Long Island Lighting Co. (Lilco) v. Imo Delaval, Inc., 668 F. Supp. 237 (S.D.N.Y. 1987) § 17.8

Marbro, Inc. v. Borough of Tinton Falls, 297 N.J. Super. 411, 688 A.2d 159 (1996) § 17.8
Martinez v. Badis, 842 P.2d 245 (Colo. 1992) § 21.6
Maryland Casualty Co. v. Bailey & Sons, Inc., 35 Cal. App. 4th 856, 41 Cal. Rptr. 2d 519 (1995) § 12.10

TABLE OF CASES

Mattco Forge Inc. v. Arthur Young & Co., 5 Cal. App. 4th 392, 6 Cal. Rptr. 781 (1992)	§ 18.6
Matyas v. Minck, 37 Conn. App. 321, 655 A.2d 1155 (1995)	§ 22.3
Maxum Founds., Inc. v. Salus Corp., 817 F.2d 1086 (4th Cir. 1987)	§ 23.5
McAninch v. Robinson, 942 S.W.2d 452 (Mo. Ct. App. 1997)	§ 6.12
McBro Planning & Dev. Co. v. Triangle Elec. Constr. Co., 741 F.2d 342 (11th Cir. 1984)	§ 5.8
MECO Sys., Inc. v. Dancing Bear Entertainment, Inc., No. 21209 (Mo. Ct. App. June 25, 1997)	§ 7.18
Metric Constructors, Inc. v. Hawker Siddeley Power Eng'g, Inc., 468 S.E.2d 435 (N.C. Ct. App. 1996)	§ 13.9
MKK Technologies, Inc./Northstar Constr. v. Scott, 63 F.3d 402 (5th Cir. 1995)	§§ 7.18, 14.6
Moler v. Melzer, 24 Kan. App. 2d 76, 942 P.2d 643 (1997)	§ 17.8
Moore v. Conliffe, 871 P.2d 204, 29 Cal. Rptr. 2d 152 (1994)	§ 18.6
Moore Eng'g v. West Fargo, 42 F.3d 452 (8th Cir. 1994)	§ 18.4
National Hydro Systems v. M.A. Mortensen Co., 529 N.W.2d 690 (Minn. 1995)	§§ 5.17, 16.3, 17.2
New Eng. Energy Inc. v. Keystone Shipping Co., 855 F.2d 1 (1st Cir. 1988), *cert. denied,* 489 U.S. 1077, 109 S. Ct. 1527, 103 L. Ed. 2d 832 (1989)	§ 23.5
North River Ins. Co. v. Philadelphia Reinsurance Corp., 63 F.3d 160 (2d Cir. 1995)	§ 23.5
Northridge Co. v. W.R. Grace & Co., 471 N.W.2d 179 (Wis. 1991)	§§ 7.10, 7.20A
O'Reilly v. Dock, 929 S.W.2d 297 (Mo. Ct. App. 1996)	§§ 5.8, 19.5, 19.9
Old Mason's Home of Ky., Inc. v. Mitchell, 304 S.W.2d 304 (Ky. Ct. App. 1995)	§ 19.9
Oriskany Cent. Sch. Dist. v. Edmond J. Booth Architects, 206 A.D.2d 896, 615 N.Y.S.2d 160 (1994)	§ 5.8
Ossining Union Free Sch. Dist. v. Anderson, LaRocca, Anderson, 73 N.Y.2d 417, 539 N.E.2d 91 (1989)	§ 12.13
Painewebber Inc. v. Fowler, 791 F. Supp. 821 (D. Kan. 1992)	§ 23.5
Paralyzed Veterans v. Ellerbe Becket Architects & Eng'rs, P.C., Civ. Action No. 96-1354 (TFH) (D.D.C. 1996)	§ 10.6
Peck v. Horrocks Eng'g, 106 F.3d 949 (10th Cir. 1997)	§§ 6.12, 13.12, 15.8
Pierce v. ALSC Architects, P.S., 890 P.2d 1254 (Mont. 1995)	§ 15.8
Playboy Enters., Inc. v. Dumas, 831 F. Supp. 295 (S.D.N.Y. 1993), *aff'd,* 53 F.3d 549 (2d Cir. 1995)	§ 11.19A
Ponderosa Ctr. Partners v. McClellan/Cruz/Gaylord & Assocs., 45 Cal. App. 4th 913, 53 Cal. Rptr. 2d 64 (1996)	§§ 12.11, 21.6
Potter-Shackelford Constr. Co. v. Law Eng'g, Inc., 1996 U.S. App. LEXIS 33368 (4th Cir. Dec. 6, 1996)	§§ 2.25, 17.8
Pratt Cent. Park Ltd. v. Dames & Moore, 60 F.3d 350 (7th Cir. 1995)	§ 17.8
P/R Clipper Gas v. PPG Indus. Inc., 804 F. Supp. 570 (S.D.N.Y. 1992)	§ 23.5

TABLE OF CASES

Priso Serena Sturm Architects, Ltd. v. Liberty Mut. Ins. Co., 1995 U.S. Dist. LEXIS 18202 (N.D. Ill. 1995)	§ 16.9
Protective Life Ins. Corp. v. Lincoln Nat'l Life Ins. Corp., 873 F.2d 281 (11th Cir. 1989)	§ 23.5
Putensen v. Clay Adams, Inc., 12 Cal. App. 3d 1062, 9 Cal. Rptr. 319 (1970)	§ 12.11
Quality Granite Constr. Co. v. Hurst-Rosche Eng'rs, Inc., 261 Ill. App. 3d 21, 632 N.E.2d 1139, *cert. denied,* 642 N.E.2d 1302 (Ill. 1994)	§§ 1.4, 6.15, 18.6
Regional Steel Corp. v. Superior Court, 25 Cal. App. 4th 525, 32 Cal. Rptr. 2d 417 (1994)	§ 12.10
Republic Contracting Corp. v. S.C. Dept. of Highways and Public Transp., 332 S.C. 197, 503 S.E.2d 761, 1998 S.C. App. LEXIS 88 (1998)	§§ 5.8, 19.5, 19.9
Riblet Tramway Co. v. Ericksen Associates, Inc., 665 F. Supp. 81 (D.N.H. 1987)	§ 6.15
Ricciardi v. Frank, 620 N.Y.S.2d 918 (1994)	§ 17.8
R.J. Longo Constr. Co. v. Transit Am., Inc., 921 F. Supp. 1295 (D.N.J. 1996)	§ 12.8
Roberts & Schaefer v. Hardaway, 1998 U.S. App. LEXIS 21252 (11th Cir. 1998)	§ 13.9
Russo Farms v. Vineland Bd. of Educ., 280 N.J. Super. 320, 655 A.2d 447 (App. Div. 1995)	§ 19.5
Santucci Construction Co. v. Baxter & Woodman, Inc., 502 N.E.2d 1134 (Ill. App. Ct. 1986)	§ 6.15
Schaffer v. Property Evaluations, Inc., 854 S.W.2d 493 (Mo. Ct. App. 1993)	§ 17.8
Scott v. City of Seymour, 658 N.E.2d 585 (Ind. Ct. App. 1995)	§ 18.2
Secretary of Labor v. CH2M Hill Cent., OSHRC No. 89-1712 (Apr. 21, 1997)	§§ 9.12, 10.5
Secretary of Labor v. Foit-Albert Assocs., Architects & Eng'rs, OSHRC No. 92-654 (Apr. 21, 1997)	§§ 9.12, 10.5
Seminole Tribe of Florida v. Florida, 116 S. Ct. 1114 (1996)	§ 11.19A
Silva v. MacLaine, 697 F. Supp. 1423, 1430 (E.D. Mich. 1988)	§ 11 14
Sinning v. Clark, 459 S.E.2d 71 (N.C. 1995)	§ 18.4
Slaught v. Bencomo Roofing Co., 25 Cal. App. 4th 744, 30 Cal. Rptr. 2d 618 (1994)	§ 23.5
Snyder v. ISC Alloys, Ltd., 772 F. Supp. 251 (W.D. Pa. 1991)	§ 9.2
Sociedad Anonima de Navegacion Petrolera v. CIA de Petroleos de Chile S.A., 634 F. Supp. 805 (S.D.N.Y. 1986)	§ 23.5
Soderberg v. McKinney, 44 Cal. App. 4th 1760, 52 Cal. Rptr. 2d 635 (1996)	§ 12.13
Somers Construction Co. v. Board of Education, 198 F. Supp. 732 (D.N.J. 1961)	§ 6.15
Stallings & Sons, Inc. v. Sherlock, Smith & Adams, 670 So. 2d 861 (Ala. 1995)	§ 23.5

TABLE OF CASES

St. Denis v. Department of Hous. & Urban Dev., 900 F. Supp. 1194 (D. Alaska 1995) §§ 7.10, 7.20A, 18.2
St. Louis Air Cargo Servs., Inc. v. City of St. Louis, 929 S.W.2d 821 (Mo. Ct. App. 1996) § 18.2
Stonecipher v. Mitchell, 655 So. 2d 1381 (La. Ct. App. 1995) § 6.9
Suriano v. City of N.Y., 658 N.Y.S.2d 654 (App. Div. 1997) § 6.12

Taramac Dev. Co. v. Delamarir, Freud & Assocs., 234 Kan. 618, 675 P.2d 361 (1984) § 12.8
Thomson v. Espey Huston & Assocs., Inc., 899 S.W.2d 415 (Tex. Ct. App. 1995) §§ 1.4, 5.7, 6.10, 7.10, 13.12, 15.1, 17.5, 19.5
Trandes Corp. v. Guy F. Atkinson Co., 996 F.2d 655 (4th Cir. 1993) § 7.23
Tommy L. Griffin Plumbing & Heating Co. v. Jordan, 463 S.E.2d 85 (S.C. 1995) § 12.8
Tommy L. Griffin Plumbing & Heating Co. v. Jordan, Jones & Goulding, Inc., Op. No. 24328 (S.C. filed Oct. 16, 1995) §§ 6.10, 7.10

United Kingdom v. Boeing Co., 998 F.2d 68 (2d Cir. 1993) § 23.5
United States v. Advance Tool Co., 902 F. Supp. 1011 (W.D. Mo. 1995) § 10.12
United States v. Days Inn of America, Inc., 1998 U.S. App. LEXIS 18159 (8th Cir. 1998) § 10.6
United States v. Ellerbe Becket, Inc., 976 F. Supp 1262 (D. Minn. 1997) § 10.6
United States v. Neifert-White Co., 390 U.S. 228 (1968) § 10.12
United States v. Winstar Corp., 116 S. Ct. 2432 (1996) §§ 18.2, 18.2
Uptergrove v. Housing Auth., No. 52098 (Mo. Ct. App. Oct. 15, 1995) § 18.2

Valhal Corp. v. Sullivan Assocs., Inc., 44 F.3d 195 (3d Cir. 1995) § 17.8
Valhal Corp. v. Sullivan Assocs., Inc., 1995 WL 2621 (3d Cir. Jan. 3, 1995) §§ 2.25, 14.7, 17.8
Vikell Investors Pacific, Inc. v. Kip Hampden, Ltd., et al., 946 P.2d 589 (Colo. Ct. App. 1997) § 9.8
Vojak v. Jensen, 161 N.W.2d 100 (Iowa 1968) § 6.15

Waldinger Corp. v. CRS Group Engineers, Inc., 775 F.2d 781 (7th Cir. 1985) § 6.14
Walker v. Bluffs Apartments, 477 S.E.2d 472 (S.C. Ct. App. 1996) § 22.2
Wamp v. Tennessee State Bd. of Architectural & Eng'g Examiners, 868 S.W.2d 273 (Tenn. 1994) § 11.19A
Weyerhauser Co. v. Western Seas Shipping Co., 743 F.2d 635 (9th Cir. 1984), *cert. denied,* 469 U.S. 1061 (1984) § 23.5

TABLE OF CASES

Yantzi v. Norton, 927 S.W.2d 427 (Mo. Ct. App. 1996) §§ 7.5, 20.14, 22.2

Yocum v. City of Minden, 649 So. 2d 129 (La. Ct. App. 1995) §§ 6.12, 13.12, 17.2

York, City of v. Turner-Murphy Co., 452 S.E.2d 615 (S.C. Ct. App. 1994) §§ 7.5, 20.14, 22.3

Zenda Grain & Supply v. Farmland Indus. Inc., 894 P.2d 890 (Kan. Ct. App. 1995) § 9.3

INDEX

ADMINISTRATION OF CONTRACTS
Detailed description of scope of designer's work, use of § 2.5
Limitations period. See STATUTE OF LIMITATIONS
Standard form specifications, disadvantages of § 2.8
–Visits and inspections § 2.12
ADR. *See* ALTERNATE DISPUTE RESOLUTION
AIR QUALITY
See INDOOR AIR QUALITY; SICK BUILDING SYNDROME
ALTERNATE DISPUTE RESOLUTION (ADR). *See also* ARBITRATION
AIA requirements re § 23.2
Consolidation of actions § 23.5
Use and results § 14.7
AMERICANS WITH DISABILITIES ACT (ADA)
Compliance issues § 10.6
Designers' liability under § 10.6
ARBITRATION
Consolidation of actions § 23.5
ATTORNEYS' FEES
Recovery of
–Violation of copyright before registration, effect of § 11.24

BONDING
Design/build arrangements § 1.10

CAUSES OF ACTION
Characterization of §§ 5.8, 19.4
CERTIFICATES OF MERIT
Claim review and § 21.6
CHANGES IN CONTRACTS
Unauthorized changes, avoiding responsibility for § 2.16
CLAIMS PROCEDURES
Use of § 7.18
COMPUTER-AIDED DESIGN AND DRAFTING (CADD) SYSTEMS
Spatial representations, inaccuracy of § 7.23
CONDOMINIUM DESIGN
Exclusion from insurance policy § 3.6
Reconstruction project § 3.6
CONTRACTS
Additional services § 2.17
Oral § 5.4
Ownership and use of documents § 2.20
Termination § 2.28
CONTRACTS, ADMINISTRATION OF
See ADMINISTRATION OF CONTRACTS
CONTRACTORS' CLAIMS
Against design professionals
–Duty to warn § 7.50
–For termination recommendations §§ 6.15, 7.18
CONVERSION
Unauthorized use of design § 11.16
COPYRIGHT PROTECTION OF DESIGNS
Architectural work § 11.7
Attorneys' fees. See ATTORNEYS' FEES
Authorized use
–Abbreviated or incomplete versions in sales brochures § 11.17
–Field revisions § 11.17
Conversion, action for § 11.16
Unauthorized use of design § 11.16
Work made for hire § 11.7

DAMAGES
–Insurance § 2.24
DEFENSES
–No Consequential Damages Clause § 17.6

INDEX

DEFICIENCIES
Assessment and statement of § 6.15
DELAYS
Inability to make decisions, effect of § 7.18
DESIGN PROFESSIONALS
As fiduciaries §§ 5.16, 9.9, 12.13

ECONOMIC LOSS
Inherently dangerous products and § 7.20A
Nature of §§ 6.10, 7.10
Risk management and § 14.4

FALSE CLAIMS ACT
Generally § 10.12
FIDUCIARY
Designer as §§ 5.16, 9.9, 12.13

GOVERNMENT AGENCIES
Reuse of designs and plans § 11.19A

INDEMNIFICATION PROVISIONS
Required and desirable § 17.2
INDOOR AIR QUALITY
Building codes, effect of § 7.20A
Industry standards § 7.20A
Sick building syndrome. See SICK BUILDING SYNDROME
Standard of care § 7.20A
Ventilation design criteria § 7.20A
INSURANCE AND SURETY
Claims-made policy § 3.4
Condominium design
–Exclusion from policy § 3.6
–Reconstruction project § 3.6
Cost of § 3.1
Cut-through endorsements § 16.9
Design activities not covered § 4.2
Design/build arrangements § 1.10
Exclusions
–Condominium design § 3.6
–Effect of § 1.10
Hold harmless agreements § 14.7
Professional liability exclusions § 16.9
Reinsurance § 16.9
Sick building syndrome § 7.20A

LIABILITY OF DESIGN PROFESSIONALS
Economic loss rule. *See* ECONOMIC LOSS RULE
Limitation of liability clauses
–Ambiguity in §§ 5.17, 17.8
–Enforcement of § 17.8
–Legality of §§ 2.25, 17.8
Under reuse statutes § 11.19A
LICENSING-RELATED CLAIMS
Failure to comply with licensing requirements, effect of § 1.10

NEGLIGENCE
Problems with electronic media § 7.22

OCCUPATIONAL SAFETY AND HEALTH ACT (OSHA)
Application to designer's services §§ 9.12, 10.5
OWNERSHIP AND REUSE OF DESIGNS
Reuse statutes § 11.19A

PRIVILEGE
For design professionals' termination recommendations § 6.15

REINSURANCE
Generally § 16.9
Cut-through endorsements § 16.9
REUSE OF DESIGNS. *See* OWNERSHIP AND REUSE OF DESIGNS RISK MANAGEMENT
Alternate dispute resolution use and results § 14.7
Client consideration § 14.6
Construction manager, effect of separate § 14.6
Designer selection, method of § 14.6
Hold harmless agreements § 14.7
Liability insurance, effect of § 14.6
Peer Review Program § 14.7
Site selection § 14.6

SAFETY
Responsibility for §§ 13.12, 15.8

INDEX

SCHEDULING OF PROJECTS
Designer's review of contractor's schedule § 1.9
Importance of § 1.10
SCHEMATIC DESIGN
–Architect responsibility for § 2.6
SICK BUILDING SYNDROME
See also INDOOR AIR QUALITY
Generally § 7.20A
Asbestos contamination § 7.20A
Causes § 7.20A
Insurance coverage § 7.20A
Sources § 7.20A
SHOP DRAWINGS
Contractor approval of § 2.15
SOVEREIGN IMMUNITY
Statutory limitations on § 18.3
Waiver of § 18.2
SPEARIN DOCTRINE
Manufacturer versus contractor liability under § 1.7
STATUTE OF LIMITATIONS
Application to subconsultants § 5.8
Government claims § 19.4

TERMINATION DECISIONS
Design professional's involvement in §§ 6.15, 7.18
TOXIC MATERIALS
Economic loss rule and §§ 7.10, 7.20A